Intellectual Property and General Legal Principles

ATRIP INTELLECTUAL PROPERTY SERIES

Series Editor: Graeme B. Dinwoodie, *Professor of Intellectual Property and Information Technology Law, University of Oxford, UK*

The ATRIP series presents the fruit of annual meetings held by the International Association for the Advancement of Teaching and Research in Intellectual Property (www.atrip.org). Yielding unique opportunities for IP scholars from a global community to explore together the different facets of one overarching topic, the essence of those meetings is captured in the edited compilation of selected contributions contained in the volumes. Rather than employing a traditional, compartmentalized view of the different areas of IP, the ATRIP series typically follow a horizontal approach, cutting across the usual boundaries of legal categorization, with the aim to uncover hidden commonalities, and accentuate the need for differentiation where that is called for. As ATRIP counts among its members leading IP scholars from all parts of the world, and actively encourages the participation of highly talented young researchers, the panel of authors contributing to the volumes not only guarantees excellence, but also represents a full and vibrant picture of contemporary, high-level IP research in an international setting.

Titles in the series include:

The Structure of Intellectual Property Law
Can One Size Fit All?
Edited by Annette Kur and Vytautas Mizaras

Individualism and Collectiveness in Intellectual Property Law
Edited by Jan Rosén

Intellectual Property at the Crossroads of Trade
Edited by Jan Rosén

Methods and Perspectives in Intellectual Property
Edited by Graeme B. Dinwoodie

Intellectual Property and General Legal Principles
Is IP a *Lex Specialis*?
Edited by Graeme B. Dinwoodie

Intellectual Property and General Legal Principles

Is IP a *Lex Specialis*?

Edited by

Graeme B. Dinwoodie

Professor of Intellectual Property and Information Technology Law, University of Oxford, UK

ATRIP INTELLECTUAL PROPERTY SERIES

Edward Elgar PUBLISHING

Cheltenham, UK • Northampton, MA, USA

Published by
Edward Elgar Publishing Limited
The Lypiatts
15 Lansdown Road
Cheltenham
Glos GL50 2JA
UK

Edward Elgar Publishing, Inc.
William Pratt House
9 Dewey Court
Northampton
Massachusetts 01060
USA

A catalogue record for this book
is available from the British Library

Library of Congress Control Number: 2014952156

This book is available electronically in the **Elgar**online
Law subject collection
DOI 10.4337/9781784714956

MIX
Paper from
responsible sources
FSC® C013056

ISBN 978 1 78471 494 9 (cased)
ISBN 978 1 78471 495 6 (eBook)

Typeset by Columns Design XML Ltd, Reading
Printed and bound in Great Britain by T.J. International Ltd, Padstow

Contents

Contributors

Abbe Brown, Senior Lecturer and Deputy Head of Law School at the University of Aberdeen, UK.

Irene Calboli, Visiting Professor at the Faculty of Law of the National University of Singapore, Professor of Law at Marquette University Law School, and Transatlantic Technology Law Forum Fellow at Stanford Law School, USA.

Giuseppina D'Agostino, Associate Professor at Osgoode Hall Law School, York University, Canada and founding director of IP Osgoode, Canada.

Graeme B. Dinwoodie, Professor of Intellectual Property and Information Technology Law, Director of the Oxford Intellectual Property Research Centre, and Professorial Fellow of St. Peter's College at University of Oxford, UK.

Séverine Dusollier, Professor at SciencesPo Paris and University of Namur, Belgium.

Brett Garrison, JD, Washington University, St Louis School of Law, USA.

Gustavo Ghidini, Professor of IP law at the University of Milan, and Luiss Guido Carli University, Rome, Italy.

Branislav Hazucha, Associate Professor at the Hokkaido University Graduate School of Law, Japan.

Torsten Bjørn Larsen, post-doctoral researcher at the University of Copenhagen, Denmark.

Hsiao-Chien Liu, Research Fellow at the Hokkaido University Research Institute for Information Law and Policy, Japan.

Charles R. McManis, Thomas & Karole Green Professor of Law at Washington University and the founder, former director and co-director of the law school's Center on Law, Innovation and Economic Growth, USA.

Caroline B. Ncube, Associate Professor in the Department of Commercial Law at the University of Cape Town, South Africa.

Begoña G. Otero, Assistant Dean at the European University Business School of Munich, Germany.

Charlotte Waelde, Professor of Intellectual Property Law at the University of Exeter, UK.

Toshihide Watabe, in-house lawyer for Voyage Group, Inc., Tokyo, Japan.

Kimberlee Weatherall, Associate Professor at the Sydney Law School, University of Sydney, Australia.

Introduction

Graeme B. Dinwoodie*

As part of the maxim *Lex specialis derogat legi generali*, the rule of *lex specialis* typically serves as an interpretative canon to determine which of two competing norms should govern.[1] Even within this narrow rubric, consideration of the maxim throws up some difficult questions: most fundamentally, what is the scope of this thing called 'intellectual property law' that constitutes a *lex specialis*, and which is the body of general law against which possible displacement by special rules is to be considered? As to the former, the vintage of the term 'intellectual property' has been the subject of some scholarly exploration.[2] At the international level, it might be thought to represent some amalgam of 'industrial property' (patents, designs and marks) dealt with by the Paris Convention and 'literary and artistic property' addressed by the Berne Convention.[3] But that undoubtedly is too simple an explanation. Even with a definition of 'intellectual property' now contained in the TRIPS Agreement, there remains debate about the borders of the concept, let alone its essence.[4] Thus, the narrow task of applying the maxim *lex specialis derogat legi generali* to such matters as copyright, patent, trade mark and their allied

* Professor of Intellectual Property and Information Technology Law, University of Oxford; Director, Oxford Intellectual Property Research Centre.

[1] *See* International Law Commission, *Fragmentation of International Law: Difficulties Arising from the Diversification and Expansion of International Law: Report of the Study Group on the Fragmentation of International Law*, Finalized by Martti Koskenniemi, UN Doc. A/ CN.4/L.682 (April 13, 2006).

[2] *See, e.g.,* Justin Hughes, A Short History of 'Intellectual Property' in Relation to Copyright, 33 Cardozo Law Review 1293 (2012).

[3] Paris Convention for the Protection of Industrial Property, July 14, 1967, 21 U.S.T. 1583, 828 U.N.T.S. 305; Berne Convention for the Protection of Literary and Artistic Works, July 24, 1971, 1161 U.N.T.S. 3.

[4] *See, e.g.,* Appellate Body Report, United States – Section 211 Omnibus Appropriations Act of 1998, WT/DS176/AB/R (August 6, 2001).

regimes (to pick a non-definitional phrase) would present plenty of opportunities for disagreement.

In this volume, the *lex specialis* label is used even more broadly, however, to connect a whole series of possible questions, including at the most abstract level: what is the relationship between intellectual property law and general legal principles? But this broader inquiry inevitably mimics some of the questions that would be at the heart of the narrower interpretative task. Most basically, to what extent are intellectual property laws exceptional? There is tendency – perhaps found in any area where a community of scholars and legal practitioners specialise – to think that what we do is special, advanced and not accessible to those not part of the specialist community. But when intellectual property comes to assume as prominent a social and economic role as it now does on a worldwide basis, it is especially important to question the costs and benefits of treating it apart from general principles of law.

Thus, several authors in this volume consider the extent to which intellectual property laws displace or conflict with generally applicable legal rules. This inquiry has perhaps been most developed in the private law sphere and that is reflected in the book. Giuseppina D'Agostino, Charles R. McManis and Brett Garrison, and Caroline Ncube each consider (in different ways) the interaction of intellectual property (especially copyright) law with principles of contract law. Branislav Hazucha, Hsiao-Chien Liu and Toshihide Watabe do the same as regards consumer protection principles in Japan.

Underlying much of the discussion in these chapters is a debate about the normative force of intellectual property principles, and the extent to which those norms should be impervious to alteration by market actors. That too is a tension underlying the contribution by Begoña Otero.

The centrality of intellectual property to contemporary society also brings it potentially into conflict with public law commitments, and such conflicts are addressed as part of a broader analysis by Gustavo Ghidini. The same is true of procedural law. Is it appropriate that disputes about intellectual property are increasingly adjudicated by specialist courts and judges, and how does it alter the development and interpretation of intellectual property law? In the US Supreme Court *Myriad* case, Justice Antonin Scalia joined the judgment of the Court, 'except,' he wrote, '[the portions] going into fine details of molecular biology. I am unable to affirm those details on my own knowledge or even my own belief.'[5] One

[5] *See* Ass'n for Molecular Pathology v. Myriad Genetics, Inc., 133 S. Ct. 2107 (2013).

wonders what this means for the rational development of patent law, or indeed for the standing of judicial decisions generally? Kimberlee Weatherall and Torsten Bjørn Larsen explore such adjectival and enforcement issues, areas where nation states have traditionally assumed greater sovereignty. If some convergence or harmonisation of such traditionally local principles is required or appropriate, is that easier if confined to matters of intellectual property law, rather than essayed with respect to procedure or enforcement generally?[6]

Exploring the purported exceptionalism of intellectual property sometimes provokes insights about the essence of intellectual property, or the need to revisit a precept that was thought to help define intellectual property (and perhaps set it apart). This lies at the heart, in particular, of the chapters by Severine Dusollier, Irene Calboli, and Abbe Brown and Charlotte Waelde.

Finally, in addition to helping us to look inward as intellectual property scholars, examining the interaction between intellectual property law and other bodies of law and critically assessing the exceptional nature of our regime allows us to look outwards and ask whether exceptionalism sacrifices law generally, learning the potential lessons of intellectual property law. Does its purportedly special nature preclude intellectual property law from contributing as fully as it might to the development of general legal principles, which may of course reinforce that suggestion that this is a narrow field, known only to, and requiring, specialists?

The question at the heart of this volume is thus a conduit for a number of different inquiries. They address the essence of intellectual property law, the role of intellectual property within broader legal institutions, and hopefully invite an engagement by legal scholars generally with a field of law that – for all its purported exceptionalism – is too significant socially and commercially to be considered only by specialists.

---

[6] *Cf.* TRIPS Agreement, art. 41(5) ('this Part does not create any obligation to put in place a judicial system for the enforcement of intellectual property rights distinct from that for the enforcement of law in general, nor does it affect the capacity of Members to enforce their law in general. Nothing in this Part creates any obligation with respect to the distribution of resources as between enforcement of intellectual property rights and the enforcement of law in general.').

1. Contract *lex rex*: Towards copyright contract's *lex specialis*

Giuseppina D'Agostino

INTRODUCTION

Intellectual property regimes, of which copyright law is generally perceived as a constitutive part, create entitlement interests, whereas contract law manages these entitlements. Copyright is thus inextricably bound to contract law. In practice, this relationship is one of subordination: contract law trumps the various entitlements copyright creates. As a result, the aims of copyright law must constantly confront the law of contract and the values on which it is premised. When this confrontation leads to tension between these two domains of law, legislatures and courts ensure that the law of contract reigns supreme, and is the *lex rex*. It may be tempting to reduce this issue to an inevitable consequence of having a *lex generalis*, such as contract law, refuse to cede ground to a *lex specialis* like copyright; indeed, one might thus question the *lex specialis* nature of copyright vis-à-vis contract law. Perhaps copyright law is the *lex generalis*, with contract law being *lex specialis* on matters of contract. But, as this speculation suggests, to engage in this kind of categorization does little to advance a solution to the tension. Ultimately, defining copyright's *specialis* status is much less consequential than explaining its relationship to contract law, and it is that hierarchical relationship that has the most bearing on creators who fuel the cultural industries, especially freelance authors. A more integrative approach is therefore vital.

I argue that there is a need for a more copyright-contract-centric *lex*: contract law should be more fully integrated into copyright in order to adequately serve the aims of copyright law, specifically those that center on providing creators with effective management and remuneration for their copyright-protected works. Indeed, without the workings of contract law, copyright law has little relevance to the needs of creators (or anyone else for that matter). From this perspective, whether copyright is a *lex specialis* seems rather beside the point. Contract law is predicated on freedom of contract, and my analysis must necessarily start to showcase the emphasis placed on this doctrine, and how it has been enshrined in both domestic legislation and jurisprudence (especially in common law countries) as well as internationally to copyright's detriment. On the international front, I discuss Berne's preoccupation in ensuring the sanctity of freedom of contract, especially as it purports to be an authors' rights statute. To further analyze the domestic shortcomings of freedom of contract, I then apply the *lex rex* status of contract law and its reliance on freedom of contract to consider the plight of the freelance author in new media as a case study. In this context, copyright law is inadequate and its objectives undermined as authors go unrewarded and unprotected, left to their own devices to engage in protracted litigation with symbolic results. Ultimately, I propose a series of mechanisms rooted in contract law, to keep freedom of contract restrained and to improve copyright law's inadequacies. Perhaps this way, copyright law or better, copyright contract can truly become a governing *lex specialis*.

A. COPYRIGHT AND CONTRACT

Copyright statutes assume a *specialis* character in that they establish a particular set of rights for authors of works: they provide entitlement interests to protect authors' "expression of their ideas".[1] Copyright law typically grants authors protection to a number of categories of works, including literary works, whether in print or digital form. Authors are the first owners of copyright in the works that they create.[2] The author is an individual who is solely responsible and exclusively deserving of the credit for the creation of a work.[3] If an author creates a work in the

---

[1] Of course, for Lord Hailsham, defining the term "the expression of ideas" depends on what is meant by an "idea." See *LB (Plastics) Limited v Swish Products Limited* (1979) RPC 551 (HL) where copyright in production drawings for knock-down furniture drawers prevented one company from copying the commercial furniture produced by a competitor. The idea/expression dichotomy may not be very useful if the concept of idea is not fully understood.

[2] Canada *Copyright Act*, RSC 1985, c C-42, s 13(1) [CCA].

[3] M. Woodmansee 'The Genius and the Copyright: Economic and Legal Conditions of the Emergence of the "Author"' Eighteenth-Century Studies 425–48, 426. Here there is no shortage of debate on who is an author; indeed many are critical of the singular classification of authorship; e.g. C.J. Craig 'Locke, Labour and Limiting the Author's Right: A Warning against a Lockean Approach to Copyright Law' (2002) 28 Queen's LJ 1.

course of his or her employment, copyright in the work vests in the employer, unless there is a contract between the two parties stating otherwise.[4] And so, via contract law, authors who are the first owners of copyright (or their stand-ins), manage their rights either via licenses or assignments, which can be made in whole or in part. The validity of these kinds of contracts is contingent on them being signed and in writing.[5] The more *generalis* body of contract law manages these entitlements. The law of contract was designed to facilitate the enforcement of private bargains arranged between parties. Without contract law, copyright law has little meaning. Copyright law is often said to be mindful of balancing a variety of interests in the public interest, among which is protecting the author.[6] Ensuring that copyright and contract law are properly working together is important to meeting copyright's objectives, especially when protecting authors' entitlement interests.

1. Contract's Freedom of Contract: The Sacred Doctrine Legally Enshrined

Contract law is premised on the doctrine of freedom of contract, which posits that individuals and organizations are free and independent to enter into private agreements within a market economy. Adam Smith in his *Wealth of Nations* (1776) offered the first sustained account of economic affairs, heralding the cause of freedom of trade against that era's prevalent economic protectionism: freedom of contract was embraced as

---

4 CCA, *supra* note 2 at s 13(3).

5 *Ibid.* at s 13(4). A mere license which does not grant an interest in the copyright need not be in writing. See JS McKeown Fox Canadian Law of Copyright and Industrial Designs (3rd edn Carswell Scarborough 2000) 388 and *Robertson v Thomson Corp*, 2006 SCC 43, [2006] 2 SCR 363, [*Robertson SCC*] interpreting this issue at para 135.

6 There is no purpose clause available in the various domestic copyright statutes, and courts have over the course of the years made different pronouncements on what copyright's purpose is; see, for instance, the often cited *Théberge v Galerie d'Art du Petit Champlain inc.*, [2002] 2 S.C.R. 336,2002 SCC 34 [30] stating, "The *Copyright Act* is usually presented as a balance between promoting the public interest in the encouragement and dissemination of works of the arts and intellect and obtaining a just reward for the creator (or, more accurately, to prevent someone other than the creator from appropriating whatever benefits may be generated)". WF Grosheide 'Copyright Law from a User's Perspective: Access Rights for Users' (2001) 23(7) EIPR 321–5, 321 discussing copyright's once idealistic "golden triangle" of interests.

an ideal of classical economic theory and classical contract law.[7] Freedom of contract featured two closely interlinked yet distinct ideas: (1) contracts were based on mutual agreement, and (2) the creation of a contract was the result of a free choice unhampered by external control such as government or legislative interference.[8] In other words, there should be no liability without the consent embodied in a valid contract. This second and negative aspect of freedom of contract narrowed the scope of the law of obligations dealing with liability imposed by law.[9] The assumption was that the parties were independently willed and sophisticated and had equal opportunity to enter such bargains to maximize their individual interests. Besides the obvious categories for which the nineteenth-century law made special provisions, such as persons below the age of capacity and lunatics, the law assumed that if a person entered into a burdensome contract, "he had only himself to blame because there was freedom of contract and he could have gone elsewhere."[10] Freedom of choice as manifested through the intention of the parties was thus at the root of freedom of contract in its classical form. And individualism was at the root of the justifications commonly advanced for freedom of contract.[11]

The ability to enter into agreements with others was thus considered a fundamental dimension of human freedom in Western liberal democracies. This private ordering played a crucial role in wealth maximization, to make commercial ventures possible. Failing to provide an individual with the ability to freely contract with others was perceived as an affront to that individual dignity. Jessel MR epitomizes this conviction in his decision for *Printing & Numerical Registering Co v Sampson*:

> [I]f there is one thing which more than another public policy requires it is that men of full age and competent understanding shall have the utmost liberty of contracting, and that their contracts when entered into freely and voluntarily should be held sacred.[12]

---

[7] J Beatson *Anson's Law of Contract* (28th edn Oxford University Press Oxford 2002) 4.

[8] PS Atiyah and S Smith *Atiyah's Introduction to the Law of Contract* (6th edn Clarendon Press Oxford 2005) 9–11.

[9] As in tort and restitution; see Beatson, *supra* note 7 at 4.

[10] Atiyah, *supra* note 8 at 16.

[11] S Wheeler and J Shaw *Contract Law* (Clarendon Press Oxford 2001) 36.

[12] *Printing & Numerical Registering Co v Sampson* (1875), LR 19 Eq 462 at 465.

While contemporary liberal democracies may not abide by as strict a commitment to freedom of contract as Jessel MR exemplifies, freedom of contract still remains a fundamental value within the law of contract, and by extension copyright law.

Modern day copyright courts still seem to echo Jessel MR's conviction. In the Supreme Court of Canada (SCC), Lebel and Fish JJ asserted that at the end of the day no matter what the law says, "parties are, have been, and will continue to be free to, alter by contract the rights established by the *Copyright Act*."[13] The *Robertson* decision, which merits attention later, as it cuts through the heart of these issues, illustrates the reverence placed on freedom of contract. And so, when contemporary courts are asked to step in and interpret copyright issues, courts should not be seen as meddling with parties' freedoms to contract.[14] Contract is the *lex rex.*

This sacrosanct status afforded to freedom of contract is not limited to courts but is also present in copyright legislation, and is most pronounced in common law jurisdictions. For instance, the UK and Canadian copyright statutes merely mandate that a contract conveying a proprietary interest must be signed and be in writing.[15] Contrast this *laissez-faire* approach with civilian statutes that impose more copyright-contract-centric restrictions.[16]

Significantly, international copyright treaties, to which states adhere, pay similar homage to freedom of contract. As an example of this preoccupation is the making of the Berne Convention for the Protection of Literary and Artistic Works[17] and ensuring that authors could contract away their rights to successors in title. In 1886, sustained pressure on the part of creators culminated with the signing of the Berne Convention.

---

13 *Robertson SCC supra* note 5 at para 58.

14 Canadian courts' equitable jurisdiction provides the judicial capacity to strike down contracts in whole, or in part, on the basis of unconscionable terms or conduct, though equity has seldom been used. See Giuseppina D'Agostino, *Copyright, Contracts, Creators: New Media, New Rules* (Cheltenham: Edward Elgar Publishing Ltd, 2010) at 72–75, 135–137 [*Copyright, Contracts, Creators*]; Giuseppina D'Agostino, "Canada's *Robertson* Ruling: Any Practical Significance for Freelance Authors?" [2007] 2 EIPR 66 [*Canada's Robertson Ruling*].

15 In the UK *Copyright, Designs and Patents Act* 1988 c 48 as amended [CDPA]; s 92(1), in CCA, *supra* note 2, s 13(4).

16 For instance, see a host of provisions in Québec and Continental Europe which are discussed at length in ch 6 at 121–129 in *Copyright, Contracts, Creators, supra* note 14.

17 Berne Convention for the Protection of Literary and Artistic Works 9 Sept 1886 168 Consol TS 185 [*Berne*].

Prior to the signing of Berne there had only been an incomplete network of bilateral agreements between nations, thus creators were drawn to Berne's broad international reach.[18] Unfortunately, Berne did not wholly turn out to be the vehicle for change that creators thought it would be.

At the heart of why the Berne Convention failed to live up to its pro-author pretensions is a conflict between two divergent perspectives on copyright, rooted in varying views of liberty and freedom of contract: the universalist/absolutist view of countries of the *droit d'auteur* tradition in civilian countries and the national pragmatic view of common law countries. Whereas the former's focus was on the "author's natural right of property in his works", the latter was much more concerned with the "author's rights in economic terms" that should be traded without restriction.[19] This divergence between legal cultures on copyright's proper conceptualization played itself out over the course of the many meetings that led up to the most recent Act of the Berne Convention.[20] The practical outcome of this tension was the preservation of freedom of contract and the slow withering away of the authors or the *droit d'auteur* as a fundamental concern of the Berne Convention.

While Berne contained a variety of pro-author provisions,[21] the promise for authors was diluted by the implicit assumption that once an author attained protection under Berne, the protection could also be enjoyed by their successors in title, such as beneficiaries and assignees.[22] This concern with protecting the assigns of authors, and thus freedom to contract, in addition to the authors themselves, became a long-standing theme in the various conferences of Berne, which was ultimately codified in Berne Convention of 1886. Including these terms in Berne solidified the presence of publishers at the negotiating tables and strengthened their status as a relevant stakeholder in international copyright legislation.

Much as one would not expect a consumers' protection act to protect sellers, one would not expect an authors' international protection statute

---

18 Sam Ricketson, 'The Boundaries of Copyright: Its Proper Limitations and Exceptions: International Conventions and Treaties' (1999) 1 IPQ 57, at 61.

19 Sam Ricketson, *The Berne Convention for the Protection of Literary and Artistic Works: 1886–1986* (London: Kluwer, 1987) at 40–41.

20 Paris Convention 1971, as amended 1979.

21 Some of the original pro-author provisions within the convention included: the recognition of authors' rights in their works across all nations irrespective of reciprocity, a limited copyright term of 50 years in addition to the author's life, no formalities in obtaining copyright protection, and the abolition or reduction of customs duties on books and works of art. See *Berne*, *supra* note 17 at 42–45.

22 *Ibid.* at 173.

to protect publishers. Instead, throughout its long history, Berne showed a preoccupation with protecting copyright exploiters. Unfortunately, this tendency persisted as subsequent international copyright treaties, including the Universal Copyright Convention, the Agreement on Trade-Related Aspects of Intellectual Property Rights, the North American Free Trade Agreement, and the WIPO Copyright Treaty, propagated Berne's validation of freedom of contract and proved themselves to be authors' assigns' statutes, more than they are authors' statutes.[23]

2. Shortcomings of Freedom of Contract for Copyright and Creators

It is with respect to copyright's reliance on parties' ability to contract with little restriction that freedom of contract begins to impede the aims of copyright law. One of copyright law's aims is to protect authors.[24] Contract law functions on the basis of *consensus ad idem* between two or more parties, free of external coercion. In other words, contracts consist of a meeting of minds between parties, and the legitimacy of a meeting of minds is contingent on the absence of undue coercion. The assumption is that parties are autonomous and sufficiently sophisticated to understand the implications of the bargain they are entering. But more often than not, power imbalances exist between parties entering into a private agreement. Significant power imbalances between parties in a contract can bring into question the legitimacy of the bargain, and thus the contract itself.

In the case of freelance authors, they often lack free choice as they are subject to power imbalances *vis-à-vis* publishers.[25] These power imbalances are largely a result of the day-to-day realities faced by freelancers who write for multinational publishing conglomerates of mainstream newspapers and magazines. The freelance author's job is to write articles that are often specialized and heavily researched. However, unlike staff writers, freelancers must do so without the help of support staff, without benefits and a pension plan, and most importantly without the security of a regular salary. In 2005 the Professional Writers Association of Canada (PWAC) executed a study and found that Canadian freelancers made an average annual income of CDN$24 035; 38 percent of freelancers made

[23] For a fuller discussion on the inadequacies of these international copyright treaties, see D'Agostino, *supra* note 14 at 99–111.

[24] See *Théberge* and Grosheide, *supra* note 6.

[25] Publishers are not all the same. I am mainly concerned with the larger publishing conglomerates such as Comcast, Time Warner, Disney and Viacom. See *Copyright, Contracts, Creators*, *supra* note 14 at 16–39.

less than CDN$10 000, while 32 percent made more than CDN$3000.[26] Freelancers thus offer publishers a cheaper source of content production compared with their employed counterparts and their average income has not increased over the last 20 years.[27]

The same freelancer hardship holds true in other nations as well. In the United States, average freelancer earnings are in the range of US$7500, and only 16 percent of full-time freelancers earn US$30 000 or above.[28] In the UK, the average annual freelance earnings hover around £16 000, with 46 percent of freelancers earning under £5000.[29] Lionel Bently provides significant context for these average annual rates of freelancer remuneration when he considers them alongside the current earnings of the cultural industries, which are approximately £110 billion per year.[30]

If these impediments were not enough, freelance jobs are also limited in number, which makes it difficult for freelancers to find work. The difficulty associated with securing a freelance contract forces them to engage in significant amounts of self-promotion and marketing, which takes time away from their writing. Freelancers live contract to contract. For staff writers, the "works made for hire" or "during course of

---

[26] The years have only added to the economic hardship faced by freelancers for in 1996 they showed an average annual income of CDN$26 000, and in 1979 CDN$25 000. Professional Writers Association of Canada (PWAC) Canadian Professional Writers Survey (Canada Magazine Fund and Department of Canadian Heritage May 2006) 27. A 2015 study in progress by G D'Agostino and commissioned by the Writers Union of Canada on authors vis-à-vis collective licensing in Canada indicates the same grim figures [on file with author].

[27] Professional Writers Association of Canada and Quantum Communications, *Canadian Professional Writers Survey: A profile of the freelance writing sector in Canada* (May 2006), online: Professional Writers Association of Canada <http://www.pwac.ca/files/PDF/PWACsurvey.pdf>.

[28] N DuVergne Smith "The Composite Writers Lot" (NWU Survey 1995); The US Bureau of Labor Statistics report on Occupational Employment and Wages (May 2007). http://www.bls.gov/oes/current/oes273043.htm does not consider self-employed workers in its statistics but the US Department of Labor recognizes that "Many writers are considered freelance writers": 'Writers and Editors' http://www.bls.gov/oco/ocos089.htm.

[29] Lionel Bently, *Between a Rock and a Hard Place: The Problems Facing Freelance Creators in the UK Media Market Place* (London: The Institute of Employment Rights, 2002) citing a study from the Society of Authors conducted in 2000 where 1171 members responded. See M Kretschmer and P Hardwick 'Authors' Earnings from Copyright and Non-Copyright Sources: A Survey of 25,000 British and German Writers' (CIPPM/ALCS Bournemouth University UK 2007).

[30] Bently *supra* note 29 at 14.

employment doctrine" applies (where copyright vests in employers) but for freelancers who base their livelihoods on each new contract, the issue is a vital one; legally, they are treated as independent contractors and meant to retain copyright, unless there is a contract stating otherwise. As authors and publishers are not on an even playing field which results in uneven bargaining, authors are less and less the owners over their works and/or lose control over the exploitation of, and gains from, their work. As a result, freedom of contract and, ultimately, copyright's lofty objectives to protect authors reduce to nothing more than illusory aspirations. The situation has grown so abysmal that some commentators have called freelancers the modern-day sweatshop workers.[31] Therefore ensuring fair copyright contracting between authors and their publishers is crucial to allowing freelancers to benefit from the copyright system. The dynamics of the freelance author-publisher relationship, and the ever escalating speed of new technologies and new platforms for publication, illustrates this persisting and worsening copyright contract problem and the need for redress.

B. NEW MEDIA AND THE PROFESSIONAL CREATOR: FREELANCERS FOR FREE

More and more copyright-protected work is born digital and publishers reuse old works in new media. More and more authors are contracted, rather than employed, by publishers.[32] The same is true for other creative industries, as OECD statistics point to a rise of independent contract work.[33]

Prior to the onset of the digital age, the publishing industry's contractual dealings with freelancers were substantially different and more salutary. Up until the early 1990s, it was common practice for publishers to have freelancers submit articles without an express written contract,

---

[31] Or as "economic refugees": Deborah Smeaton, 'Self-employed Workers: Calling the Shots or Hesitant Dependents? A Consideration of the Trends' (2003) 17(2) Work, Employment and Society 379 at 381.

[32] As a result, freelancers do not enjoy the benefits of having a support staff, sick leave, a pension, and a consistent and reasonable wage. See *Copyright, Contracts, Creators*, *supra* note 14 at 22–24.

[33] See OECD, 'Partial Renaissance of Self-Employment' in *OECD Employment Outlook* (2000), online: OECD <http://www.oecd.org/els/emp/2079593.pdf>.

and those submissions were generally for one-time print publishing.[34] Freelancers experienced less delay with respect to payment; writers' fees were agreed upon and paid soon after their article was published. In the event that a publisher sought to make a change to the original publication, such as a reprint or a translation, the freelancer would customarily receive additional fees on top of the original flat fee they were paid for the first publication.[35]

In more recent times, publishers have relied on previous oral contracts, silent on digital uses, and have repurposed freelance works in electronic databases, websites and CD-ROMS, often with third parties without due notice, consent or remuneration to authors. In doing so, publishers have secured a new avenue to profit from authors' works to authors' disapproval.

1. Copyright Contract Litigation

Over the course of the last decade, various cases have been litigated across the globe as freelancers have sued publishers for copyright infringement. Freelancers argue that they receive no notice, give no consent, and obtain no payment for the exploitation of their works through new digital uses. Publishers justify: (1) there is no difference between the media, (2) even if they are infringing, contracts previously made with their freelancers allow them to exploit new uses of such works and (3) assuming they have to pay the authors, they want a wait and see approach, as they reorganize their business models to stay afloat.

The central issue is one of copyright contract: whether the authors' contracts, through which copyright was licensed/transferred, contemplated electronic publication rights. There exists ambiguity in the ownership and control of future works largely because many pre-dated new technologies. At issue is the period pre-dating electronic publication (before 1990s) when there were no written contracts; only key terms such as submission date and word count were agreed upon. While many cases were litigated in continental Europe, I highlight the twin common law

[34] National Union of Journalists and Contributors, *Freelance Briefing Paper*, online: National Union of Journalists <http://media.gn.apc.org/ar/briefing.html> indicating increasing attempts to formalize the relationship. Absent fieldwork, it is difficult accurately to gauge the specific types of agreements between authors and publishers; Laurie A Santelli, 'Notes and Comments: New Battles between Freelancer Authors and Publishers in the Aftermath of *Tasini v New York Times*' (1998) 7 JL & Policy 253 at 262.

[35] *Ibid.*

cases of *Tasini* in the US and *Robertson* in Canada as they best illustrate the copyright licensing issues.[36]

In *Tasini v New York Times Co*,[37] the United States Supreme Court was faced with deciding whether 21 articles written for The New York Times Company, Newsday Inc., and Time Inc. by six freelancer authors, represented by Jonathan Tasini, could be reproduced in electronic media without their consent. The majority ultimately held that reproducing the articles in the electronic media fell outside the publisher's privilege conferred by section 201(c) of the Copyright Act 1976, which reads:

> In the absence of an express transfer of copyright or of any rights under it, the owner of copyright in a collective work is presumed to have acquired only the privilege of reproducing and distributing the contribution as part of that particular collective work, any revision of that collective work, and any later collective work in the same series.[38]

Taking a purposive approach to interpreting the provision, the majority held that collective rights owners could only reproduce constituent parts of their collective work in context and not standing alone.[39] Because the reproductions of the articles in question were capable of being individually accessed through the electronic media, and publishers had not explicitly bargained for the ability to individually reproduce the articles in this way, the Supreme Court found the publishers liable of copyright infringement.

Tasini is arguably a significant triumph for freelance authors, but is far from a panacea solution to the copyright contract problems that gave rise to the litigation in the first place, which were no longer an issue by the time the case made its way to the Supreme Court.[40] None of the *New York Times*' freelancers had any written agreement with the publisher. However, at the District Court, it was argued by *Newsday* and *Time* that

---

[36] For the continental European jurisprudence see *Copyright, Contracts, Creators, supra* note 14 at 164–176.

[37] *Tasini v New York Times Co* 533 US 483, 121 S Ct 2381 (2001) [*Tasini*].

[38] Copyright Act 1976 17 USC [USCA].

[39] Often referred to as the "decontextualization" test. *Tasini supra* note 37 at 496; 2389. See discussion in *Copyright, Contracts, Creators, supra* note 14 at 141–151.

[40] In *Tasini v New York Times Co* 972 F Supp 804 (NYSD Ct 1997) [*Tasini* DT] the District Court released a ruling for summary judgment in favour of the defendant publishers, and in *Tasini v New York Times Co* 981 F Supp 841 (NYSD Ct 2001) the Appeals Court denied the authors' motion for reconsideration [*Tasini* CA].

their freelancers had "expressly transferred" the electronic rights in their articles, and as a result were not open to the benefits of section 201(c).[41] For instance, *Time*, relying on a motion picture decision,[42] argued that language in its contractual agreement with Whitford, the freelancer, included no "media-based limitation", implying that its first publication rights within the agreement should be interpreted to publish the freelancer's work in LexisNexis' electronic database.[43] The District Court ultimately ruled in *Time*'s favor, but was later reversed on appeal. Interestingly, *Time* could have made an alternative argument on the basis of seeking to enforce its rights under clauses (b) and (c) of the Whitford Contract. Doing so would have allowed them to validate their electronic rights, and defend themselves against the copyright infringement claim. In *obiter*, the District Court took the opportunity to ask why *Time* had not done so.[44] This seemingly rhetorical question was answered by the Appeals Court: if *Time* had enforced these rights under clauses (b) and (c) of the freelancer agreement, then they would have had to abide by its license and compensate the freelancer for putting his work to a new use.[45]

Time's opportunistic approach to the contractual issue is symptomatic of how publishers approach freelancer contracts more generally. They will enforce contracts at their convenience and expect to own the copyright in freelancers' works as a matter of course. They fail to seek permission for additional uses, and when they do, they avoid compensating freelancers. After their defeat in *Tasini*, the *New York Times* adopted a new policy to only accept freelance articles for which authors were willing to surrender all of their copyright. The *New York Times* also thought it appropriate to blacklist the *Tasini* plaintiffs from ever publishing with them.[46] Collectively, these measures undermine any of the freelancers' judicial success and suggest more of a pyrrhic victory.

---

41 *Tasini DT*, *ibid.* at para 809.

42 *Bartsch v Metro-Goldwyn-Mayer Inc* 391 F2d 150, 154–5 cert denied 393 US 826, 89 S Ct 86 (1968) holding that the right to "exhibit" a motion picture included the right to exhibit movies on television.

43 *Tasini DT*, *supra* note 40 at para 811.

44 It is important to keep in mind that *Time* had only alleged "first publication rights" pursuant to Whitford Contract clause 10(a).

45 *Tasini CA*, *supra* note 40 at para 171.

46 M Williams 'Memo to News Executives re Tasini Plaintiffs' (18 Sept 2001) www.nwu.org referring to Tasini, discussed in *Copyright, Contracts, Creators*, *supra* note 14 at 27, 151.

Post *Tasini*, there were a number of class actions launched by the Authors Guild, the American Society of Journalists and Authors (ASJA) and several freelancers against LexisNexis, Dow Jones Interactive and other publishers. These lawsuits, also known as *Tasini* No 2, claim copyright infringement for works dating back to 1978, and were joined and ordered into mandatory mediation and to date have met unsuccessful results.[47] The US Appeals Court for the Second Circuit rejected the settlement of US$18 million and further litigation continues.[48] Ultimately, in Yuri Hur's words, what the *Tasini* disputes highlight is the "continuing struggle between freelance writers and publishers over compensation for the electronic publication of copyrighted material."[49]

Robertson v Thomson Corp[50] is Canada's version of *Tasini*, which displays a similar decision-making approach and has also fuelled ongoing litigation. Before discussing the appellate and Supreme Court of Canada decisions, I examine the first instance decision, as it more appropriately introduces the issues, especially those concerning the copyright licenses between the parties. Like *Tasini*, *Robertson* is a copyright infringement case dealing with the issues of: (1) whether electronic reproduction violates the individual copyright of the owner or whether such reproduction falls within the copyright of the collective author and, in the alternative, (2) although the newspaper company may have infringed the plaintiff's copyright, whether it may have an implied license or implied term defense.[51] However, unlike *Tasini*, where there were individual joined plaintiffs, in *Robertson*, Heather Robertson headed a class of plaintiffs. Robertson is a well-known Canadian writer who contributed

---

47 *Reed Elsevier and others v Muchnick and others* (US Ct of Appeals 2nd Ct, docket 08-103). For comment see: http://lawprofessors.typepad.com/civpro/2010/03/commentary-on-reed-elsevier-v-muchnick-a-win-for-jurisdictional-clarity.html

48 *In re Literary Works in Electronic Databases Copyright Litigation* MDL 1379; F 3d 2007 WL 4197413 (2d Ct 2007). The Supreme Court granted the case a hearing on 2 March 2009 in order to decide whether the USCA s 411(a) restricts the subject matter jurisdiction of the federal courts over copyright infringement. In August 2011, the US Supreme Court dismissed the action. See Andrew Albanese, 'Second Circuit Rejects "Freelance" Settlement' http://www.publishersweekly.com/pw/by-topic/digital/copyright/article/48401-second-circuit-rejects-freelance-settlement.html

49 Y Hur 'Tasini v New York Times: Ownership of Electronic Copyrights Rightfully Returned to Authors' (2000) 21 Loyola LA Ent LJ 65.

50 *Robertson SCC*, *supra* note 5.

51 *Ibid.* para 2; against *Robertson*'s trial case, *Tasini* argued the statutory action of copyright infringement in the alternative.

two individual works to the newsprint edition of *The Globe & Mail* (*The Globe*).[52] These works were subsequently stored electronically and made available to the public for a fee by various electronic media, including CD-ROM and Internet databases.[53] Similar to the publishers in *Tasini*, Thomson Corporation is a large multimedia company with various subsidiaries in the business of publishing newspapers such as *The Globe*.

In contrast to *Tasini*, where there were no written agreements except for the plaintiff Whitford's, in *Robertson*, *The Globe* entered into a letter agreement with Robertson's publisher McClelland & Stewart in August 1995 for one-time usage of one of her works for a fee, which made no reference to electronic rights. Beginning in February 1996, *The Globe* entered into a written contract with numerous freelancers, which it revised in December 1996 in order to expand the electronic rights clause, which read:

> for perpetual inclusion in the internal and commercially available databases and other storage media (electronic and otherwise) of *The Globe* or its assignees and products (electronic and otherwise) derived therefrom.[54]

The first instance court determined that *The Globe* had infringed Robertson's copyright by including her two articles into the databases and CD-ROM, but found the licensing issues problematic and thus could not grant summary judgment as there was a genuine issue for trial. Section 13(4) of the *Act* provides that assignments and proprietary licenses must be made in writing, but a mere license that grants no interest in the copyright need not be in writing. *The Globe* argued that it possessed a license to the electronic rights to the articles based on implied terms in the contract entered into by Robertson, or an implied license. *The Globe* claimed entitlement to a "continuing right of perpetuity to reproduce the plaintiff's freelance articles throughout the world through electronic on-line databases via the Internet."[55] Robertson, on the other hand, contended that a grant of the kind envisioned by *The Globe* implied the

---

[52] According to the Statement of Claim, the class has been defined as: "anyone who created literary or artistic work published in Canada in the print media and which has been reproduced through computer databases since April 24, 1979" (the launch date of Info Globe Online, one of the online databases to which Robertson's works were posted). T Down 'Suing Thomson: It's a Classic David and Goliath Story' (1999) 5(4) Media 14–15. See *Canada's Robertson Ruling*, *supra* note 14.

[53] *Robertson* SCC *supra* note 5, para 2.

[54] *Ibid.* at para 22.

[55] *Ibid.* at para 168.

granting of a proprietary interest in her copyright, and so *The Globe* would need to comport with section 13(4) of the *Act*.

The court ultimately held that *The Globe*'s license did not need to be in writing because it was non-exclusive, and thus does not convey a proprietary interest in Robertson's copyright. The fact that Robertson retained the rights to publish and further exploit her work suggests that the implied license was non-exclusive.[56] On account of the conflicting evidence in the case, the court did not ultimately resolve the licensing issues and left the question open. However, the court did seem to suggest that *The Globe* likely could have contracted with Robertson more transparently about electronic rights given that its electronic database had been operational since 1977.[57] Moreover, prior to entering into the original agreement with Robertson for her work, *The Globe* had adopted the custom of only accepting articles that could be digitally distributed, which gave all the more reason to believe that they could have contracted more expressly, but actively chose not to do so.[58] Instead, *The Globe* chose to rely on their unstated, unilateral custom as a safeguard in its dealings with its freelancers, with Robertson being only one among many.

In the hope of resolving the scope of the implied license issue left undecided by the trial court, Robertson took the issue to the Ontario Court of Appeal. In addition to dismissing Robertson's appeal, the Court also dismissed *The Globe*'s cross-appeal with respect to copyright infringement. According to the appeal court, Robertson provided *The Globe* with a valid oral license, although it did not outline the full extent of the license. In other words, the court refused to address whether the reproduction of her work in the new media fell within the purview of the oral license allowing them to print and archive her articles on microfiche and microfilm. Throughout the proceedings, Robertson maintained that she had never contracted with *The Globe*, either orally or in writing, to use any of her works in new media.

At the SCC, the licensing issue remained unresolved as the court refused to go beyond agreeing with the appellate court's determination that an exclusive license need not be in writing.[59] Additionally, the court made it clear that licensing issues are best reserved for determination at trial. While the court found the publishers to have infringed the authors' electronic rights, it could still be found that freelancers had implied to

---

[56] *Ibid.* at para 77.
[57] *Ibid.* at para 23.
[58] *Ibid.* at paras 23–24.
[59] *Ibid.* at para 58.

forfeit all their digital rights to their publishers. For the SCC, "this decision will, of course, be of less practical significance. Parties are, have been, and will continue to be free, to alter by contract the rights established by the Copyright Act."[60] As noted, this pronouncement epitomizes the lasting status of freedom of contract within contract law, and the strong role that it can play within copyright law as a trump to the entitlement interests created by the statute. In the aftermath of the SCC decision, Robertson found herself pursuing another class-action lawsuit on similar grounds against a different set of publishers.[61] That case ultimately settled, signaling no judicial answer to the copyright contract issues to authors' ongoing ambiguous new media litigation.

2. Ongoing Litigation and Standard-form Contracts

Ongoing litigation persists in other creative sectors. For instance, a more recent decision in Canada's Federal Court also involved a freelancer and her digital rights.[62] At issue was whether a photographer, Catherine Leuthold, was entitled to remuneration from the Canadian Broadcasting Corporation (CBC) for making use of her photographs in ways that she had not explicitly consented to in a prior license she had granted to the CBC. The court's ultimate concern was to avoid "commercially absurd" interpretations of the contract: Leuthold contended that the license she had originally signed with the CBC allowed the use of her photographs in only one television broadcast per time zone because there was no explicit term in the contract that dictated otherwise.[63] For the court, the CBC could not have possibly sought such a limited license. The court privileged industry custom by considering the CBC's more reasonable interpretation of the contract over the less reasonable expectations of the creator.

Publishers often impose their industry custom and standard-form contracts to the authors' disadvantage.[64] Consider that since the high-profile freelance author litigation, publishers have "contracted around" the problem: they unilaterally enforce standard-form contracts, ensuring

---

60 *Ibid.*

61 See *Robertson v ProQuest Information and Learning LLC*, 2011 ONSC 2629, 18 CPC (7th) 406.

62 *Leuthold v Canadian Broadcasting Corporation*, 2012 FC 748, 413 FTR 162

63 *Ibid.* at para 89.

64 W Gordon 'Fine-Tuning Tasini: Privileges of Electronic Distribution and Reproduction' (2000) 66 Brooklyn LRev 473–500, 475.

that they possess all future reuse rights. These contracts, and often letter agreements (as observed in the UK, post *Tasini*),[65] say they give freelancers "copyright" but then allow publishers to reproduce freelancers' works, worldwide, in any media now known or unknown in perpetuity. The *modus operandi* of publishers seems premised on the simple philosophy of extracting all the possible rights that they can from their freelancers, waiting for their article or work to gain popularity, and then capturing the windfall if it comes to pass.[66] Or more alarmingly, some bypass these copyright contract issues altogether. For instance, other creative exploiters are changing the freelancer category of employment. Consider that the American Society of Media Photographers notes that new agreements are being written to cast freelancers as creating "works made for hire" (without the actual benefits of employment) so as to bypass any copyright issues that would be associated with independent contractors.[67]

C. TOWARDS A COPYRIGHT CONTRACT *LEX SPECIALIS*

Copyright law needs to evolve and embrace less its commitment to a dated mold of contract law, with freedom of contract at its roots, and more a modernized version of contract law. In the twentieth century, contract law itself evolved to protect the weaker parties. Atiyah notes the devolution of freedom of contract and rise of specialized bodies of law. Some important examples of government-imposed restrictions that evidence this recalibration of contract law include: landlord and tenant statutes, employment standards legislation, statutory restrictions on discrimination on the grounds of sex and race, and consumer protection law.[68] These restrictions suggest that contract law has become much more cognizant of inequalities between contracting parties than ever before. As

---

[65] Large daily newspapers such as the *Guardian*, *The Times*, the *Daily Telegraph* and the *Independent*. Sample letters provided in ch 2 *Copyright, Contracts, Creators*, *supra* note 14 and discussed at 178–179.

[66] See Lionel Bently, *Between a Rock and a Hard Place: The Problems Facing Freelance Creators in the UK Media Market Place* (London: The Institute of Employment Rights, 2002) at 6.

[67] 'Copyright, Creativity, and Commercialization,' Center for the Protection of Intellectual Property (Roundtable, June 20–21, 2013 Laguna Cliffs Marriott Resort, Dana Point, California).

[68] *Copyright, Contracts, Creators*, *supra* note 14 at 254.

such, copyright law may also stand to benefit in considering contract law's sensitivities in its perception of power relations between contracting parties. In what follows I will outline a series of potential paths that may lead towards a more copyright-contract-centric *lex* in its treatment of freelance authors.

1. Copyright Contract Legislative Intervention

Copyright and contract law should (and could) work better together to account for the imbalanced position of freelancers in the bargaining process. Here contract law is salutary when freedom of contract is put in check. Copyright law should contain more copyright-contract-centric provisions that restrict freedom of contract. Many continental jurisdictions already feature a variety of copyright contract clauses.[69] As such, legislative intervention is more sorely needed in common law countries which, as seen, embrace a *laissez-faire* ideology to private ordering.

As I have argued elsewhere,[70] attaining the copyright contract reform freelancers need may begin with legislating a pro-author default rule within copyright statutes. This rule would function similarly to the *contra proferentem* rule to interpret any ambiguity in the contract against the drafter. Further, besides it being used in contract law, such a rule was part of past UK legislation and case law; is used in current UK new-use jurisprudence and contract interpretation; is currently found in copyright statutes of other nations, such as Belgium (and these could be used as a template for drafting one into other copyright statutes); it can deal with inequalities of bargaining power and informational asymmetries, as it incentivizes the more informed publisher to reveal information to the less informed freelancer, else risk having the contract interpreted against them.

Should legislatures be averse to include more copyright-contract-centric provisions, a tailor-made freelance author Act may be a viable alternative. The policy objective underlying this Act would be to remedy the imbalanced power relationships that exist between freelancers and publishers at the bargaining table, and would do so by spelling out clearly defined rules on contract formation between the two parties. In addition to mandating a pro-author default rule, drawing from the many provisions found in continental European statutes, the Act could also

---

69 For example, France, Holland, Germany, and Spain's "purpose of grant rule", or Belgium's "pro-author interpretation". See *Copyright, Contracts, Creators*, *supra* note 14 at 167–170.

70 *Ibid.*, see discussion in 261–267.

consist of provisions that copyright assignments and licenses (1) specify use, scope and duration, (2) be interpreted narrowly in favor of the author, (3) include a duty to exploit works within a period of time or risk termination, and (4) provide reversion and other termination possibilities and equitable or guaranteed remuneration.[71]

The "guaranteed payment" provision is embedded already in some civilian provisions and was found in the UK's Copyright Act of 1842.[72] Under the 1842 Act, specifically section 18, contributors to collective works were conferred considerable protection.[73] The 1842 Act provided that while collective work authors did not maintain complete copyright control over their works, they had at least (1) guaranteed payment, (2) the right to refuse consent to additional uses of their works, (3) reversion of copyright after 28 years, and (4) the ability to publish their own work if bargained for.[74] There were therefore some useful restraints preventing the collective copyright owner from doing as he pleased.

The UK 1911 Act repealing the 1842 Act provided a new provision on collective works and is equally appealing to emulate. Section 5 on copyright ownership provided that before the owner of a collective work obtained copyright there must have been (1) giving or promising of some valuable consideration, and (2) no agreement to the contrary.[75] If it was inferred from the mutual intention of the parties that the author should retain copyright, "it ought to be so held."[76] Moreover, according to section 5(2) copyright reverted to the author's estate after the expiry of 25 years and the publisher was entitled to reproduce the author's work on

---

71 s 3(1) Copyright Act of 30 June 1994, 27 Moniteur Belge 1994 (Belgium); see also Central Station Tribunal de première instance de Bruxelles (Brussels Court of First Instance), 16 October 1996, Auteurs & Media 1996, 426; Cour d'appel de Bruxelles (Brussels Court of Appeals), 28 October 1997, Auteurs & Media 1997, 383.

72 5&6 Vict c 45 [the 1842 Act]. The bill received royal assent 1 July 1842; (1842) 64 Hansard Parl Debates 858.

73 EJ MacGillivray *A Digest of the Law of Copyright* (John Murray London 1902) 12–13.

74 The 1842 Act, *supra* note 72 at s 18; *ibid.* at 14–15.

75 EJ MacGillivray *The Copyright Act 1911 Annotated* (Stevens & Sons London 1912) 55; though the first proviso of the 1911 Act s 5(a) only applied to engravings, photographs and portraits.

76 *Ibid.*

payment of a 10 percent royalty.[77] These provisions serve as useful legal precedents to re-craft a more copyright-contract-centric law.

International mechanisms should also be considered as a means for addressing the power imbalances in contractual negotiations between freelancers and publishers. These mechanisms could take the form of codified copyright contract rules. The difficulty here lies in creating a unified approach because, as argued by Sterling, disparate provisions on fundamental issues "can only lead to chaos" and result in an inefficient international system.[78] Codifying these rules could need to begin with preexisting international copyright statutes, such as the Berne Convention.[79] When international revisions or new treaties are scheduled, their agendas need to take seriously creators' issues for redress.

Ultimately, as an alternative (and ideally complementary) approach to national and international legislative intervention, it may be possible to establish a voluntary code or non-binding statement of principles to improve publisher and freelancer relations. There is no reason why publishers should resist this cooperative, less intrusive approach. Many authors' groups also generate these codes of practice at a national level but typically restrict these to members.

2. Copyright Contract Judicial Principles

Irrespective of legislative intervention, courts could also do better to embrace a more creator-friendly copyright-contract-centric approach. Historically in the UK, nineteenth-century courts were more attuned to authors' copyright contract struggles. Ambiguous copyright transfers were generally interpreted in favor of authors.[80] Interestingly, these cases have not been overturned, and therefore provide legal grounds for following a more pro-author approach to ambiguous contract resolutions between authors and publishers. Some of the ways in which courts

---

[77] And, under the 1956 Act, employed authors, in particular, retained copyright in their works unless there was an agreement to the contrary. But under the CDPA this last "anomaly" was removed. Bently *supra* note 29 at 117.

[78] JAL Sterling *World Copyright Law* (London: Sweet & Maxwell, 2003) 923.

[79] *Ibid.*

[80] See *Hole v Bradbury*, (1879) LR 12 886 (Ch D)(Fry J); *Re Judes' Musical Compilations* [1906] 2 Ch 595; *Reade v Bentley*, (1857) 3 K & J 271; *Sweet v Cater*, (1841) 11 Sim 572. For discussion see, Giuseppina D'Agostino, 'The History of Copyright Contract in Relation to the Freelancer' (2010) 22 I.P.J. 2.

managed (and many still do)[81] to engage in this pro-author decision-making included following the *contra proferentem* rule; using restrictive interpretative approaches to contracts, especially in regards to publishers asserting industry custom as grounds for finding an implied granting of rights; and avoiding a foreseeability rule with respect to new technology for determining whether a freelancer could have granted the rights claimed by the publisher.[82] *Mayhew v Maxwell*, which was decided in 1860, presents an issue somewhat similar to *Robertson* with the layering of the freelancer's and the publisher's copyrights in the individual articles, and the newspaper compilation, respectively. However, in stark contrast to the holding in *Robertson*, the British court decided that just because the newspaper publisher was the registered proprietor of the copyright in the newspaper, that did not mean that they were free to lay claim to the individual copyright of the articles it consisted of, unless this grant had been expressly negotiated for.[83]

3. Other Copyright Contract Mechanisms

In addition to legal mechanisms in the legislatures and the courts, there are also a myriad of other tools worth exploring for contract law to work more meaningfully with copyright law in order to ameliorate authors' imbalanced relationship. One example is the establishment of, and support of, authors' groups to promote fairer contracting and model agreements. Authors could emphasize the need to have provisions similar

---

[81] Common law and civilian courts have considered factors such as intent of parties' industry custom, purpose of grant, unfairness in bargaining, and generally favored a restrictive interpretative approach; in the UK, albeit in other freelancer contexts, see for instance *Robin Ray v Classic FM plc* [1998] ECC 488 (Ch D), *Saphena Computing Ltd v Allied Collection Agencies Ltd* (1988)[1995] FSR 616 (QB) appeal dismissed (1989)[1995] FSR 649 (CA); for a full summary of the various factors and approaches see *Copyright, Contracts, Creators*, supra note 14 at 199.

[82] *Hospital for Sick Children (Board of Governors) v Walt Disney Productions Ltd* [1968] Ch 52, *Union of French Journalists and National Syndicate of Journalists v SDV Plurimédia* (3 February 1998) (Tribunal de Grande Instance de Strasbourg – Ordonnance de Référé Commercial) (tr) (1998) 22 Columbia-VLA JLA 199; *Netherlands Association of Journalists v De Volkskrant* No D 3.1294 (24 September 1997) (DCt of Amsterdam) (tr) (1998) 22 Columbia-VLAJLA 181, and Robertson, *supra* note 5. I discussed the foreseeability principle and its pitfalls at length in *Copyright, Contracts, Creators*, *supra* note 14 at 137, and 164–167.

[83] See analysis in *Copyright, Contracts, Creators*, *supra* note 14 at 63.

to those proposed in the freelance author Act previously mentioned, with particular emphasis placed on requiring copyright contracts to expressly state the scope of the agreement, duration, uses and remuneration. Engaging in this kind of group mobilization could confer freelancers significant bargaining power during negotiations with publishers. Moreover, these groups could also serve a pedagogic function by providing freelancers with logistical information with respect to copyright contracts that it is in their fundamental interests to know.[84] One way of doing this would be to provide members of authors' groups a "black list" of contract clauses that they should be wary of while at the bargaining table, and another list of preferable contract clauses that speak to their interests.[85]

The kind of information freelancers need to improve their position *vis-à-vis* publishers is becoming more readily available. One example is the *Contract Watch* newsletter, which is published by the Contracts Committee of the American Society of Journalists and Authors (ASJA). This newsletter serves as an information center for freelancers with respect to contractual relationships, and provides ASJA members with up-to-date information about the current trends in the publishing industry with regards to contractual negotiations.[86] The Professional Writers Association of Canada (PWAC) provides a similar service through its website where it disseminates to its members, and the public, information on copyright, professional practices, standard agreements between authors and publishers, and what to pay a professional writer.[87] Other examples include the website "Freelance Writing", which provides freelancers with a free ebook on how to retain the copyright in their work, and the American National Writers Union's "contract advice services", which offers freelancers a review service to have their freelance contracts evaluated before giving them final assent.[88]

---

[84] For instance, the National Union of Journalists London, through its website, provides its members with model response letters for freelancers to send to their publishers.

[85] Tim Perrin, 'Publishing Contract Checklist' (2004), online: Right-Writing <http://www.right-writing.com/checklist.html>.

[86] See ASJA member news, ASJA http://www.asja.org/index.php.

[87] See PWAC 'Best Practices' online: http://www.pwac.ca/eventsandresources/bestpractices

[88] See Freelance Writing, 'Online Copyright for Writers', online: Freelance Writing <http://ia601205.us.archive.org/11/items/OnlineCopyrightForWriters_976/copyright-book-for-writersFIN.pdf>; National Writers Union, 'Contract Advice', online: National Writers Union <https://nwu.org/contract-advice>.

Grievance boards, particularly those empowered by legislation, may be another effective way for freelancers to improve their bargaining disadvantages. Grievance boards offer a cheaper alternative to litigation, as court battles raise serious access-to-justice issues for authors. Moreover, grievance boards provide a more personalized and less formal avenue for redress than does a courtroom. An example of this kind of initiative is the American National Writers Union's (NWU) grievance-resolution process, which is both confidential and available at no cost to NWU members in good standing.[89]

Authors' groups can also work more closely with publishers' and users' groups. One way to work together would be for scale agreements to be negotiated between them (though these would work better if mandated via legislation). Collective bargaining could ensure at least minimum terms and provisions for authors. Some jurisdictions have these mechanisms in place but are limited in scope.[90] Ultimately, without some type of joint collective effort, it may be difficult for freelancers to bolster their bargaining position.

Finally, education needs to be emphasized further as a complementary means for any solution advanced. Educating freelancers is of the utmost importance because they are ultimately the ones who will need to represent their interests during negotiations. Similarly, it is also important to educate the public, particularly with respect to the distribution of gains in the publishing and wider cultural industries. The public should be made aware of creators' unsavory dealings that make their consumption of these industries possible. The more informed the public is of these issues, the more effective it can be at exerting pressure on policy-makers and industry actors to bring this type of undue exploitation of freelancer work to an end. Similar lopsided power imbalances for "users" in copyright law have been brought to public prominence more recently. Via

---

[89] See NWU 'Grievance Assistance' online: https://nwu.org/grievance-assistance.

[90] See for example in Canada, *The Status of the Artist Act*, SC 1992 c 33 applying only to freelancers of federal institutions. The Status of the Artist Act received royal assent on 23 June 1992 and was brought into force in stages until 9 May 1995 when it became fully in force. For discussion see: E Lefebvre 'Les rapports collectives en milieu artistique et la production multimedia' Barreau du Québec vol 192 (2003) 173; E Lefebvre 'Du droit d'auteur au status de l'artistes: étude comparative des législations applicable dans un context de droit civil et examen comparatif des pouvoirs de leur forum décisionnel' Institutions administrative du droit d'auteur, (2002) 161; JA Francais 'Eléments de protection canadienne de l'activité créatrice des artistes-interprètes du domaine sonore' (Etude pour le ministère du Patrimoine canadien 23 mars 2006).

social media and other tools of engagement, there has been a push-back by increasingly vocal user groups demanding fairer "rights."[91] In Canada, this push has been manifested on many levels, but perhaps most forcefully against government, calling for "fair" copyright reform for more user rights.[92] Ultimately with more public awareness, the public will be in a better position to evaluate the precarious position of creators who are gradually becoming less important to the law of copyright.

CONCLUDING REMARKS

In 1968, Roland Barthes, the French literary theorist and continental philosopher, published his famous essay "The Death of the Author", in which he sought to reconceptualize the notion of meaning as applied to literature, and writing more generally.[93] It was Barthes' contention that too great an emphasis is placed on what authors intend to convey when they write, and their "situatedness."[94] Underlying Barthes' conviction was the belief that this approach to meaning was far too restrictive, and, as such, fails to do justice to the independent life taken on by a text upon being written down and left open to interpretation. According to Barthes, writing is never closed because meaning is something disentangled from a text, not deciphered, and when we "give an Author to a text" we begin to close the writing with an illusory monolithic meaning.[95] It is on these grounds that Barthes calls for the death of the author in the context of literary interpretation. The author may soon be in the grips of death: not so much in the way Barthes envisioned, but by the grips of contract.

Freedom of contract allows for the stronger party to thrive while relegating the weaker party to a position of contractual subordination (either through their status as an independent contractor or via "work made for hire"). There are solutions available for reforming copyright

---

91 For a Canadian example, see Fair Copyright for Canada Groups on Facebook currently springing up from June 2008 online: http://www.facebook.com/group.php?gid=6315846683 [Fair Copyright for Canada]. See discussion in Giuseppina D'Agostino 'Healing Fair Dealing? A Comparative Copyright Analysis of Canada's Fair Dealing to U.K. Fair Dealing and U.S. Fair Use' (2008), 53 McGill L.J. 309.

92 Fair Copyright for Canada, *ibid.*

93 See Roland Barthes, 'The Death of the Author' in *Image-Music-Text*, translated by Stephen Heath (London: Fontana Press, 1977) 143.

94 *Ibid.* at 144.

95 *Ibid.* at 147.

law with a more copyright-contract-centric approach that entails restricting freedom of contract and mandating rules from contract formation to interpretation to enforcement.

Redressing this lopsided copyright system matters for a number of reasons, and here some points merit underscoring. Current "entrepreneurial copyright" challenges copyright's said objectives.[96] Authors go vastly unrewarded and suffer a loss of control of their works. And while time and space did not permit a fulsome discussion, users have decreased diversity and access to works.[97] This outcome cannot be in the public interest. As the cases illustrate, freelancers are a vulnerable group. They have inferior bargaining power, which resonates to nineteenth-century UK copyright. Freelancers are a growing category of creative workers as more and more firms are outsourcing work. So they will constitute the wave of future employment. The ownership of works in new media is a problem that will persist as it implicates copyright law and its future. Anytime there is a new technology, there is a new means of exploitation and renewed challenges to the existing business models, and ultimately copyright law. Witness this renewed problem from the onset of the printing press to the 1920s, when silent picture films became talkies. These types of "disruptive" technologies will continue to persist and will continue to open up new markets of exploitation and, with this, renewed challenges to copyright law. Ultimately, the wider creative and social context is implicated. The issue of authors' copyright contract dealings is not limited to the publishing industry but the wider cultural industries (for example as seen with freelance photographers in the *Leuthold* case) and any social context where there is a new technology and there are issues of ownership, control and access to works. And here in the context of freelance writing, the user-generated online phenomena, where the Internet might be seen to allow anyone with a computer to be a creator and monetize this work, may not pose a viable solution or at best cannot be the only solution. In the context of freelancers, online citizen journalism is already seen to duplicate some of the very issues my work takes issue with: unfriendly content-provider arrangements against the creators. As Dan Gilmour, US citizen media expert, says in reference to YouTube's commercialization initiative of Citizen News, he would not

[96] Grosheide *supra* note 6.

[97] See analysis in *Copyright, Contracts, Creators supra* note 14 at 9–11.

want it to adopt the motto: "you do all the work and we'll take all the money, thank you very much."[98]

In order to rebalance the unfairness in bargaining creators face, copyright's reliance on freedom of contract needs to be in check. Doing so means codification of a variety of contract-based rules in copyright to address a worsening problem. Perhaps in doing so, copyright – or better, copyright contract – can truly attain a *lex specialis* status. Whether we call it so is less important than ensuring that copyright and contract work better together, towards a more copyright-contract-centric *lex*.

---

[98] D Gilmour *We the Media: Grassroots Journalism by the People, for the People* (O'Reilly Media Inc Sebastopol 2006) and Y Benkler *The Wealth of Networks: How Social Production Transforms Markets and Freedom* (University Press New Haven 2006).

2. The enforceability of mass-market e-commerce licenses and social networking agreements: Is copyright or contract law the new *lex specialis*?

Charles R. McManis and Brett Garrison

As many commentators have noted, the Internet is rapidly undergoing a shift from a "read-only" web (Web 1.0) to an increasingly interactive web (Web 2.0) in which social networks vie with e-commerce for prominence and user-generated content (UGC) is becoming an ever more prominent feature.[1] A common feature of both eras has been reliance on mass-market licenses to control the uses that can be made of Internet content. This chapter will compare the contractual phenomenon of mass-market licensing in both the e-commerce and social networking contexts and examine the extent to which such licenses are enforceable or preempted, or might constitute copyright or "license" misuse in the United States.

[1] *See* http://en.wikipedia.org/wiki/Web_2.0, which notes that the term Web 2.0 "was coined in 1999 by Darcy DiNucci and was popularized by Tim O'Reilly at the O'Reilly Media Web 2.0 conference in late 2004." A Web 2.0 site "may allow users to interact and collaborate with each other in a social media dialogue as creators of user-generated content in a virtual community, in contrast to websites where people are limited to the passive viewing of content." *Ibid. See also* Brian Getting, "Basic Definitions: Web 1.0, Web 2.0, Web 3.0," 2007, *available at* http://www.practicalecommerce.com/articles/464-Basic-Definitions-Web-1-0-Web-2-0-Web-3-0, noting that Web 1.0 could be considered the "read-only web."

I. MASS-MARKET LICENSING IN E-COMMERCE (WEB 1.0 ERA)

Software and digital content are distributed by mass-market licenses, which typically contain terms that restrict licensee uses of the content. Mass-market licensing in e-commerce has evolved with recent advances in technology. When computer software was primarily sold in boxes, distributors typically used "shrink-wrap" licenses, which took effect when the purchaser tore open the shrink-wrap on the box.[2] With subsequent advancements in computing and Internet speed, software has been distributed digitally through "click-wrap" licenses, where a user clicks a button on the screen to indicate acceptance of the license.[3] These "click-wrap" licenses are also used in the burgeoning field of e-books.[4]

The debate in the United States over mass-market licensing arose in the 1990s, sparked by a proposed U.C.C. Article 2B (Licensing), which eventually morphed into a proposed stand-alone Uniform Computer Information Transactions Act (UCITA).[5] The debate was also fueled by decisions under existing law in *ProCD v Zeidenberg*[6] and *Bowers v Baystate Technologies*[7] upholding mass-market licensing terms.

Collectively, these developments seemed to envision U.S. copyright law as a set of default rules, or *lex generalis*, various provisions of which, such as the first sale doctrine[8] and the fair use privilege,[9] could be varied

---

[2] *See* Charles McManis, *The Privatization (or "Shrink-Wrapping") of American Copyright Law*, 87 CAL L. REV. 173 (1999).

[3] Mark A. Lemley, *Terms of Use*, 91 MINN. L. REV. 459, 459 (2006).

[4] Matthew Chiarizio, *An American Tragedy: E-Books, Licenses, and the End of Public Lending Libraries?*, 66 VAND. L. REV. 615, 622 (2013).

[5] For an online version of UCITA, *see* http://www.steptoe.com/assets/attachments/2359.pdf.

[6] 86 F.3d 1447 (7th Cir. 1996).

[7] 320 F.3d 1317 (Fed. Cir. 2003).

[8] *See* 17 U.S.C. § 109(a), which states in part.

> Notwithstanding the provisions of section 106(3), the owner of a particular copy or phonorecord lawfully made under this title, or any person authorized by such owner, is entitled, without the authority of the copyright owner, to sell or otherwise dispose of the possession of that copy or phonorecord.

[9] *See* 17 U.S.C. § 107, as amended in 1992:

> Notwithstanding the provisions of section 106 and 106A, the fair use of a copyrighted work, including such use by reproduction in copies or phonorecords or by any other means specified by that section, for purposes such as criticism, comment, news reporting, teaching (including multiple copies for

by license, including mass-market license. This stance effectively made contract law the *lex specialis*.

But Article 2B was widely criticized[10] and was not widely adopted.[11] Moreover, the debate over mass-market licensing continues under existing law.[12] Recently, the American Law Institute published the *Principles of the Law of Software Contracts*, which states three limiting principles that apply to mass-market licenses: "A term of an agreement is unenforceable if it conflicts with a mandatory rule of federal intellectual property law, conflicts impermissibly with the purposes and policies of federal intellectual property law, or would constitute federal intellectual property misuse in an infringement proceeding."[13] The last two of these concepts implicate federal preemption and copyright misuse as tools to address these practices. The practices to be addressed by these concepts are: (1) precluding the user from making fair uses of the work; (2) banning or limiting reverse engineering; (3) restricting copying or dissemination of factual information; or (4) forbidding the transfer of the software. As this chapter will illustrate, copyright preemption, misuse, and unconscionability potentially serve as a *lex specialis* to limit these license terms.

A. Copyright Misuse

Copyright misuse provides a tool to maintain U.S. copyright law as a *lex specialis*. Copyright misuse is a defense to copyright infringement where

---

classroom use), scholarship, or research, is not an infringement of copyright. In determining whether the use made of a work in any particular case is a fair use the factors to be considered shall include –

(1) the purpose and character of the use, including whether such use is of a commercial nature or is for nonprofit educational purposes;
(2) the nature of the copyrighted work;
(3) the amount and substantiality of the portion used in relation to the copyrighted work as a whole; and
(4) the effect of the use upon the potential market for or value of the copyrighted work.

The fact that a work is unpublished shall not itself bar a finding of fair use if such finding is made upon consideration of all the above factors.

10 *See, e.g.*, McManis *supra* note 2.

11 Only Maryland and Virginia passed similar legislation to UCITA. For the text of their legislation *see* http://mlis.state.md.us/2000rs/billfile/hb0019.htm and http://leg1.state.va.us/cgi-bin/legp504.exe?001+ful+SB372ER, respectively.

12 *See, e.g.*, ALI Principles of the Law of Software Contracts (2010).

13 *Ibid.*

a copyright holder uses copyright law to reach subject matter outside of the scope of the rights granted by Congress.[14] A particularly important illustrative case is *Assessment Technologies of WI, LLC v WIREdata, Inc.*,[15] which addressed the "attempt of a copyright owner to use copyright law to block access to data that not only are neither copyrightable nor copyrighted, but were not created or obtained by the copyright owner."[16] The information in question concerned real estate data – the address, name of the owner, the assessed value, and so forth. As Judge Posner emphasized, to "try by contract or otherwise to prevent the municipalities from revealing *their own* data, especially when … the complete data are unavailable anywhere else, might constitute copyright misuse."[17] Judge Posner explained that the doctrine of misuse prevents copyright holders from leveraging their limited monopoly to allow them control of areas outside the scope of protection provided by the copyright law.

Although Judge Posner had previously expressed skepticism that an IP misuse defense is distinguishable from and broader than an underlying antitrust claim, in *WIREdata* he states: "The argument for applying copyright misuse beyond the bounds of antitrust … is that for a copyright owner to use an infringement suit to obtain property protection, here in data, that copyright law clearly does not confer, hoping to force a settlement or even achieve an outright victory over an opponent that may lack the resources or the legal sophistication to resist effectively, is an abuse of process."[18] In short, the attempt of the copyright owner to use a software license to control data that the licensee generated and that copyright law itself does not protect is contrary to the underlying policies of copyright law and thus a misuse.

Much like the company misused copyright law to protect data in *WIREdata*, copyright misuse could handle mass-market licenses that restrict dissemination of factual information.

---

14 *See Lasercomb Am., Inc. v Reynolds*, 911 F.2d 970, 973 (4th Cir. 1990). For a full discussion on copyright misuse, *see* Lydia Pallas Loren, *Slaying the Leather-winged Demons in the Night: Reforming Copyright Owner Contracting with Clickwrap Misuse,* 30 OHIO NORTHERN U. L. REV. 495 (2004); Kathyrn Judge, Note, *Rethinking Copyright Misuse,* 57 STAN. L. REV. 901 (2004); JuNelle Harris, *Beyond Fair Use: Expanding Copyright Misuse to Protect Digital Speech,* 13 TEX. INTELL. PROP. L. J. 83 (2004).

15 350 F.3d 640, 646-7 (7th Cir. 2003).

16 *Ibid.* at 641.

17 *Ibid.*

18 *Ibid.* at 647.

B. Federal Preemption of Mass-Market Licenses

In addition to the doctrine of copyright misuse, federal copyright law may preempt mass-market licenses.[19] Preemption addresses the situations where the license forbids rights granted by copyright law such as the fair use privilege, reverse engineering and the first sale doctrine.

Federal copyright preemption can arise either through express or implied preemption.[20] Congress may explicitly preempt state law in any field in which it has constitutional power to regulate, including its constitutional authority to grant (or withhold) federal copyright and patent protection. Even in the absence of explicit federal statutory preemption of state law, however, the Supremacy Clause of the U.S. Constitution, which declares that the Constitution and the laws of the United States made in pursuance thereof are the supreme law of the land, binding on state courts, notwithstanding any contrary state law, has been construed to give federal courts the power to determine whether state law "stands as an obstacle to the accomplishment and execution of the full purposes and objectives of Congress."[21] What remains unclear is whether the Supremacy Clause has a role to play where Congress has exercised its power to preempt state law, as it has in the Copyright Act of 1976.[22]

i. Express statutory preemption

With the Copyright Act of 1976, Congress did exercise its express preemption power to some extent. In section 301(a), Congress declared

---

[19] *See generally* Kathleen K. Olson, *Preserving the Copyright Balance: Statutory and Constitutional Preemption of Contract-Based Claims*, 11 COMM. L. & POL'Y 83 (2006). In addition to implied and express preemption, two additional bases for preempting state law arise where the federal statutes either occupy a field as to give rise to a "reasonable inference that Congress left no room for the states to supplement it" or "touch[] a field in which the federal interest is so dominant that the federal system will be assumed to preclude enforcement of state law on the same subject," *see English v General Electric Co.*, 496 U.S. 72, 79 (1990), quoting *Rice v Santa Fe Elevator Corp.*, 331 U.S. 218, 230 (1947). However, in *Goldstein v California*, 412 U.S. 546 (1972), the Supreme Court held that neither the Copyright Clause of the U.S. Constitution nor the federal statutory copyright law then in effect triggered these two bases for preemption of state law. Because the Copyright Act of 1976 includes a provision expressly purporting to preempt state law, neither of the tests alluded to in *English* are relevant to the subject of this chapter.

[20] *See* Olson, *supra* note 19.

[21] *Hines v Davidowitz*, 312 U.S. 52, 67 (1941).

[22] The express preemption provision in the Copyright Act of 1976 is contained in § 301(a), 17 U.S.C. § 301(a).

that on and after the effective date of the Act, all rights that are "equivalent" to any of the exclusive rights within the general scope of copyright[23] and come within the subject matter of copyright,[24] whether created before or after that date and whether published or unpublished, are governed exclusively by federal copyright law: "Thereafter, no person is entitled to any such right or equivalent right in any such work under the common law or statutes of any State."[25] The specific purpose of section 301, which is described in the legislative history as "one of the bedrock provisions of the bill," was to accomplish a "fundamental and significant change" in U.S. copyright law, by replacing a dual system of "common law copyright" for unpublished works and statutory copyright for published works with a single system of federal statutory copyright from the moment of creation (i.e. fixation).[26] The House Report on the bill stated that in section 301, Congress intended to state "in the clearest and most unequivocal language possible, so as to foreclose any conceivable misinterpretation of its unqualified intention" to act preemptively, and to "avoid the development of any vague borderline areas between State and Federal protection."[27]

Unfortunately, Congress did not altogether succeed in that effort, as the statutory preemption test does not specify what result courts should reach when mass-market licenses are made enforceable under state contract law and used either to abrogate certain statutorily permissible uses of copyrighted works, such as the "fair use" privilege, or to extend protection to subject matter, such as ideas, procedures, processes, systems, methods of operation, concepts, principles, or discoveries (i.e. facts), that are explicitly excluded from the subject matter of copyright,[28] though potentially protectable under the more exacting standards of federal patent law.

---

[23] Described in § 106, 17 U.S.C. § 106.

[24] Specified in §§ 102 and 103, 17. U.S.C. §§ 102 & 103.

[25] 17 U.S.C. § 301(a).

[26] H.R. REP. NO. 94-1476, at 129, *reprinted in* 5 U.S. CODE, CONG. & ADMIN. NEWS 5659, 5745 (1976).

[27] *Ibid.* at 130, 5 U.S. CODE, CONG. & ADMIN. NEWS at 5746.

[28] *See* 17 U.S.C. § 102(b), which states that:

> In no case does copyright protection for an original work of authorship extend to any idea, procedure, process, system, method of operation, concept, principle, or discovery, regardless of the form in which it is described, explained, illustrated, or embodied in such work.

The courts have considered whether copyright law expressly preempts mass-market licenses, notably in *ProCD v Zeidenberg*.[29] The *ProCD* court held that section 301 did not expressly preempt the software license, because the contract did not create an "exclusive right," but rather only affected the parties to the contract.[30] Similarly, in *Bowers v Baystate Technologies, Inc.*,[31] the Court of Appeals for the Federal Circuit held that a shrink-wrap prohibition against reverse engineering was enforceable and not preempted by federal copyright law.[32]

While the subsequent decision in the Seventh Circuit in *WIREdata* seems to be at odds with, and to some extent marks a retreat from, the *ProCD* and *Bowers* decisions,[33] the two cases nevertheless demonstrate that the express statutory preemption test contained in section 301 of the Copyright Act of 1976 may simply be too blunt an instrument to distinguish the circumstances in which mass-market license terms should be enforced from those in which they should be held to conflict with the overriding policies of federal copyright law. For a more nuanced

---

[29] 86 F.3d 1447 (7th Cir. 1996).

[30] *Ibid.* at 1454. However, as the court itself noted in its recitation of the facts of the case, the plaintiff's restrictive licensing terms were embodied not only in a shrink-wrap license accompanying the product but also in a click-wrap license built into the product's startup sequence and appearing on a user's screen every time the software runs. *Ibid.* at 1450. Thus, someone who finds a copy of the product on the street will inevitably confront a click-wrap license and be required to agree to the terms as a condition of using the product. Except for those who altogether forgo using the plaintiff's product, there are no strangers to the contract. As a practical matter, the built-in licensing terms function to create a *de facto* right against the world.

[31] 320 F.3d 1317 (Fed. Cir. 2003).

[32] *Ibid.* at 1323–1326. This ruling stimulated a sharp dissent, in which Judge Dyk charged that by allowing a shrink-wrap license to override the fair use defense, the majority decision "permits state law to eviscerate an important copyright policy reflected in the fair use defense, and … threatens other federal copyright policies as well." *Ibid.* at 1335. While Judge Dyk agreed that a state can permit parties to contract away a fair use defense or to agree not to engage in uses of copyrighted material that are permitted by the copyright law, if the contract is freely negotiated, he went on to liken state law enforcement of shrink-wrap licenses to a state law that allows a copyright holder to bar fair use of copyrighted material by placing a black dot on each copy of the work offered for sale or simply labeling its products so as to eliminate a fair use defense: "Like any other contract of adhesion, the only choice offered to the purchaser is to avoid making the purchase in the first place." *Ibid.* at 1336–1337.

[33] *See* Part I(A), *supra*, discussing *Assessment Technologies of WI v WIREdata, Inc.*, 350 F.3d 640 (7th Cir. 2003).

approach to that question, some combination of implied Supremacy Clause preemption and/or a customized concept of public policy unconscionability or copyright misuse will arguably be required.

ii. Implied Supremacy Clause preemption

While some have argued that implied Supremacy Clause preemption has no role to play where Congress has expressly chosen to preempt state law, the legislative history of the Copyright Act of 1976 suggests that Congress did not intend for section 301 to altogether supplant the implied Supremacy Clause preemption doctrine in copyright cases. Likewise, certain language in the Copyright Act itself, particularly when construed in light of two later amendments to the Act and accompanying legislative history, suggests that Congress did not intend to permit routine contractual overrides of the statutory fair use privilege enunciated in section 107, at least not through the mechanism of mass-market licenses lacking any indications of having been freely negotiated.

As has been noted, the specific purpose of section 301(a) of the Copyright Act was to preempt common-law copyright protection for unpublished fixed works of authorship, and to "avoid the development of any vague borderline areas between State and Federal protection."[34] The legislative history also reveals that the purpose of companion section 301(b) – which as ultimately enacted simply represents the obverse of section 301(a) by providing that the Act does not preempt state law not falling within the preemptive scope of section 301(a) – was "to make clear, consistent with the 1964 Supreme Court decisions in *Sears, Roebuck & Co. v Stiffel Co.*,[35] and *Compco Corp. v Day-Brite Lighting, Inc.*,[36] that preemption does not extend to causes of action, or subject matter outside the scope of the revised Federal copyright statute."[37] The *Sears* and *Compco* cases, in turn, have functioned as the cornerstone for the Supreme Court's modern implied Supremacy Clause preemption jurisprudence in cases involving Congressional exercise of its power under the Patent and Copyright Clause of the U.S. Constitution, as the cases enunciated the principle that "when an article is unprotected by a patent or a copyright, state law may not forbid others to copy that article."[38] In view of an apparent Congressional intent to formulate an

---

34 *See supra* notes 24–26.

35 376 U.S. 225 (1964).

36 376 U.S. 234 (1964).

37 *See* H. R. REP. NO. 94-1476 at 131, 5 U.S. CODE, CONG. & ADMIN. NEWS at 5747 (1976).

38 376 U.S. at 237.

express preemption rule that is "consistent with" the Supreme Court's decisions in *Sears-Compco*, it is difficult to argue that Congress in section 301 intended to altogether supplant the Supreme Court's implied preemption jurisprudence in copyright cases, even where state law seems to create "vague borderline areas" between state and federal protection and the express statutory preemption test functions as too blunt an instrument to achieve an effective balance between competing federal and state policies.

Specific language in the Copyright Act suggests that Congress had no intent to permit routine contractual overrides of the statutory fair use privilege contained in section 107 of the Act, at least not through the mechanism of essentially unilaterally imposed mass-market licenses. This legislative intent can be extrapolated by construing the language of section 107 in light of its own legislative history and that of two subsequent amendments to the Copyright Act.

To begin with, the four-factor balancing test enunciated in section 107 for determining fair use virtually invites the federal courts to continue engaging in interstitial policymaking in copyright cases, subject to very general legislative oversight. The legislative history offers strong support for that construction, as it emphasizes that section 107 of the Act was designed to "restate the existing judicial doctrine of fair use, not to change, narrow, or enlarge it in any way."[39] Indeed, the legislative history goes on to state that:

> The bill endorses the purpose and general scope of the judicial doctrine of fair use, but there is no disposition to freeze the doctrine in the statute, especially during a period of rapid technological change. Beyond a very broad statutory explanation of what fair use is and some the criteria applicable to it, the courts must be free to adapt the doctrine to particular situations on a case-by-case basis.[40]

Two subsequent amendments to the Copyright Act offer support for the proposition that Congress did not intend to permit routine mass-market contractual overrides of the statutory fair use privilege. Ironically, the first relevant amendment originated as a misguided effort on the part of the computer software industry to obtain explicit Congressional approval of the practice of employing mass-market licenses to modify the permissible uses to which computer programs could be put. The original

---

[39] H.R. REP. NO. 94-1476, at 66, U.S. CODE, CONG. & ADMIN. NEWS at 5680.

[40] *Ibid.*

statutory language of a proposed 1980 amendment confirmed that computer software was indeed protected under the Copyright Act of 1976, but would be subject to a limitation spelled out in a revised section 117, permitting a "person in rightful possession" of a copy of a computer program to make additional copies or adaptations (1) as an essential step in using the computer program in conjunction with a machine, or (2) for archival purposes.[41] However, the software industry prevailed upon Congress at the eleventh hour to change the section 117 limitation so as to apply only to "the owner of a copy of a computer program."[42] The evident purpose of the substitute language, which was nowhere explained or discussed in the legislative history of the amendment, was to enable the software industry to contract around the section 117 limitation through the simple expedient of "licensing" the use of software without transferring ownership of specific copies. This conclusion can be extrapolated from the fact that the substitute language is identical to that contained in section 109 of the 1976 Act, the statutory embodiment of the so-called "first sale" doctrine, which permits the "owner" of a particular copy of a copyrighted work to sell or otherwise dispose of the possession of that copy,[43] but can be obviated by the simple expedient of "licensing" specified uses of the copyrighted work, without transferring ownership of any particular copies of the copyrighted work.

In lobbying through this eleventh hour amendment, however, the software industry may have inadvertently shot itself in the foot, as it only serves to highlight that other user safe havens contained in the Copyright Act of 1976, and indeed the broad fair use privilege itself, are not limited to the "owner" of a particular copy of the copyrighted work, but apparently extend to any person in rightful possession of a copy of the work. For example, section 108 of the Act specifies that it is not an

---

[41] *See* Charles R. McManis, *Intellectual Property Protection and Reverse Engineering of Computer Programs in the United States and the European Community*, 8 HIGH TECH. L. J. 25, 77 78 (1993).

[42] *Ibid.* at 79.

[43] Section 109(a) states that:

> Notwithstanding the provisions of section 106(3) [conferring on copyright owners an exclusive right to distribute copies or phonorecords of the copyrighted work to the public by public sale or other transfer of ownership, or by rental, lease, or lending], the *owner* of a particular *copy* or phonorecord lawfully made under this title, or any person authorized by such owner, is entitled, without the authority of the copyright owner, to sell or otherwise dispose of the possession of that copy or phonorecord.

17 U.S.C. § 109(a) (emphasis added).

infringement of copyright for a qualifying library or archive to reproduce a copy or phonorecord of a work or to distribute the copy or phonorecord under the conditions specified in the section for a variety of purposes, including responding to a request of a user of that or another library or archives for a copy of no more than one article or other contribution to a copyrighted collection or periodical issue or a copy or phonorecord of a small part of any other copyrighted work (the so-called interlibrary loan exception).[44]

Nothing in section 108 indicates that libraries or archives must be the "owner" of the copy reproduced in order to invoke the interlibrary loan exception, thus suggesting that this safe haven, unlike sections 109 and 117, may not be subject to a contractual override, at least not by means of a unilaterally imposed mass-market license. Any other construction of section 108 could quickly convert public libraries and archives into unwilling arms of the sound recording industry and/or photocopy collection agencies such as the Copyright Clearance Center,[45] as copyright owners could deploy mass-market licenses on publications and phonorecords to simultaneously divest libraries and archives of ownership of any copies or phonorecords of copyrighted works purchased for their collections and strip them of their interlibrary loan privilege and their statutory privilege to make photocopy machines available for public use.[46] Likewise, section 107 itself states that the "fair use" of a copyrighted work, including such use by reproduction in copies or phonorecords, for purposes such as criticism, comment, news reporting, teaching (including multiple copies for classroom use), scholarship, or research, is not an infringement of copyright,[47] thus suggesting that one

---

[44] 17 U.S.C. § 108(a)–(b) & (g). Section 108(c), in turn, permits qualifying libraries and archives, under certain conditions, to duplicate published works solely for the purpose of replacement of a copy or phonorecord that is damaged, deteriorating, lost, or stolen, while § 108 (d) permits qualifying libraries and archives to make available photocopy machines for public use, so long as the library has had no notice that any copies made will be used for any purpose other than private study, scholarship, or research, and the library or archive displays prominently, at the place where orders are accepted, and includes on its order form a warning of copyright in accordance with requirements that the Register of Copyrights prescribes by administrative regulation. 17 U.S.C. §§ 108(c), 108(d).

[45] For a description of the services provided by the Copyright Clearance Center, *see* http://www.copyright.com/.

[46] *See supra* note 44, discussing the privilege of qualifying libraries and archives to make photocopy machines available for public use.

[47] For the text of §107, *see supra* note 9.

need not be the "owner" of a copy of copyrighted work in order to raise the defense of fair use.

That reading of section 107 finds further support in a 1992 legislative amendment to the Copyright Act of 1976, which amended section 107 itself by adding a concluding sentence stating that, "The fact that a work is unpublished shall not itself bar a finding of fair use if such finding is made upon consideration of all the above factors."[48] The amendment was described in an accompanying House Report[49] as a response to concerns by some biographers, historians and publishers that their ability to use unpublished primary source material had been compromised by two decisions of the U.S. Court of Appeals for the Second Circuit, in *Salinger v Random House, Inc.*,[50] and *New Era Publications, International ApS v Henry Holt & Co.*,[51] which suggested that unpublished works "normally enjoy complete protection against copying any protected expression."[52] Significantly, the first of these two cases involved unpublished letters that had been donated to universities' libraries (which thus owned the tangible copy of the letters, though not their copyright, which remained vested in the author or the author's heirs or assignees) and were made available to researchers subject to various standard form agreements restricting the use researchers could make of the letters. At least one of these access agreements specifically required researchers to obtain permission of the library and the owner of the literary property rights "to publish the contents of the manuscript or any excerpt therefrom."[53]

In explaining why a legislative amendment of section 107 was necessary, even though the Second Circuit had subsequently backed away from its holding in *Salinger* and *New Era Publications*, the House Report accompanying the bill proposing the amendment cited with approval a third decision of the Court of Appeals for the Second Circuit, in *Wright v Warner Books, Inc.*[54] The Report describes *Wright* as having taken "major steps in the direction of ending the Second Circuit's flirtation

---

48 106 Stat. 3145 (1992).

49 H. R. REP. NO. 102-836, at 4 (1992), *reprinted in* 5 U.S. CODE, CONG. & ADMIN. NEWS 2553, 2555–2556 (1992).

50 811 F.2d 90 (2d Cir. 1987).

51 873 F.2d 576 (2d Cir. 1989).

52 811 F.2d at 97, *cited in* H. R. REP. NO. 102-836, at 6 (1992), 5 U.S. CODE, CONG. & ADMIN. NEWS 2553, 2557 (1992) (noting that "the *Wright* opinion properly balanced all the fair use factors").

53 811 F.2d at 93.

54 953 F.2d 731 (2d Cir. 1991). *See* H. R. REP. NO. 102-836, at 7 (1992), 5 U.S. CODE, CONG. & ADMIN. NEWS 2553, 2559 (1992).

with a per se rule [barring fair use of unpublished works]," but notes that it "did not disavow certain troublesome language in the *Salinger* opinion, in particular [the] statement that unpublished works 'normally enjoy complete protection against copying any protection expression'."[55] The proposed amendment was designed to "reiterate Congress's intention in codifying fair use that in evaluating a claim of fair use, including claims involving unpublished works, the courts are to examine all four statutory factors set forth in Section 107, as well as any other factors deemed relevant in the court's discretion."[56]

Although not explicitly mentioned in the House Report, the *Wright* opinion likewise quoted with approval from the trial court's opinion in *Salinger*, which said of the standard contractual restrictions governing access to the unpublished letters involved in that case:

> [T]he intention and scope of [the] agreements are to protect the literary property interests of the owner and not to give the copyright owner an arbitrary power to block legitimate non-infringing use. … [The contractual restrictions] should be understood as applying only to quotations and excerpts *that infringe copyright*. To read them as absolutely forbidding any quotation, no matter how limited or appropriate, would severely inhibit proper, lawful scholarly use and place an arbitrary power in the hands of the copyright owner going far beyond the protection provided by law.[57]

In other words, the trial court in *Salinger* construed the contractual restrictions imposed by the libraries in a manner that was arguably contrary to the actual intent of at least one of the agreements (which clearly required permission "to publish the contents of the manuscript *or any excerpt therefrom*"[58]), but did so precisely in order to avoid striking down the contractual provision as contrary to the underlying policies of federal copyright law, much as a federal court might narrowly construe a federal or state statute in order to avoid striking it down as unconstitutional. The appellate court in *Wright* likewise rejected the argument that the defendant in that case violated a contractual restriction specifying that the archived materials "may not be published in whole or in part unless such publication is specifically authorized,"[59] and noted that, unlike the defendant in *Salinger*, the defendant in *Wright* had merely paraphrased

---

55 H. R. Rep. No. 102-836, at 8 (1992), 5 U.S. Code, Cong. & Admin. News 2553, 2560 (1992).

56 *Ibid.* at 9, 5 U.S. Code, Cong. & Admin. News 2553, 2561 (1992).

57 953 F.2d 731, 741 (2d Cir. 1991).

58 *See* 811 F.2d at 93 (emphasis added).

59 *See* 953 F.2d at 740.

the archived material – and not even closely in most instances. In the court's view, it would be "particularly paradoxical to construe the agreement as conferring greater protection on the copyright holder than that provided by the Copyright Act."[60]

That the 1992 amendment of section 107 and the judicial decisions prompting it bear on the question of the enforceability of mass-market licensing restrictions on reverse engineering of computer software publicly distributed in object code only is amply illustrated by the fact that several senators went out of their way to state in legislative debate that the amendment "applies to uses of letters, diaries and other unpublished works" but does not "broaden the fair use of unpublished computer programs …"[61] How these senators managed to derive this conclusion from the language of the proposed amendment is unclear,[62] but to the suspicious eye their statement appears to be a dubious attempt, prompted no doubt by lobbyists for the software industry, to plant in the legislative history of the amendment a limitation on the fair use privilege that does not appear in the language of the amendment itself. Once again, however, the software industry may have outfoxed itself in this lobbying effort, as the statement of the senators simply serves to highlight that members of Congress were well aware that this statutory clarification of the applicability of the fair use privilege to unpublished works could have an adverse impact on the enforceability of mass-market licensing restrictions on permissible uses of software publicly distributed in object code only. At the same time, nothing in the language of the amendment or the more authoritative committee reports accompanying it indicates that the amended section 107 would not apply to arguably "unpublished" computer software, such as software publicly distributed in object code only and accompanied by mass-market licensing terms purporting to prohibit reverse engineering that would otherwise constitute fair use.

---

60 *Ibid.* at 741.

61 S.Rep. 102-141, 102nd Cong., 1st Sess. 5, 6 (1991).

62 *See* 4 MELVILLE & DAVID NIMMER, NIMMER ON COPYRIGHT § 12.05[A][2][b] n. 195 (quoting the statement of the senators, but going on to state that "How they derived this distinction is unclear."). One possible (albeit hairsplitting) explanation is that, because the purpose of the proposed amendment was not to "broaden," but rather to clarify, the applicability of the fair use doctrine with respect to unpublished works, it is technically true that the amendment would not "broaden" the fair use of unpublished computer programs. On the other hand, the proposed clarification clearly seems to have been worded so as to apply to *all* unpublished works, and not simply to letters, diaries and the like.

In short, in light of the language and legislative history of the twice-amended Copyright Act of 1976, it is difficult to sustain the argument that Congress had any intent to permit routine mass-market contractual overrides of the statutory fair use privilege. This conclusion finds additional support in the increasing public recognition of the need for a customized concept of public policy unconscionability and/or intellectual property misuse.[63]

II. MASS LICENSING IN SOCIAL NETWORKING (WEB 2.0 ERA)

The rise of social networking has propelled an abundance of mass licenses. These licenses are similar to the aforementioned mass-market licenses in e-commerce, but social networking licenses have important differences from licenses in e-commerce. The licenses do present issues relating to overriding copyright through contract, but these issues concern the intellectual property created by the social network's users. User-generated content (UGC) is distributed pursuant to mass licenses in which the social network site as a licensee imposes terms on the user as a licensor. Here, an analogous "license misuse" (unconscionability) doctrine should serve as a *lex specialis* limiting the scope of these license terms.

Social networks present a fundamentally different licensing relationship, and the nature of this relationship affects how these licenses should be controlled. With the now conventional mass-market e-commerce licenses, the software or digital content producer is the licensor, and the user is the licensee. License terms restrict the licensee's use of the software or other digital content. Intellectual property misuse and federal statutory preemption provide defenses to enforcement of the license and/or underlying intellectual property rights. In social networking, the

[63] *See generally* Mark A. Lemley, *Beyond Preemption: The Law and Policy of Intellectual Property Licensing,* 87 CAL. L. REV. 111 (1999); Jerome H. Reichman & Jonathan A. Franklin, *Privately Legislated Intellectual Property Rights: Reconciling Freedom of Contract with Public Good Uses of Information,* 147 U. Pa. L. Rev. 875 (1999); Brett Frischmann & Dan Moylan, *The Evolving Common Law Doctrine of Copyright Misuse: A Unified Theory and Its Application to Software*, 15 BERKELEY TECH. L. J. 865 (2000); Lydia Pallas Loren, *Slaying the Leather-winged Demons in the Night: Reforming Copyright Owner Contracting with Clickwrap Misuse,* 30 OHIO NORTHERN U. L. REV. 495 (2004); Kathyrn Judge, Note, *Rethinking Copyright Misuse,* 57 STAN. L. REV. 901 (2004); JuNelle Harris, *Beyond Fair Use: Expanding Copyright Misuse to Protect Digital Speech,* 13 TEX. INTELL. PROP. L. J. 83 (2004).

licensing relationship is reversed. Users of social networking sites become licensors of their user-generated content (UGC), but social networking sites set the terms of the license. The users are unable to freely negotiate the terms of the license as it relates to their intellectual property rights. Where the concern with e-commerce is that the software or digital content producer uses the license terms to provide more protection to their products, the concern with social network licensing is that the social networks are taking too much control over the user's intellectual property.

To be sure, social networking intellectual property licenses are not objectionable *per se*. Social networks inevitably deal with user-created intellectual property (i.e. copyrights and/or rights of publicity), so the websites include clauses in their terms of use to receive licenses to that content. With this license, the social network can transmit the UGC to other users of the social network. While a license is necessary for such networks to operate, the scope of the license raises some concerns.

Social network license terms are typically quite broad,[64] granting social networks more than they need to operate the site at a potentially significant cost to the user. These licenses need to be subject to some limiting principle in order to adequately protect the user's intellectual property (i.e. copyright and/or rights of publicity). This requires distinguishing between direct and indirect uses of user-generated content.

Uses in direct connection with the social network include activity such as copying to the server, distributing to other users, and so on. But even here, contributors of user-generated content should arguably have some control over the scope of its use. Facebook provides this control through its privacy settings.[65] For example, a user can limit access of his or her page to only his or her friends.

Indirect uses of user-generated content are, for example, terms that grant social networks a qualified right to distribute user-generated content to third parties.[66] This use is not necessary for the social network to

---

64 *See e.g.* note 32.

65 *See e.g.* note 32.

66 *See* Facebook Statement of Rights and Responsibilities, ¶ 2 (https://www.facebook.com/legal/terms). Facebook's license states that "You own all of the content and information you post on Facebook, and you can control how it is shared through your privacy and application settings.

> "In addition: For content that is covered by intellectual property rights, like photos and videos (IP content), you specifically give us the following permission, subject to your privacy and application settings: you grant us a non-exclusive, transferable, sub-licensable, royalty-free, worldwide license to

function, though it may provide revenue, and is thus an indirect use.[67] Indirect uses have generated much public concern. Recently, Facebook settled a class action lawsuit regarding its "Sponsored Stories" tool, which takes a user's profile picture and places it inside an advertisement for a product that the user has "liked." In the settlement, Facebook agreed to propose a new Statement of Rights and Responsibilities[68] and offered a $20 million settlement.[69] Facebook subsequently posted and eventually adopted a proposed Statement of Rights and Responsibilities.[70]

With licenses granting social networks substantial control over UGC, a limiting principle to confine the scope of these licenses becomes necessary. The concept of "license misuse" is arguably analogous to copyright misuse in the e-commerce context. Generally understood as the doctrine of unconscionability, license misuse should prevent inequitable conduct on the part of social networks in imposing overbroad and/or difficult to understand intellectual property license terms.[71] In this sense, unconscionability will serve to elevate copyright law as the *lex specialis*.

Commentators such as Steven Hetcher have noted the concerns surrounding Facebook's intellectual property licenses.[72] Although many of the terms Hetcher objected to as unconscionable have been modified since his 2008 publication, Facebook's terms of use still retain the same

---

use any IP content that you post on or in connection with Facebook (IP License). This IP License ends when you delete your IP content or your account unless your content has been shared with others, and they have not deleted it."

[67] *See, e.g.*, Facebook's Sponsored Stories advertising product, where if you click "Like" on a branch such as Target, your friends might start seeing Target-related ads with your face next to them.

[68] For the current Statement of Rights and Responsibilities, *see supra* note 66.

[69] Ari Melber, Woodrow Hartzog and Evan Selinger, *Fighting Facebook, a Campaign for a People's Terms of Service*, THE NATION, May 22, 2013.

[70] For the proposed changes, see https://www.facebook.com/legal/proposedsrr. For the final Statement of Rights and Responsibilities, see https://www.facebook.com/legal/terms. The IP License remains the same: "[Y]ou grant us a non-exclusive, transferable, sub-licensable, royalty-free, worldwide license to use any IP content that you post on or in connection with Facebook." *Ibid.*

[71] *See, e.g.*, Steven Hetcher, *User-Generated Content and the Future of Copyright: Part Two – Agreements Between Users and Mega-Sites*, 24 SANTA CLARA COMP. & HIGH TECH. L. J. 829 (2008), arguing that an earlier version of Facebook's terms of use amounted to offering unconscionable contracts to millions of people, especially to the millions of minors who spend time on the site.

[72] *See, e.g.*, Hetcher, *supra* note 71.

basic intellectual property license. This license states that for a user's content covered by intellectual property rights "you grant us a non-exclusive, transferable, sub-licensable, royalty-free, worldwide license to use any IP content that you post on or in connection with Facebook (IP License)."[73] This IP License retains the same language in Facebook's proposed changes to its Statement of Rights and Responsibilities.[74]

Facebook's IP License poses significant issues when minors use the service. Facebook's Statement of Rights and Responsibilities excludes some minors, stating that "[y]ou will not use this service if you are under 13."[75] This clause creates two classes of minors using Facebook: (1) minors under 13 who use Facebook despite this clause and (2) minors between the ages of 13 and 18 who use Facebook.

The first set of minors presents a puzzling scenario. Minors under age 13 are clearly in violation of Facebook's terms of use and subject to termination of their accounts.[76] Facebook deletes around 20 000 under-age user accounts a day.[77] The Copyright Act does not require a minimum age to receive copyright protection of a work, so these minors are creating a significant amount of UGC. Facebook nevertheless copies and distributes this material to its users until the accounts are deleted.

Meanwhile, Facebook is considering opening the website to users of all ages in the United States.[78] Such action would require significant changes to the website, and would not solve the problems with the minor's UGC.[79] In India, however, a court recently ruled that Facebook is

---

73 Facebook, n 31.

74 *See* n 34.

75 Facebook, n 31.

76 The 13 age requirement is not an arbitrary figure. The Children's Online Privacy Protection Act of 1998 (COPPA) requires websites to establish certain procedures for the collection of information, marketing and parental consent for children under 13. 15 U.S.C. §§ 6501–6506 (Pub. L. 105-277, 112 Stat. 2581-728, enacted October 21, 1998).

77 http://www.huffingtonpost.com/2011/03/23/facebook-underage-users_n_839437.html. Furthermore, "an estimated 3.6 million of Facebook's 153 million monthly visitors in [the United States] are under 12." http://www.nytimes.com/2011/03/12/technology/internet/12underage.html?_r=2&.

78 http://www.cp24.com/news/facebook-considers-opening-site-to-users-under-13-1.1505734. Opening Facebook to children under 13 would present many challenges to Facebook. *See* COPPA, n 39. But Facebook may think that these problems are easier to overcome than its current situation.

79 Instead, these minors would fall into a similar category as those currently between the ages of 13 and 18, addressed in note 82 and accompanying text.

not for minors below 13.[80] To comply with this ruling, Facebook is to add a prominent disclaimer on the homepage notifying everyone that minors under 13 are not allowed to open an account.[81]

The second set of minors, persons between the ages of 13 and 18, presents a different problem. These individuals are not in violation of the terms of use. But they might not be old enough to license their UGC.[82] Facebook does provide specific user settings, typically in the form of restrictions, for minors.[83] These restrictions, however, address privacy issues and minor protection and do not indicate any changes for a minor's UGC.

The examples of public outcry over social network terms of use indicate that there is a potential for some negotiation with these licenses. Thus, just as the Web 1.0 "New Economy" (i.e. Internet companies and users) in 2012 collectively confronted the "Old Economy" (i.e. the established copyright content industries) over the latter's attempt to lobby through ACTA and implementing legislation,[84] so now we see the "New Economy" itself being confronted by the "New (i.e. interconnected) Consumer" that the Web 2.0 era of the Internet has unleashed. Mass licenses may be metamorphosing from contracts of adhesion into something more akin to socially negotiated mass licenses.[85] These socially negotiated mass licenses have the effect of championing copyright law as a *lex specialis* over contract law.

---

[80] http://indiatoday.intoday.in/story/facebook-not-for-kids-below-13-years-rules-delhi-court/1/291689.html.

[81] *Ibid.*

[82] *See* Hetcher at 856.

[83] *See* https://www.facebook.com/help/473865172623776/.

[84] *See* Charles R. McManis, *The Proposed Anti-Counterfeiting Trade Agreement (ACTA): Two Tales of a Treaty*, 46 HOUS. L. REV. 1235 (2009).

[85] Consumers have begun to post (probably futile) disclaimers to the Facebook terms and conditions. *See, e.g.*, http://www.tbennettlaw.com/createprotect/2014/12/2/do-i-need-a-facebook-disclaimer.

3. Fair is as fair does: Contractual normative regulation of copyright user contracts in South Africa

Caroline B. Ncube

INTRODUCTION

This chapter considers the regulation of copyright user contracts by contract and consumer protection law in South Africa. The normative regulation of copyright contracts was identified as a significant research gap by Kretschmer et al., who specifically list the following questions as being worthy of investigation:[1]

- How should 'fairness' be defined for the context of copyright contracts?
- Are existing contracts really 'unfair'?
- Do alternative contracts, within the current copyright law, exist that can be perceived as being 'fairer'? If they do exist, do those contracts sacrifice efficiency?
- To what extent does any perceived 'unfairness' depend upon copyright law?
- Can copyright law be altered in order that the balance of bargaining positions be changed and the resulting contracts are 'fair'?

This chapter engages with some of these questions, which will be posed with regard to user contracts for the reprographic reproduction of copyright-protected works concluded between copyright-holders (represented by a reprographic rights organisation) and higher educational institutions. Here, the main concern is whether such blanket or transactional licenses override statutory exceptions and limitations. If so, is this fair? If it is not fair, how may copyright law be amended to ensure fairness?

[1] Martin Kretschmer, Estelle Derclaye, Marcella Favale and Richard Wyatt, *The Relationship between Copyright and Contract Law* (2010) 9 and 28.

The key methodology will be doctrinal. The discussion will unfold within an access to knowledge framework, which seeks an equitable treatment of copyright-holder and user interests based on the public interest and constitutional principles. Specifically it will focus on how a lack of fairness or equity would fall foul of consumer protection legislation and thwart South Africa's constitutional imperative to provide education for its citizenry.

Copyright law frames the contracting space in which a copyright-holder contracts with third parties. It endows the copyright-holder with exclusive rights, which he can then license to users.[2] As noted by Derclaye and Favale,[3] these rights are limited by eligibility[4] and substantive[5] criteria for protection, the exclusion of certain works from copyright protection,[6] the limited duration of copyright, the exhaustion of rights and exceptions and limitations. Exceptions and limitations provide users with limited permission and royalty-free uses of copyright-protected works. Both user and copyright-holder then negotiate a contract for use of the work that exceeds usage covered by exceptions and limitations. It is in this contracting space that fairness needs to be achieved – and more so when contracts seek to erode existing permissible uses and thus expand the right-holder's monopoly in an environment where digital distribution is widespread.[7]

---

[2] Niva Elkin-Koren, 'Copyright Policy and the Limits of Freedom of Contract', (1997) 12 Berkeley Tech. L.J. 93, 105.

[3] Estelle Derclaye and Marcella Favale, 'User Contracts' in Martin Kretschmer et al *The Relationship between Copyright and Contract Law* (2010) 71, 71.

[4] Section 2 (1) of the Copyright Act provides for the following exhaustive list of copyright-eligible subject matter: (1) literary, musical and artistic works; (2) cinematograph films; (3) sound recordings; (4) broadcasts; (5) programme-carrying signals; (6) published editions and (7) computer programs.

[5] Copyright will subsist automatically in eligible works if the three requirements for protection are met, namely that the work is reduced to a material form (ss 2(2)–2(2A)) and is created by a qualified person (ss 3(1) and 37) or is first published in South Africa or another country to which protection is extended (ss 4(1) and 1(5)).

[6] See for example s (8) (a), which provides: 'No copyright shall subsist in official texts of a legislative, administrative or legal nature, or in official translations of such texts, or in speeches of a political nature or in speeches delivered in the course of legal proceedings, or in news of the day that are mere items of press information.'

[7] Elkin-Koren (supra note 2) 113.

To the extent that copyright law defines the baseline for both rightholders and users, it is a *lex specialis*. The delimitation of the rightholder's exclusive rights and the exceptions and limitations upon which a user can rely are the domain of this body of law. General contractual principles are relevant to the extent that they regulate the conduct of both parties in the negotiation and conclusion of a copyright contract. Additionally, as discussed below, consumer protection legislation is also applicable.

As a precursor to this discussion, a brief overview of reprographic licensing in South Africa is given.

REPROGRAPHIC RIGHTS LICENSING IN SOUTH AFRICA

The only reprographic rights organisation in South Africa is the Dramatic, Artistic and Literary Rights Organisation (DALRO). It is a member of both the International Confederation of Copyright Societies (Confédération Internationale des Sociétés d'Auteur et Compositeur) (CISAC) and the International Federation of Reproduction Rights Organisations (IFRRO). DALRO states that its main mandate is the administration of 'reprographic reproduction rights (from published editions), public performance rights (including stage rights for book musicals and dramas) and reproduction rights (granted for both publishing and copying) in works of visual art'.[8]

DALRO issues two types of reprographic reproduction rights licenses, namely blanket and transactional licenses. The Universities of Cape Town, Stellenbosch and the University of the Witwatersrand have entered into blanket licenses with DALRO. These licenses permit licensees to make the copies it requires over an agreed period, after which the licensee reports on the copies made. Licensees are required 'to pay a once off invoice before the end of May each year'.[9] No additional payment will be required provided the blanket license copying parameters are maintained. These parameters limit copying up to a maximum of one chapter or 10 per cent of a book; one article from a journal issue;

---

[8] DALRO 'About us' <http://www.dalro.co.za/index.php/about-us> (last accessed 8 November 2013).

[9] University of the Witwatersrand 'Blanket License agreement with DALRO' <http://libguides.wits.ac.za/content.php?pid=227586&sid=2361879> (last accessed 8 November 2013).

a full case study and a full law report.[10] Copying more than 10 per cent of a book will fall within the parameters if it consists of one full chapter.[11] Where a licensee wishes to copy more than these parameters, DALRO would negotiate licensing with South African publishers, but where the publisher is foreign the licensee has to negotiate with that publisher directly.[12] Of concern to this chapter is whether these parameters adequately take exceptions and limitations for educational purposes into account. The DALRO explanatory guide asserts that they have been taken into account.[13] This point is addressed further below in the section entitled 'Fairness under copyright law'.

Transactional licensing, used by the University of Pretoria,[14] is described by DALRO as 'a pay-per-use service where institutions, businesses, schools and organisations pay for the re-use of specific selections. These selections are: a specific published work to be distributed to a specific group of people enrolled in a specific course or workshop held at a specific time.'[15] DALRO's 2013 rates for higher education institutions were ZAR0.63 per page and were significantly lower for state secondary and primary schools.[16]

Both licenses are administered through a copyright clearance system that has been put in place to facilitate this. Details of its implementation are available on the websites of several institutions.[17] In the financial year

---

[10] *Ibid.* Cape Higher Education Consortium (which administers licenses for universities in the Western Cape province of South Africa) User Manual: The Request Process <http://plo.uct.ac.za/help/user/usr_00_main.php> (last accessed 8 November 2013).

[11] DALRO Information Brochure March 2013, 5. <http://www.dalro.co.za/index.php/repository/Downloads/DALRO-Information-Brochure/> (last accessed 8 November 2013).

[12] *Ibid.*

[13] DALRO *Reprographic Reproduction of Copyright Material for Educational Purposes* (undated) <http://www.wsu.ac.za/library/DALRO.pdf> (last accessed 8 November 2013).

[14] University of Pretoria 'How to apply for copyright permission' <www.ais.up.ac.za/copyright/permission.htm> (last accessed 8 November 2013).

[15] DALRO 'Copyright Access for Institutions of Higher Learning: Transactional Licenses' <http://www.dalro.co.za/index.php/lincences> (last accessed 8 November 2013).

[16] DALRO 'Default rates April 2013' <http://www.dalro.co.za/index.php/repository/Downloads/DEFAULT-RATES-APRIL-2013/> (last accessed 8 November 2013).

[17] University of the Witwatersrand (supra note 9), the University of Pretoria (Transactional License) <http://www.ais.up.ac.za/copyright/permission.htm>. The University of Cape Town, University of the Western Cape, Cape Peninsula

ending 30 June 2010 DALRO collected license and royalty revenue for reprographic reproduction of ZAR26 842 183.[18]

FAIRNESS UNDER COPYRIGHT LAW

There are several ways to rationalise copyright law, such as natural justice, economic, cultural and social arguments.[19] Whatever one's philosophical persuasion, it is indisputable that one of the purposes or aims of copyright law, since its inception, has been to serve the public interest. This purpose requires a balance between right-holder and user interests, particularly those underpinned by fundamental freedoms or public policy. As noted by Helfer and Austin:[20]

> Conceptually and textually, there exist venerable connections between education and intellectual property. These connections are particularly clear in the copyright context ... The first copyright statute, the English Statute of Anne of 1709, was entitled 'An Act for the Encouragement of Learning.' Similarly, the Copyright Clause of the U.S. Constitution empowers the U.S. Congress to 'to promote the progress of science' (or, in modern parlance, 'knowledge') by creating a national copyright system. In the early years of the French Revolution, responsibility for the development of copyright law passed to the 'Committee for Public Instruction,' and by 1793, it was accepted that 'enacting a copyright law formed part of a grander scheme of public education'.

The Berne Convention, 1886[21] out of this understanding of the need to balance contesting stakeholder interests in the public interest, provides for exceptions and limitations to secure unremunerated user access to

---

University of Technology and the University of Stellenbosch use the Cape Higher Education Consortium's Public Liaison Office's Copyright Clearance System < http://plo.uct.ac.za/user.php> (all last accessed 8 November 2013).

[18] DALRO 'About us' <http://www.dalro.co.za/index.php/about-us> (last accessed 8 November 2013).

[19] Tana Pistorius, 'Copyright Law' in Hennie Klopper et al., *The Law of Intellectual Property in South Africa* (Lexis Nexis 2011) 143 at 144.

[20] Laurence R Helfer and Graeme W Austin, *Human Rights and Intellectual Property: Mapping the Global Interface* (Cambridge Univ. Press 2011) 316.

[21] Berne Convention for the Protection of Literary and Artistic Works, 9 September 1886, amended 28 September 1979, Art 2*bis*, 1161 UNTS 3 (Berne Convention).

protected works in specified circumstances.[22] In addition, it provides that member states may permit certain exceptions to the reproduction right subject to the so-called three-step test.[23] This provision has been broadened to apply to other exclusive rights in more recent intellectual property (IP) agreements, namely article 13 of the Agreement on Trade Related Aspects of IP Rights (TRIPS)[24] and article 10 of the World IP Organisation (WIPO) Copyright Treaty (WCT).[25] Fairness and the balancing of interests are therefore often said to be a fundamental concern of this body of law. However, using the metaphor of balance raises several vexed questions, which have been discussed by several scholars.[26] For present purposes it will suffice to mention three of these. Firstly, what exactly does the concept mean or entail? Secondly, which measure should be used to gauge such balance?[27] Thirdly, even if one knows what it means and how to measure it, how is it to be attained on international and domestic levels?[28] In some instances, the concept of balance is often used without full appreciation of its complex and 'multidimensional nature'.[29] In relation to the second aspect, I have suggested elsewhere that 'the twin pillars of human rights and socio-economic conditions

---

[22] Daniel J Gervais, 'Making copyright whole: a principled approach to copyright exceptions and limitations' 2008 University of Ottawa Law & Technology Journal 1.

[23] Berne Convention, Article 9(2). For a discussion of the three-step test see Gervais (supra note 22) and Martin Senftleben, *Copyright, Limitations, and the Three-step Test: An Analysis of the Three-step Test in International and EC Copyright Law* (2004); Martin Senftleben, 'The International Three-Step Test: A Model Provision for EC Fair Use Legislation' 1 (2010) JIPITEC 67, para. 1.

[24] Agreement on Trade-Related Aspects of Intellectual Property Rights, including Trade in Counterfeit Goods, adopted 15 December 1993, entered into force 1 January 1995, (1994) 33 ILM 81.

[25] WIPO Copyright Treaty, adopted 20 December 1996, entered into force on 6 March 2002 36 ILM 65.

[26] For example see William Patry, *How to Fix Copyright* (Oxford Univ. Press 2010) 134–140; Graeme B Dinwoodie 'The WIPO Copyright Treaty: A Transition to the Future of International Copyright Lawmaking?' (2007) 57 Case Western Reserve Law Review 751; Abraham Drassinower 'From Distribution to Dialogue: Remarks on the Concept of Balance in Copyright Law' (2008–2009) 34 Journal of Corporation Law 991.

[27] Carys J Craig, 'The Evolution of Originality in Canadian Copyright Law: Authorship, Reward and the Public Interest' (2005) 2 U. Ottawa L. & Tech. J. 425, 441.

[28] Dinwoodie (supra note 26) 753.

[29] Dinwoodie, ibid. For other discussions see also Patricia Akester, 'The New Challenges of Striking the Right Balance Between Copyright Protection and

could be used to attempt to break the deadlock between creators and users' interests'.[30] Another concern raised by using this metaphor is its tendency to distill the interests at stake into two sides, namely right-holders and users, which raises the risk of overlooking the highly nuanced positions of those who fall into neither group.[31] In particular, the interests of users are distinct from those of society generally as are the interests of authors and creators from those of intermediaries and publishers who may hold copyright in the works in question. Further, the interests of members of each of these constituencies are diverse. For example, not all users have the same interests. Indeed the balance metaphor has been dismissed as a 'fallacy'[32] and suggestions have been made for its replacement with other turns of phrase.[33] In view of these considerations, this chapter uses the concept of balance whilst acknowledging its limits.

The other rhetorical device used in this chapter – that of the 'public interest' – is also used advisedly because it is similarly fraught and has been critiqued for being vague.[34] It has been appropriated by different agendas over time and identified or conflated with the interests of a specific copyright constituency.[35] However, in reality, the public interest in copyright is multidimensional and consists inter alia of authorship interests and access interest.[36] Although it continues to draw debate about its meaning, the concept of the public interest in copyright remains in usage because of the potential it represents as it evokes the hope of

---

Access to Knowledge, Information and Culture', (2010) 32:8 European Intellectual Property Review 372.

[30] Caroline B Ncube, 'Harnessing Intellectual Property for Development: Some Thoughts on an Appropriate Theoretical Framework' (2013) 16(4) Potchefstroom Electronic Law Journal 369, 374. A discussion of this question is beyond the scope of this chapter and for present purposes, it will suffice merely to raise it.

[31] Teresa Scassa, 'Interests in the Balance' in Michael Geist ed., *In the Public Interest: The Future of Canadian Copyright Law* (Irwin Law 2005) 41–65, 41.

[32] Patry (supra note 26) 134.

[33] For example Drassinower (supra note 26) suggests that dialogue is a more apt term.

[34] Isabella Alexander, *Copyright Law and the Public Interest in the Nineteenth Century* (2010) 16.

[35] Rebecca Giblin and Kimberlee Weatherall, 'What would copyright law look like if it was actually in the public interest?' Working Paper (2014) 5–7.

[36] Guan H Tang, *Copyright and the Public Interest in China* (Edward Elgar 2011) 50.

justice and fairness for the common good.[37] As noted above, this chapter's purpose is not to engage in an excursus of the debates surrounding copyright rhetoric but rather to consider the substantive fairness of licenses for the reprographic reproduction of copyright-protected works. It is to this task, that the rest of the chapter turns.

South African copyright legislation, post-1910, has been based on English law[38] and is thus imbued with the imperatives of the Statute of Anne and subsequent English legislation. Further, South Africa has ratified both Berne and TRIPS and incorporated their provisions relating to exceptions and limitations, together with other limitations on copyright into domestic legislation. Therefore, it can also be said that South African copyright law is also fundamentally concerned with the public interest goals of achieving fairness and the balancing of stakeholder interests.

The balancing mechanisms employed by the South African Copyright Act are the same as those adopted globally, which are listed above, and include its provisions for exceptions and limitations. Indeed, three of these provisions – the fair dealing,[39] quotation[40] and illustration in

---

[37] Gillian Davies, *Copyright and the Public Interest* PhD thesis Aberystwyth University (1997) 1.

[38] Tana Pistorius (supra note 19) 148.

[39] Section 12(1) provides 'Copyright shall not be infringed by any *fair dealing* with a literary or musical work –

(*a*) for the purposes of research or private study by, or the personal or private use of, the person using the work;
(*b*) for the purposes of criticism or review of that work or of another work; or
(*c*) for the purpose of reporting current events –
  (i) in a newspaper, magazine or similar periodical; or
  (ii) by means of broadcasting or in a cinematograph film:

Provided that, in the case of paragraphs (*b*) and (*c*) (i), the source shall be mentioned, as well as the name of the author if it appears on the work'. (my emphasis)

[40] Section 12(3) provides 'The copyright in a literary or musical work which is lawfully available to the public shall not be infringed by any quotation therefrom, including any quotation from articles in newspapers or periodicals that are in the form of summaries of any work: Provided that the quotations shall be compatible with *fair practice*, that the extent thereof shall not exceed the extent justified by the purpose and that the source shall be mentioned, as well as the name of the author if it appears on the work.' (my emphasis)

teaching[41] exceptions – expressly refer to fairness. However, the Copyright Act does not provide any guidance as to how the fairness of user conduct is to be assessed. An express stipulation of the relevant factors to be considered in such an assessment would have been beneficial similar to those contained in the United States Copyright Act's fair use provision.[42] In other common law jurisdictions, such as Canada, which have a fair dealing exception, the courts have pronounced extensively on the relevant factors. However, in South Africa there is no case law elucidating the concept of fairness generally in copyright law or clarifying the contours of the quotation, illustration in teaching and fair dealing exceptions.

In addition to the above exceptions, domesticating Berne article 9(2), s 13 of the South African Copyright Act, provides:

> In addition to reproductions permitted in terms of this Act reproduction of a work shall also be permitted as prescribed by regulation, but in such a manner that the reproduction is not in conflict with a normal exploitation of the work and is not unreasonably prejudicial to the legitimate interests of the owner of the copyright.

---

[41] Section 12(4) provides 'The copyright in a literary or musical work shall not be infringed by using such work, to the extent justified by the purpose, by way of illustration in any publication, broadcast or sound or visual record for teaching: Provided that such use shall be compatible with *fair practice* and that the source shall be mentioned, as well as the name of the author if it appears on the work.' (my emphasis)

[42] Section 107 of the US Copyright Act provides 'Notwithstanding the provisions of sections 106 and 106A, the fair use of a copyrighted work, including such use by reproduction in copies or phonorecords or by any other means specified by that section, for purposes such as criticism, comment, news reporting, teaching (including multiple copies for classroom use), scholarship, or research, is not an infringement of copyright.

In determining whether the use made of a work in any particular case is a fair use the factors to be considered shall include –

(1) the purpose and character of the use, including whether such use is of a commercial nature or is for non profit educational purposes;
(2) the nature of the copyrighted work;
(3) the amount and substantiality of the portion used in relation to the copyrighted work as a whole; and
(4) the effect of the use upon the potential market for or value of the copyrighted work.

The fact that a work is unpublished shall not itself bar a finding of fair use if such finding is made upon consideration of all the above factors.'

The relevant Regulations permit copying of one copy of *a reasonable portion* of the work, having regard to the totality and meaning of the work and provided 'the cumulative effect of the reproductions does not conflict with the normal exploitation of the work to the unreasonable prejudice of the legal interest and residuary rights of the author'.[43] The issue that this provision raises is: What exactly constitutes a reasonable portion? In other jurisdictions, a quantitative indicator is given which cannot be reduced by a license. For example, the UK's recent amendments[44] to the Copyright, Designs and Patents Act, 1988 provide that up to '5% of a work may be copied … by or on behalf of an educational establishment in any period of 12 months'.[45] Any license terms that seek to reduce the proportion of a work which may be copied whether subject to a fee or not are void.[46] South African courts have not pronounced on the extent of what would be considered a reasonable portion, so uncertainty on this point exists.

Two further regulations permit copying, subject to regulation 2, which is quoted above. The first of these, regulation 7, permits the making of 'multiple copies (not exceeding one copy per pupil per course)… by or for a teacher for class-room use or discussion'. The second, regulation 8, allows a 'single copy [to] be made by or for a teacher, at his request, for research, teaching or preparation for teaching in a class'. It goes without saying that these two regulations are marred by the uncertainty of regulation 2 to which they cross-refer.

In the absence of clear legislative provisions and judicial guidelines on factors to determine fairness and as to what constitutes a reasonable portion of a work, users are likely to err on the side of caution, to their detriment.[47] This is probably even more so in the case of 'public-interest institutions like libraries and universities [which] generally stay clear of activities that might bring about litigation'.[48] They are likely to exercise

---

[43] Regulation 2, Copyright Regulations, 1978, GNR.2530 of 22 December 1978.

[44] The Copyright and Rights in Performances (Research, Education, Libraries and Archives) Regulations 2014, SI 1372, 2014.

[45] Section 36(5).

[46] Section 36(7).

[47] For a discussion of this issue in the context cultural institutions, see E. Hudson, *Drafting Copyright Exceptions: An Empirical Study* (Cambridge Univ. Press 2015) (forthcoming).

[48] Chris Armstrong, Jeremy de Beer, Dick Kawooya, Achal Prabhala and Tobias Schonwetter 'Summary and conclusions' in Chris Armstrong et al., *Access to Knowledge in Africa: The Role of Copyright* (UCT Press 2010) 317, 322.

their entitlement to permission-free uses of copyright-protected works to a minimal or negligible extent. It is true that less risk-averse users may liberally interpret the exceptions. However, the fairness of copyright cannot be left to depend on the risk-aversion levels of users.

The lack of certainty as to the extent of permissible license-free use of copyright-protected works negatively affects the contractual bargaining space because the user approaches negotiations with uncertainty as to the parameters of their permission-free use of the work. Consequently, the resultant licensing agreement may be unfair because it requires the user to pay for uses that should have been permission-free. Such licenses effectively override exceptions and limitations through their failure to take them into account in setting the boundaries of permitted copying or in setting the licensing fee.

To that extent it is reasonable to assert that some unfairness in licensing contracts is due to deficiencies in copyright law. Copyright law can, and should, be amended to change the balance of bargaining positions which would result in fair contracts. There are two kinds of fairness being contemplated here. The first is that the permission free uses of protected works provided for by copyright legislation ought to be fair to the user. If the relevant provisions do not adequately cater for user interests and needs then the playing field is uneven as users start off on the back foot, trying to compensate contractually for legislative short-comings. This is inherently unfair because contractual uses have to be paid for and in economically disadvantaged contexts, they may become unattainable for those who are unable to afford license fees. Secondly, fairness is being considered in relation to licensing contracts relating to use of the work beyond that permitted by copyright legislation. This aspect is discussed in the second half of this chapter.

The concept of fairness is of significance in relation to the first aspect, that of permission free uses of protected works, primarily due to its incorporation in the fair dealing, quotation and illustration in teaching exceptions, which have been discussed above. As already stated, the meaning of fairness in these contexts is unclear. To provide the necessary clarity, the Copyright Act ought to be amended to provide for factors that ought to be considered in determining fairness. To this end, lessons can be drawn from the interpretation of similar legislative provisions in other jurisdictions. The Canadian Supreme Court in *CCH Canadian Limited v Law Society of Upper Canada*[49] held that the following factors are to be considered in determining the fairness of the dealing: the

[49] [2004] 1 SCR 339, 2004 SCC 13.

purpose of the dealing, the character of the dealing, the amount of the dealing, the nature of the work, available alternatives to the dealing, and the effect of the dealing on the work. These factors have been consistently applied and were most recently re-iterated by the Supreme Court in 2012.[50]

In addition, the Copyright Act and its Regulations can also be amended to give quantitative guidelines as to permitted reproduction for educational purposes, as has been done in the United Kingdom. As stated above, DALRO has set royalty-free copying parameters at 10 per cent or one chapter of a book for its blanket licenses. This raises the question of whether this constitutes a reasonable portion. The rationale behind setting this limit at 10 per cent rather than any other figure is not publicly available, making it difficult to interrogate it. However, the fact that it sets a fixed limit that does not permit a consideration of individual circumstances engenders some discomfort. Under transactional licenses, license fees are paid for each copy. There is no royalty-free threshold. This raises the question of how the license takes exceptions and limitations into account. In its publications, DALRO asserts that the portions of copyright-protected works that it licenses are not covered by exceptions and limitations. It states:

> Finally, it is most important to note that the concessions dealt with above are explicitly stated in Regulation 7 to be intended for 'class-room use or discussion'. They do not permit the making of compilations commonly referred to as 'course packs', 'study packs', 'course readers', 'study guides' or 'student hand-outs' in which extracts from various publications are reproduced with or without notes by the lecturer, and then made available to students.[51]

CAN, AND SHOULD, COPYRIGHT EXCEPTIONS AND LIMITATIONS BE OVERRIDDEN BY CONTRACT?

Exceptions and limitations can be justified on two main grounds, namely fundamental rights and market failure.[52] Private copying exceptions may be seen as a way of dealing with market failure.[53] Exceptions for satire,

---

[50] *Alberta (Education) v Canadian Copyright Licensing Agency (Access Copyright)* 2012 SCC 37.

[51] DALRO *Reprographic Reproduction of Copyright Material for Educational Purposes* 5.

[52] Derclaye and Favale (supra note 3) 72.

[53] Derclaye and Favale (supra note 3) 73.

parody, criticism and quotation can be justified on the freedom of expression.[54] South Africa's Copyright Act currently does not provide for satire or parody exceptions but provides for fair dealing for purposes of criticism and reporting current events. It is argued that it ought to be amended to provide for parody and satire exceptions to give effect to constitutional imperatives. The Constitutional Court has considered the freedom of expression in a trademark infringement matter[55] where it was alleged that the parodic use of trademarks tarnished the marks under s 34(1) (c) of the Trademarks Act, 194 of 1993.[56] The court did not make a finding on fair use of the mark under that section and freedom of expression because it held that the trademark holder had failed to prove economic harm.[57] The court noted that:

> unlike the US, in our jurisprudence there are no enclaves of protected expression such as parody or satire and therefore the mere characterisation of an expression as such would not be decisive of what is fair use under our

---

[54] Section 16 of the Constitution of South Africa, 1996 which provides:

'(1) Everyone has the right to freedom of expression, which includes –
- (*a*) freedom of the press and other media;
- (*b*) freedom to receive or impart information or ideas;
- (*c*) freedom of artistic creativity; and
- (*d*) academic freedom and freedom of scientific research.'

[55] 2006 (1) SA 144 (CC). For commentary, see Jason Brickhill, 'Breaking Down the Boardroom Doors with A Snigger and A Smirk – Laugh It Off Laughs Last: Case Note' (2006) 21 SA Public Law 214; J Deacon and I Govender, 'Trade Mark Parody in South Africa – The Last Laugh!' (2007) 32 Journal for Juridical Science 18; George Devenish, 'We are Amused: *Laugh it Off Promotions CC v SAB International (Finance) BV t/a Sabmark International*: notes' (2005) 122 SALJ 792; Tana Pistorius 'Trade-mark Tarnishment: Should We "Laugh it Off" All the Way to "Telkomsucks" and "Hellcom"?' (2004) 16 SA Merc LJ 727; and C Ncube, 'From the law reports: *Laugh It Off Promotions CC v South African Breweries International (Finance) BV t/a Sabmark International*' 2005 (1) Codicillus 82.

[56] The section provides:

> 'The rights acquired by registration of a trade mark shall be infringed by the unauthorised use in the course of trade in relation to any goods or services of a mark which is identical or similar to a trade mark registered, if such trade mark is well known in the Republic and the use of the said mark would be likely to take unfair advantage of, or be detrimental to, the distinctive character or the repute of the registered trade mark, notwithstanding the absence of confusion or deception: Provided that the provisions of this paragraph shall not apply to a trade mark referred to in section 70(2)'.

[57] At para 65.

> anti-dilution protection of section 34(1)(c) because ordinarily all categories of expression, save those excluded by the Constitution itself, enjoy constitutional shield and may be restricted only in a way constitutionally authorised.[58]

The Copyright Act's exceptions for educational purposes clearly can be justified on the constitutionally protected right to education.[59] It is not possible to exercise this right without access to learning materials. Such access is not entirely dependent on copyright but it is indisputably a key factor. Current copyright law is not optimal for meaningful access to learning materials due to uncertainties such as those pointed out above and its failure to cater for digital and distance learning models, access to orphan works and exceptions to cater for the conversion of works to formats that are accessible to the visually impaired.[60] Despite such limitations, these exceptions are so crucial to achieving access to learning materials that South Africa cannot continue to risk them being overridden by contract. In addition, if they were strengthened in the future, one would want them to be protected from abrogation by agreement.

There is support for the view that exceptions and limitations based on fundamental rights ought to be imperative and thereby protected from contractual abrogation. Indeed, some jurisdictions make exceptions and limitations imperative and nullify any contractual clauses that seek to reduce or minimise them. The examples cited by Derclaye and Favale[61] of such jurisdictions are Belgium,[62] Ireland[63] and Portugal.[64]

The approach of these jurisdictions has been faulted for making all exceptions and limitations mandatory, rather than protecting only those

---

58 Ibid.

59 Section 29 of the Constitution of South Africa, 1996 provides: 'Everyone has the right to a basic education, including adult basic education and further education, which the State, through reasonable measures, must progressively make available and accessible'.

60 Caroline B Ncube 'Key copyright issues in African distance education: a South African case study' (2011) 32(2) *Distance Education* 269; Tobias Schonwetter and Caroline B Ncube, 'New hope for Africa? Copyright and access to knowledge in the digital age' (2011) 13(3) Info 64–74; Tobias Schonwetter, Caroline B Ncube and Pria Chetty 'South Africa Country Report' in Chris Armstrong et al (ed.) *Access to Knowledge in Africa: The Role of Copyright* (2010) UCT Press, 231–280.

61 (supra note 3) 83–87.

62 Art 11 of the Belgian Database Act, Law 31 of 1998 makes all exceptions relating to the *sui generis* database right imperative and art 23 *bis* makes similar provision in relation to copyright exceptions.

63 s2(10) Copyright Act n.38 of 2000.

64 Code of Author's Rights and Related Rights, 14 March 1985.

relating to fundamental rights and public policy.[65] Hence the suggestion has been made that not all exceptions and limitations be made imperative but that careful choices must be made about which of them to make imperative. It is argued that this critique is assailable because as all exceptions and limitations have a justiciable public interest basis, they should be mandatory. Exposing some or all of them to contractual arbitrage would not be in the public interest.

Currently there are no provisions in the South African Copyright Act that invalidate any contractual clauses that attempt to override such exceptions and limitations. It would therefore appear that contractual clauses might reduce or eliminate them altogether. The following section of this chapter considers whether, in the face of the inadequacy of copyright law, South African users can look to consumer protection law for any protection. At the outset, it is important to note that resorting to consumer protection law is an acceptable alternative, which has been lauded by some because it is a body of law that aims to 'promote and advance the social and economic welfare of consumers'.[66] For example, Consumers International has identified the use of consumer protection law to prohibit or reduce the exclusion of user rights as a best practice because it provides avenues of redress 'against big companies that use their IP to infringe upon consumers' rights.'[67]

FAIRNESS UNDER THE CONSUMER PROTECTION ACT

1. Applicability of Consumer Protection Legislation to Copyright Licenses

The South African Consumer Protection Act, 2008 came into force in April 2011. It 'applies to every transaction[68] occurring within South

---

65 Derclaye and Favale (supra note 3) 84.

66 Section 3(1) Consumer Protection Act.

67 Consumers International *IPWatchlist 2012*, 4.

68 Defined by s1 as –

'(a) in respect of a person acting in the ordinary course of business –
  (i) an agreement between or among that person and one or more other persons for the supply or potential supply of any goods or services in exchange for consideration; or
  (ii) the supply by that person of any goods to or at the direction of a consumer for consideration; or

Africa, which has not been exempted by the Act, and to the promotion and supply of any goods or services within South Africa'. Goods are defined as 'any literature, music, photograph, motion picture, game, information, data, software, code or other intangible product written or encoded on any medium, or a license to use any such intangible product'. These are copyright-eligible goods and copyright will subsist automatically in them if the three requirements for protection are met, namely that the work is original,[69] it is reduced to a material form[70] and is created by a qualified person[71] or is first published in South Africa or another country to which protection is extended.[72]

The Consumer Protection Act will not apply to contracts, which pertain to these goods if any exemptions apply. The relevant exemptions are:[73]

1. transactions under which goods and services are promoted or supplied to the state, and
2. transactions where the consumer is a juristic person that had an annual turnover of more than ZAR 2 million at the time of the transaction.

The second exemption is subject to the exception that juristic persons, regardless of turnover, are entitled to benefit for the protection provided for in sections 60–61 of the Act, which pertain to product recalls.[74] These exemptions are quite significant. They would apply where a government department (that is the state) or an institution of higher education which has an annual turnover that is above the above-stated threshold enters into licensing contract with regard to the reprographic reproduction of books. This means that any normative regulation of contracts provided for in the Consumer Protection Act will not apply. They would only apply where the educational institution has an annual turnover of less than ZAR 2 million.

(iii) the performance by, or at the direction of, that person of any services for or at the direction of a consumer for consideration; or

(b) an interaction contemplated in section 5 (6), irrespective of whether it falls within paragraph (a).'

69 Section 2(1) Copyright Act.
70 Section 2(2) Copyright Act.
71 Section 3(1) Copyright Act.
72 Section 4(1) Copyright Act.
73 Section 5(2) (a)–(b) Consumer Protection Act.
74 Elizabeth de Stadler *Consumer Law Unlocked* (2013) 8.

The applicability of consumer protection legislation to copyright-protected goods distinguishes South Africa from the United Kingdom, where the Unfair Contract Terms Act 1977 and its regulations do not apply to copyright contracts which create or transfer rights or an interest.[75] Another distinction between the two jurisdictions is that the Unfair Contract Terms Act focuses on limitation clauses in pro forma or standard form contracts, whereas the South African Consumer Protection Act is much broader in its ambit. It also considers unfairness in contracts that have been negotiated by the parties. To that extent, its approach is closer to Australian Consumer Law (ACL).[76] In particular, the ACL regulates 'misleading and deceptive conduct, unconscionable conduct, unfair practices, consumer guarantees, unsolicited consumer agreements and consumer product safety'.[77] All these aspects are also covered by South African consumer protection legislation.

2. Normative Regulation of Fairness

The concept of fairness is well developed in South African contract[78] and consumer protection law, where it has a multi-dimensional character which addresses substantive, procedural, abstract and contextual fairness.[79] Existing statutory provisions seek to achieve a balance between contractual parties' freedom of choice and the need to eliminate or reduce inequities due to the differences in the parties' bargaining power, knowledge of the law and their ability to enforce their rights.

---

[75] Schedule 1, s1(c) provides that Sections 2 to 4 of the Act do not extend to 'any contract so far as it relates to the creation or transfer of a right or interest in any patent, trade mark, copyright, registered design, technical or commercial information or other intellectual property, or relates to the termination of any such right or interest'.

[76] Schedule 2 Competition and Consumer Act 2010.

[77] Jeannie Paterson *Unfair Contract Terms in Australia* (Thomson Reuters 2012) 11.

[78] For example, see AM Louw, 'Yet Another Call for a Greater Role For Good Faith in the South African Law of Contract: Can We Banish the Law of the Jungle, While Avoiding the Elephant in the Room?' (2013) 16(5) Potchefstroom Electronic Law Journal 44; Philip J Sutherland, 'Ensuring contractual fairness in consumer contracts after Barkhuizen v Napier 2007 5 SA 323 (CC) – part 1' (2008) 19(3) Stellenbosch Law Review 390; Philip J Sutherland, 'Ensuring contractual fairness in consumer contracts after Barkhuizen v Napier 2007 5 SA 323 (CC) – part 2' (2009) 20 Stellenbosch Law Review 50.

[79] Philip N Stoop, *The Concept of 'Fairness' in the Regulation of Contracts under the Consumer Protection Act 68 of 2008,* Thesis LLD University of South Africa, 2012, 32–49.

The South African Consumer Protection Act seeks to provide protection for consumers[80] in accordance with its stated purposes and policy.[81] For this chapter, the most relevant purpose is:

> protecting consumers from –
>
> (i) Unconscionable, *unfair*, unreasonable, unjust or otherwise improper trade practices; and
> (ii) deceptive, misleading, *unfair* or fraudulent conduct (my emphasis).[82]

This chapter focuses on substantive fairness.[83] The goal of substantive fairness is achieved through a number of statutory provisions. The most pertinent of these for this discussion is use of black lists, which prohibit certain clauses and render them *void ab initio*, and grey lists, which create a rebuttable presumption that other clauses are unfair, unreasonable or unjust. The black list is contained in s 51 of the Act and the grey list is contained in reg 44 of the Regulations.[84] A full discussion of the use of these lists is beyond the ambit of this chapter and readers are

---

[80] Defined by s1 'in respect of any particular goods or services' as:

'(a) a person to whom those particular goods or services are marketed in the ordinary course of the supplier's business;
(b) a person who has entered into a transaction with a supplier in the ordinary course of the supplier's business, unless the transaction is exempt from the application of this Act by section 5 (2) or in terms of section 5 (3);
(c) if the context so requires or permits, a user of those particular goods or a recipient or beneficiary of those particular services, irrespective of whether that user, recipient or beneficiary was a party to a transaction concerning the supply of those particular goods or services; and
(d) a franchisee in terms of a franchise agreement, to the extent applicable in terms of section 5 (6) (b) to (e).'

[81] s 3.

[82] s 3(1) (d).

[83] The reader is referred elsewhere for a nuanced discussion of the other related concepts such as unconscionability which goes to procedural fairness. For example, see Graham Glover, 'Section 40 of the Consumer Protection Act in Comparative Perspective' (2013) 4 TSAR 289; Jacques Du Plessis, 'Protecting consumers against unconscionable conduct: Section 40 of the Consumer Protection Act 68 of 2008' (2012) THRHR 26.

[84] Consumer Protection Regulations, GNR.293 of 1 April 2011: Regulations (Government Gazette No. 34180).

referred to other writing on these points.[85] Section 48 of the Act contains the 'general fairness criterion for consumer contracts'[86] that is also referred to as 'the general right to fairness'.[87]

The threefold approach of s 48 (1) is of particular relevance to this discussion First, s 48(1) (a) prohibits the inclusion of unfair, unreasonable or unjust terms in contracts. It provides:

> A supplier must not offer to supply, supply, or enter into an agreement to supply, any goods or services at a price that is unfair, unreasonable or unjust; or on terms that are unfair, unreasonable or unjust.

Secondly, s 48(1) (b) prohibits the marketing of any goods or services, or the negotiation, conclusion or administration of a transaction or an agreement in a manner that is unfair, unreasonable or unjust. Thirdly, s 48(1) (c) prohibits suppliers from requiring 'a consumer, or other person to whom any goods or services are supplied at the direction of the consumer, to waive any rights; assume any obligation; or waive any liability of the supplier, on terms that are unfair, unreasonable or unjust, or impose any such terms as a condition of entering into a transaction.'

The Consumer Protection Act then sets out a list of unfair, unreasonable or unjust transactions or agreements, terms or conditions and notices which includes the following:[88]

(a) 'excessively one-sided in favour of any person other than the consumer or other person to whom goods or services are to be supplied'; and
(b) 'so adverse to the consumer as to be inequitable.'

One may argue that clauses in licensing agreements that override, or take no account of exceptions and limitations in setting license fees, are unreasonable, unfair and unjust because they render the contract excessively one-sided in favour of the licensor and are so adverse to the licensee as to be inequitable. In addition one could argue that licensors who conclude such contracts have not negotiated in good faith. Such an argument should stand despite the lack of provisions in the Copyright Act

[85] Tjakie Naudé, 'The use of black and grey lists in unfair contract terms legislation in comparative perspective' (2007) 124 South African Law Journal 128.
[86] Stoop (supra note 79) 113.
[87] De Stadler (supra note 74) 114.
[88] s 48(2).

that make such exceptions imperative. This is because of the constitutional imperatives that underpin some exceptions, such as the right to education and freedom of expression which have been briefly canvassed above.

These two factors – (a) and (b) – above are the substantive equivalent of Regulation 5(1) in the UK Unfair Terms in Consumer Contracts Regulations, which refer to terms that cause 'a significant imbalance in the parties' rights and obligations under the contract to the detriment of the consumer'.[89] Accordingly, an assessment of the entire contract in question would be necessary to weigh rights and obligations of both parties to ascertain if an excessive imbalance exists. There is as yet no case law in South Africa on this point relating to copyright user contracts. For its part, DALRO reports that it has reviewed its licenses to ensure compliance with the Consumer Protection Act.[90]

There certainly seems to be scope to challenge unfair blanket and transactional licenses on the basis of consumer protection law. However, the statutory provisions are not applicable where the licensee has a turnover of more than ZAR 2 million, and would thus exclude many institutions of higher learning and perhaps some government departments that take out licenses on behalf of schools. In order to mount a successful challenge, it would be necessary to prove that exceptions and limitations have been unfairly discounted in setting license terms and fees and, consequently, the resultant contract is either excessively one-sided or is so adverse that it is inequitable.

However, to the extent that some inequities are due to the inadequacy of current copyright law, is it necessary to effect some amendments of copyright law to broaden and entrench exceptions and limitations. This underscores the *lex specialis* nature of copyright, which defines the baseline for both right-holders and users. The need to return to the bascline is inevitable because doing so will benefit all users and particularly those who are excluded from the ambit of the Consumer Protection Act.

---

[89] Stoop (supra note 79) 115, citing *Director General of Fair Trading v First National Bank* [2002] 1 Lloyd's Rep 489; [2001] 3 WLR 1297 and *Sasfin (Pty) Ltd v Beukes* 1989 (1) SA 1 (A).

[90] DALRO Annual Report, 2011 <http://www.dalro.co.za/index.php/about-us> (last accessed on November 2013).

4. Compelling disclosure of software interoperability information: A risk for innovation or a balanced solution?

Begoña G. Otero

The first part of this chapter explores how and why certain provisions of the Software Directive influence disclosure of software interoperability information. This inquiry is prompted by Actions 23 and 25 of the Digital Agenda for Europe 2010–2020 (DAE). There, the European Commission (in a study of licensing) proposed a compulsory licence approach as the most suitable way to achieve *ex ante* disclosure of interoperability information from significant market players in the ICT sector.[1] Additionally, the Study reached two central conclusions: first, interoperability information needs to be treated differently than software generally; and, second, compelling the disclosure of interoperability information, though important for reasons of competitiveness, must also be done with awareness of the broader effects of innovation.

As to the former, it has to be recognised that software interoperability information involves a number of strategic choices for players in the ICT sector. This information is embodied in a very specific part of software systems, namely its interfaces. Where to put interfaces and whether to make them "open" or "closed" is a fundamental strategic choice for firms.[2] From the legal perspective, this strategic choice has raised considerable concerns both for the fields of intellectual property rights (IPRs) and competition law. However, approaches differ. From the perspective of intellectual property law, whether tackling patents on

[1] Report from workshop 3 of the Digital Agenda Assembly "Interoperability and Standards: Making it happen", Digital Agenda for Europe, Actions 23 and 25, 16–17 June 2011, available at: http://ec.europa.eu/digital-agenda/sites/digital-agenda/files/03.pdf (last accessed November 2013).

[2] Report from workshop 3, op.cit., p. 19.

computer-implemented inventions,[3] copyright protection of the programs[4] or even trade secrets covered by software licences,[5] the main question is to what extent interoperability information should be protected? Nonetheless, from the perspective of competition law, the question is to what extent control over interoperability information might jeopardise free competition.[6] Without losing sight of the paramount importance of licensing nowadays, the relevance that copyright in computer programs has for interoperability and licensing is remarkable. The first definition of the concept of interoperability in a legal text is found in the Software Directive, and this instrument contains a specific provision (Article 6 – Decompilation) devoted to promoting interoperability between competitors.[7] Furthermore, the great importance of copyright claims in standards was illustrated by a "clarification" of the International Organisation for Standardisation (ISO) intellectual property policy published in July 2003.[8] That clarification would have required all software developers and commercial data resellers who embedded data elements from the ISO's

---

[3] See EPO Dec. T 2217/08 (Executable code/MICROSOFT) of 10.04.2013 and EPO Dec. T 1415/07 (Converting graphical programs/NATIONAL INSTRUMENTS) of 17.11.2011.

[4] See ECJ Case C-393/09 – *Bezpečnostní softwarová asociace – Svaz softwarové ochrany v Ministerstvo kultury* (22 December 2010) OJ C 63, p. 8; ECJ Case C-406/10 – *SAS Institute Inc. v World Programming Ltd.* (2 May 2012) OJ C 174, p. 5.

[5] See CFI Case T-201/04 *Microsoft Corp. v Commission of the European Communities* (17 September 2007) Rec 2007 II-03601. In this case, opening the source code was not sufficient; what was required was documentation anyone else could use on top of developing the source code.

[6] See Merger decisions such as Intel/McAfee M.5984, OJ C 329 of 7 December 2010; Atos Origin/Siemens IT Solutions & Services M.6127, OJ C 68 of 3 March 2011; Microsoft/Skype M.6281, OJ C 268 of 10 September 2011, and Antitrust decisions such as CFI Case T-201/04 *Microsoft Corp. v Commission of the European Communities* (17 September 2007) Rec 2007 II-03601; *Décision 04-D-54 du 9 novembre 2004, relative à des pratiques mises en œuvre par la société Apple Computer, Inc. dans les secteurs du téléchargement de musique sur Internet et des baladeurs numériques*; investigation Case no. 39840 The MathWorks (closed in September 2014 without further explanation).

[7] See Proposal for a Council Directive on the legal protection of computer programs, OJ C91, vol. 32, 12.4.1989, p. 16.

[8] R. Maginnis, Dir. Of Elec. Sales & Mktg., ANSI, Summary Regarding the Use of ISO Codes 3-4 (9 July, 2003) Available at: http://www.incits.org/archive/2003/in030912/in030912.pdf (Accessed November 2013).

standard country and currency codes to pay an annual fee (or a one-off fee plus regular maintenance fees) for doing so.[9]

Regarding how interoperability is regulated by the Software Directive, it is important to remark that by essentially protecting interoperability information under the same regime as computer programs in general, the Directive fails to explicitly recognize that, as a result of network effects and standardization, the optimal balance between openness and control of interoperability information may well be different from that of programs at large. On the one hand, the manner in which the Software Directive protects computer programs extends beyond source and object code.[10] Translations of programs from one programming language to another and any other type of adaptation, arrangement or alteration to programs are assuredly within the scope of protection.[11] Likewise, detailed preparatory design materials, such as flowcharts, are manifestations of program design that copyright law protects according to the Software Directive.[12] This means the copyright holder controls access to all program information. On the other hand, Article 6 of the Software Directive permits decompilation in order to access interoperability information that supports the functionality built into an existing program when the independently created program incorporates a corresponding functionality. But functional behaviour of computer programs is not part of the literary expression for which copyright protection is available.[13] Providing protection to functional elements via copyright would lead to a thicket of IP rights which could seriously deprive markets of the general advantages of competition.[14]

As to the latter conclusion, the European Commission's proposal for compulsory licensing of interoperability information is supported by the

---

[9] R. Cover, "Standard Organizations Express Concern about Royalty Fees for ISO Codes" [online] (2003); P. Samuelson, "Questioning Copyright in Standards" in L. DeNardis (ed.), *Opening Standards: The global politics of interoperability*, MIT Press, Cambridge, Massachusetts, 2011, p. 135.

[10] Article 1 (Object of protection) and Article 4 (Restricted Acts) Directive 2009/24/EC of the European Parliament and the Council of 23 April 2009 on the legal protection of computer programs (5 May 2009) OJ L 111, pp. 16–22 (Software Directive).

[11] See Article 4.1(b) Software Directive.

[12] See Article 1(1) Software Directive.

[13] See ECJ Case C-406/10 – *SAS Institute Inc. v World Programming Ltd.* (2 May 2012) OJ C 174, p. 5, para 39.

[14] P. Samuelson, T. Vinje and W. Cornish, "Does Copyright Protection Under the EU Software Directive Extend to Computer Program Behaviour, Languages and Interfaces?", EIPR, 34(3), 2012, p. 165.

fact that companies in the ICT sector do not easily provide interoperability information about their products. When this refusal to disclose comes from a significant market player and there are no standards, the Commission considers that innovation in the ICT sector will be at risk.[15] However, due to the copyright protection and the complicated regime established by Article 6 of the Software Directive, an application of the framework of the Microsoft case (the essential facilities doctrine) could risk ignoring the particular issues that arise when access is sought to proprietary standards and specifically interoperability information. As some scholars have affirmed, the limitation contained in Article 6 of the Software Directive tries to provide a mechanism whereby it would be more advantageous to both parties to avoid decompilation and negotiate the supply of interoperable information.[16] However, as the Microsoft case has revealed, this negotiation imposes abundant costs on the copyright holder which causes them to decline a voluntary licensing negotiation route. These costs are mainly three: the mere passive nature of the reverse engineering instruments; the discrepancy between static legal conditions and a dynamic state of the art in reverse engineering; and, the particular conditions established in the wording of Article 6.[17] If the parties seem to be unwilling to determine the terms of access to the key information, how may the Commission and courts determine and monitor the terms of access to that information? This could put in risk innovation by inadequately balancing incentives and increasing legal uncertainty.

It should not be forgotten that dominance itself does not contravene Article 102 TFEU, and a refusal to license in the ICT sector based on the grounds of abuse of dominant position has to comply with the conditions detailed by the CFI in the Microsoft case.[18] Compelling disclosure of interoperability information as a general solution is very unlikely to work

---

[15] Action 25 of the Digital Agenda for Europe (DAE), available at: https://ec.europa.eu/digital-agenda/en/pillar-ii-interoperability-standards/action-25-identify-and-assess-means-requesting-significant (Accessed November 2013).

[16] B. Czanorta and R.J. Hart, *Legal Protection of Computer Programs in Europe: A guide to the EC Directive*, Butterworths, London, 1991, p. 80.

[17] A. van Rooijen, *The Software Interface between Copyright and Competition Law: A legal analysis of interoperability in computer programs*, Kluwer Law International, Alphen aan der Rjin, 2009, p. 86.

[18] For a commentary about the Microsoft case see: F. Lévêque, "Innovation, Leveraging and Essential Facilities: Interoperability licensing in the EU Microsoft Case", World Competition 28, 2005, p. 71–91; M.A. Dizon, "Decompiling the Software Directive, the Microsoft CFI case and the i2010 strategy: How to reverse engineer an international interoperability regime", CTLR 14, 2008, 213–228.

as a balanced solution for the ICT industry. It will only be used in exceptional circumstances, as under Article 102 TFEU.

In June 2013, the European Commission released a Working Document titled "Analysis of measures that could lead significant market players in the ICT sector to license interoperability information"[19] (hereinafter, Commission SWD). Some of the proposals contained in this document bring about greater uncertainty about the costs for the Commission when trying to foster licensing of interoperability information. The EC is focusing again on compulsory licensing. But the impact of copyright on encouraging both licensing and access to interoperability information has been underestimated and the importance of pursuing EU ICT standard reform has not been taken into consideration. After exploring what software interoperability means in practice and what problems it creates in the ICT sector, this chapter examines the measures proposed in that working document and suggests some recommendations aimed at achieving more motivation, innovation and competition, and enhancing *ex ante* disclosure of software interoperability information.

1. WHAT SOFTWARE INTEROPERABILITY MEANS IN PLAIN ENGLISH

There is no general agreement on the definition of software interoperability, whether one looks at definitions in technology, business, policy or legal literature. On the one end of the spectrum, some definitions focus only on technological aspects, while broader frameworks distinguish and very broadly define interoperability at various levels, including, for instance, legal, organisational and political levels. An apparent conclusion is that interoperability is a very context-specific concept. However, when it comes to software interoperability, all definitions pivot around the same

[19] Commission Staff Working Document (SWD) of the European Commission "Analysis of measures that could lead significant market players in the ICT sector to licence interoperability information" SWD (2013) 209 final, 6 June, 2013, p. 3. This chapter is the result of an investigation performed in the framework of the Digital Agenda for Europe, specifically Actions 23 and 25, which refer namely to standards and interoperability, mostly through the study of compulsory licensing of interoperability information owned by significant market players in the absence of standards.

idea: "the ability of two pieces of software to exchange information and mutually use the information that has been exchanged".[20]

However, over the last few years software interoperability has not been regarded as a phenomenon that should be studied and developed as a rigorous mathematical and scientifically lawful phenomenon. The current means of dealing with software interoperability is much the same as the way mechanical problems were handled prior to Newton: ad hoc trial-and-error constructions that were completely restricted to the present problem, and with no sense that each problem is an example of a set of globally valid laws that are expressible in mathematical equations that directly reveal the real structure of the problem and the means of solving it.[21] The word "interoperability" is generally being abused and it is not an all-or-nothing concept.[22] In fact, from a strictly software perspective, interoperability is not so hard to define.

It is common nowadays to read that software interoperability and software compatibility are synonymous terms.[23] It is also argued that any software interoperability failure can be solved through a solution designed to ensure compatibility. Although the second statement is true, its main consequence leads us to an "intraoperability" framework and not to an interoperability one. It is a matter of degree; the latter is part of the former. However intraoperability only focuses in achieving good level of connectivity with a dominant system. Full or true interoperability means

---

20 Recital 12 of Directive 2009/24/EC of the European Parliament and the Council of 23 April 2009 on the legal protection of computer programs (5 May 2009) OJ L 111, pp. 16–22 (Software Directive). Almost identical is the definition given by the Institute of Electrical and Electronics Engineers (IEEE): "the ability of two or more systems or components to exchange information and to use the information that has been exchanged". IEEE Standard Computer Dictionary: A Compilation of IEEE Standard Computer Glossaries, Inst of Elect & Electronic Engineers, New York, 1990.

21 M. Leyton, "Institute Mission Statement of the International Institute of Interoperability Science for Large-Scale Engineering Systems Integration, DIMACS Center for Discrete Mathematics & Theoretical Computer Science, Rutgers University" [online], 2002. Available at: https://www.rci.rutgers.edu/~mleyton/Interoperability_Institute.html (Accessed November 2013).

22 U. Gasser and J. Palfrey, *Interop: The promise and perils of highly interconnected systems*, Basic Books, New York, 2012, p. 21.

23 See for instance "Microsoft Interoperability Principles" [online]. Available at http://www.microsoft.com/openspecifications/en/us/programs/interop/interoperability-principles/default.aspx, or the topic "Interoperability, Connectivity, and Compatibility" of Microsoft [online]. Available at: http://technet.microsoft.com/en-us/library/exchange-online-interoperability-connectivity-compatibility.aspx (Accessed November 2013).

software success does not exclusively depend on who controls the conditions of connectivity but because the application is faster, more reliable, more secure, it has a better user interface and more generally provides a better quality of service. The problem of abuse consists of using "interoperability" when the facts prove "intraoperability". In plain English: software compatibility means that we could make two software products, which mutually exchange and use information, work together without knowing why or how. Software interoperability allows two pieces of software to work together as they do with any two others (and we know why and how).

In a compatibility or *intraoperability* situation, one piece of software is central and dominant, by reason of market share, consumer attitude or acquiescence. Connectivity is supported by protocols and data formats that favour the central software and those are often prescribed by the provider, which do not meet the definition of open as set by neutral organizations such as IDABC (European Union's programme for Interoperable Delivery of European eGovernment Services to public Administrations, Businesses and Citizens). The goal is to absorb all important data and process into the central software ecosystem; thus it is, in this sense, that the prefix "intra" is used.[24] In this situation, to solve an interoperability failure, we may need licences to use the protocols or formats, and the central vendor may even try to standardise the specifications with rules stating that one cannot break compatibility with their products. Licences might even prevent the use of the formats, protocols or even a user interface from competitors or creators of open-source software. It may be in the immediate economic interest of the other players to participate, but they do so with the tacit agreement that they are agreeing to play in an asymmetric environment where the primary advantages go to the one in the centre.

Consequently, some market players provide a high level of *intraoperability* by allowing users to transfer content from one device to another without restriction; other competitors create and operate in a closed environment that is tightly controlled by digital rights management and low levels of interoperability.[25]

---

[24] R. Sutor, "Software Standards, Openness, and Interoperability", in L. DeNardis (ed.), *Opening Standards: The global politics of interoperability*, MIT Press, Cambridge, Massachusetss, 2011, p. 214.

[25] *See inter alia*: Adobe Personal Computer Software License Agreement, terms 8 and 16 [online], available at: http://www.adobe.com/products/eulas/reader/x/eula_en_gb.html; Software License Agreement Apple iBooks Software,

For full software interoperability to work, the key factor is open standards. Open standards do not favour any software provider or developer; they only allow for two pieces of software to work together as they do with any other two. From a market perspective, open standards do not prevent one of the software providers from holding a dominant position. Reaching a dominant position in an open standards context depends on the broader merits, not in having used (or abused) an (asymmetrical) *intraoperability* situation.

The problem of creating a robust and high-quality software open standard – one that meets the needs of vendors and customers, users and implementers, public and private sectors, now and over time – is complex and context-dependent. Because of the peculiarities of the ICT sector itself, there are any number of reasons why a particular open standard for software may succeed or fail in the market, and meeting the open standards requirements is no guarantee that the standard will magically succeed by that fact alone. In addition to this, open standards initiatives are purely a voluntary effort, and anecdotal evidence suggests that companies with patent portfolios might easily interfere or even block such initiatives.[26] Furthermore, standard-setting processes are normally complex, time-consuming and relatively expensive when compared with unilateral or bilateral approaches; arguably, their cost-efficiency is comparatively low.[27]

As will be explained below, any given level of interoperability is likely to be the result of a complex interplay between different factors. However, we should not overlook the fact that software is a functional work. This means a program may succeed in the market because the application or service is faster, more reliable, more secure and more scalable, has a better user interface or, more generally, provides a better quality of service. It should not succeed because a provider abuses the

---

term 2.A and 2.B [online], available at: http://www.apple.com/legal/sla/docs/iBooks.pdf (accessed November 2013).

26 M, Dolmans, "A Tale of Two Tragedies – A plea for open standards", *IFOSS L. Rev.*, Vol. 2, No. 2, 2010, p. 115; Bridges, "Open IT Standards Would Benefit Developing Countries", *ICTSD,* Vol. 11, No. 7, November [online] 2007, available at: http://ictsd.org/i/news/bridges/3171/ (Accessed November 2013).

27 HM Government, "Open Standards Principles. For software interoperability, data and document formats in government IT specifications", [online] 2012, p. 6, available at: https://www.gov.uk/government/uploads/system/uploads/attachment_data/file/78892/Open-Standards-Principles-FINAL.pdf (accessed November 2013); OSPT Alliance, "Why Open Standards for Transit?" [online] 2013, available at: http://www.osptalliance.org/the_standard/why_open_standards (accessed November 2013).

word "interoperability" and convinces others that they are on a level playing field.

2. THE SOFTWARE INTEROPERABILITY PROBLEM IN THE ICT SECTOR

It is generally accepted that higher levels of interoperability help to achieve economic growth through innovation, competition and trade.[28] Several theoretical models of innovation support this statement.[29] From an empirical perspective, cloud computing, bar codes, identity management systems, the Internet, and web services are just a few examples of how high levels of interoperability can benefit society. On the other side of the coin, however, high levels of interoperability bring high levels of standardisation, and the presence of too many industrial standards in a market sector is capable of stifling innovation because of the lack of plural and diverse competitive tenders.[30]

From an economic perspective, it should not be forgotten that switching costs in the ICT sector is the general rule, not the exception, and this is a double-edged sword: software companies have large incentives to innovate and to be the first to market when, by achieving strong network effects, they are competing for the entire market and not just for a share of it.[31] When the new software technology developed by a company becomes a standard as a result of exploitation of strong network effects rather than for its real value for society, together with the refusal to allow

---

28 U. Gasser and J. Palfrey, op. cit., p. 125.

29 J. Zittrain, *The Future of the Internet – And How to Stop It,* Yale University Press, New Haven, CT, 2008, p. 176; B. van Schewick, *Internet Architecture and Innovation*, MIT Press, Cambridge, MA, 2010, p. 285; E. von Hippel, "Open Source Projects as Horizontal Networks – by and for Users", *Industrial and Corporate Change*, Vol. 16, 2007, pp. 2–30; C.M. Christensen, *The Innovator's Dilemma. The revolutionary book that will change the way you do business*, Harper Collins, New York, 2003, p. 10.

30 M. Lehmann, "Standardization and the EC Directive of 14 May 1991 on the Legal Protection of Computer Programs", in W.F. Korthal et al. (eds), *Information Law Towards the 21st Century*, Kluwer Law and Taxation, Deventer, Boston, MA, 1992, p. 368.

31 A. Slowak, "Standard-Setting Capabilities in Industrial Automation: A collaborative process", *Journal of Innovation Economics*, Vol. 2, 2008, pp. 147–169; G. Surblytė, *The Refusal to Disclose Trade Secrets as an Abuse of Market Dominance – Microsoft and Beyond*, Stampfli Publishers Ltd, Berne, 2011, p. 161.

interoperability of its technology to other market players (that is, when taking advantage of a mismatch) can the reward given to the market player through the standard be considered to be excessive?[32]

As a result, the ICT industry is on an evolution continuum of essential non-interoperability to interoperability. The maturity of a given technology, market structure (for example number of market players, presence of network effects, lock-in situations) and market incentives (for example consumer demand, new market niches) as well as the boundaries of protection as determined by the legal regime, especially intellectual property and competition law, all affect any given level of interoperability.[33]

There are various common means used by market players to achieve software interoperability:

1. Developing and designing out-of-the-box (OOTB) products[34] with little need for customisation or integration services, such as Microsoft with Microsoft Office, Apple with iTunes or Amazon with Kindle.
2. Informal community collaboration among manufacturers and other industry constituents to develop technologies necessary to create interoperability between related products, product families and services. Within these types of means of ensuring interoperability there are different levels of it. The most straightforward means will be for a provider voluntarily to provide unilateral openness that allows others to achieve interoperability with its products or services.[35] Beneath this will be negotiation and licensing of intellectual property rights by the

---

[32] C. Shapiro and H.R. Varian, *Information Rules: A strategic guide to network economy*, Harvard Business School Press, Boston, MA, 1999, p. 103; J. Farrell and M.L. Katz, "The Effects of Antitrust and Intellectual Property Law on Compatibility and Innovation", *Antitrust Bulletin*, Vol. 43, 1998, p. 46.

[33] U. Gasser and J. Palfrey, op. cit., p. 124.

[34] An out-of-the-box (OOTB) product is a term used in the ICT sector to refer to a software or hardware feature or functionality that works immediately after installing without any configuration or modification. *See* http://searchcio.techtarget.com/definition/out-of-the-box; http://h30499.www3.hp.com/t5/Discover-Performance-Blog/You-want-to-implement-software-out-of-the-box-Here-s-how/ba-p/6070403#.UoOPSj9fYVc (Accessed November 2013).

[35] This is the case of Facebook or Google, which voluntarily created an open application programming interface (API) to allow anyone to develop interoperable APIs for their web services, without the need for further approval or cooperation. *See* https://developers.facebook.com/ and https://developers.google.com/ (accessed November 2013).

parties involved.[36] And finally, when no unilateral openness or licensing is possible, interoperability may be achieved by the use of reverse engineering techniques.[37]

3. Developing and implementing technical standards, whether formal standards established by consortiums (that is, adopted for standardisation by a Standards Development Organisation (SDO), such as the International Standards Organisation) or informally adopted by users as *de facto*; this second category includes both closed and open standards.[38]

Depending on the business model, a market player may emphasise one or more of these approaches over others and, in many cases, take more than one avenue to interoperability. However, when negotiating and licensing is not possible because one of the parties refuses to do so, the range of possibilities to achieve interoperability decreases to mainly two means. The first is to appeal to the use of reverse engineering techniques in order to develop new products, and the second is to request compulsory licensing before the competition authorities if the refusal constitutes an abuse of a dominant position. Neither of these two ways are the most desirable from a business perspective. And, besides, neither really guarantees achievement of interoperability. In the first case, reverse engineering is a difficult and expensive process and the Software Directive does not provide legal certainty about the scope of the

---

[36] For the agreements between Microsoft and Red Hat to enable cross-certification of the companies' virtualisation platforms, *see*: http://www.redhat.com/promo/svvp/ (accessed November 2013). About the collaboration between Microsoft and Intel to develop Plug and Play, *see*: http://software.intel.com/en-us/vcsource/samples/application-sample-using-microsoft-multimedia-framework-plug-ins (Accessed November 2013). More recently, the Tolino initiative in the e-book sector in Germany; *see*: http://www.tolino.de/de/service/ (Accessed November 2013).

[37] Examples of this practice are cases such as *Atari, Inc. v Nintendo of America, Inc.*, 975 F.2d 832, 24 U.S.P.Q.2d (BNA) 1015 (Fed. Cir. 1992) or *Sega Enterprise, Ltd. v Accolade, Inc.*, 977 F.2d 1510, 24 U.S.P.Q.2d (BNA) 1561 (9th Cir. 1992) in the United States; the WPL software which ended up in the ECJ C-406/10 or the case between RealNetworks and Apple that never reached a court decision. A comment on this case is found in B. Gonzalez Otero, *The Software Interoperability Debate on European Copyright*, Unpublished Ph.D. thesis, Department of Commercial Law, Industrial Law Institute, Universidad de Santiago de Compostela, 2013, pp. 30–31, available at: http://dspace.usc.es/handle/10347/10620 (accessed November 2013).

[38] Examples of software standards are TCP/IP, MPEG, HTTP, HTML, Open Document Format, Open XML, PDF, VGA, ISA, MP3.

decompilation exception.[39] In the latter, enforcing competition law is meant to be an exceptional tool. Cases such as Apple with iTunes in France, or Microsoft with Windows in the EU, revealed that, even when the conditions established by Article 102 of the Treaty on the Functioning of the European Union are met, mandating disclosure of software interoperability information is not a real guarantee of achieving it.[40]

As the EC working document suggests,[41] and as has been pointed out by many scholars in the past,[42] market players of closed platforms are fairly reluctant to negotiate the supply of interoperability information. The source of poor software interoperability is not technical but primarily comes from business decisions in large platforms designed to keep their ecosystems closed. This should not be a problem at first sight, but when business practices of one or some market players lead to a situation where the lack of interoperability prevents competition in the market, those companies will have few incentives to innovate at a high pace. Intervening then might indeed be too late to repair the damage or it might force public authorities to twist the law in order to salvage the situation.[43]

---

[39] B. Gonzalez Otero, "Compelling to Disclose Software Interoperable Information: A Risk for Innovation or a Balanced Solution?", JWIP, Vol. 16, Issue 1-2, 2013, p. 8.

[40] B. Gonzalez Otero, *The software interoperability debate*, op. cit., p. 294.

[41] Commission SWD, op. cit., p. 3.

[42] A. van Rooijen, *The Software Interface between Copyright and Competition Law: A legal analysis of interoperability in computer programs*, Kluwer Law International, Alphen aan den Rjin, 2009, p. 84; J. Bartmann, *Grenzen der Monopolisierung durch Urheberrechte am Beispiel von Datenbanken und Computerprogrammen: Eine rechtsvergleichende Studie des europäischen, deutschen und US-amerikanischen Rechts*, Carl Heymanns, Cologne, 2005, p. 125; P. Samuelson et al., "A Manifesto Concerning the Legal Protection of Computer Programs", *Columbia Law Review*, Vol. 94, No. 8, 1994, p. 2341; B. Czarnota and R.J. Hart, *Legal Protection of Computer Programs in Europe: A Guide to the EC Directive*, Butterworths, London, 1991, p. 78.

[43] See CFI Case T-201/04 *Microsoft Corp. v Commission of the European Communities* (17 September 2007) Rec 2007 II-03601, and some of the comments on the case criticising the application of the Essential Facilities Doctrine by the Commission and the European Court of Justice such as D. Spulber, "Competition Policy and the Incentive to Innovate: The dynamic effect of Microsoft v. Commission", *Yale J. on Reg.*, Vol. 25, No. 2, 2008, p. 247; A. Devlin et al., "Success, Dominance and Interoperability", *Ind. L.J.*, Vol. 84, 2009, p. 1168; S. Anderman, "Microsoft v. Commission and the interoperability issue", in L. Rubini (ed.), *Microsoft on Trial. Legal and Economic Analysis of a Transatlantic Antitrust Case*, Edward Elgar, Cheltenham, 2010, p. 258; E. Fox, "The EC Microsoft case and duty to deal: the transatlantic divide", in L. Rubini

The software interoperability problem lies in the fact that these business practices are completely supported by the legal regime. Software interoperability information can be controlled or restricted through three main forms of intellectual property rights, namely patents, trade secrets and copyright. And, as stated above, providing protection to a program's functional elements via copyright would lead to a thicket of IP rights which could seriously deprive markets of the advantages of general competition.

3. THE COMMISSION STAFF WORKING PAPER

The document released by the European Commission in June 2013 is the result of research conducted in the framework of Action 25 of the Digital Agenda for Europe, on the feasibility of measures that could lead significant market players to license interoperability information in the absence of standards.[44] It is structured around two different types of measures: non-legislative and legislative.

Under the first category, the Commission explored "soft" measures that could encourage negotiation between market players, such as model licences to facilitate licensing, especially for small actors; a code of best practices for dealing with licensing requests; guidelines for assessing the value of interoperability information; and the inclusion of optional interoperability clauses in grant agreements for research and innovation projects. Basically, all these measures relate, to a greater or lesser extent, to software licensing.

I agree with the conclusion of the Working Paper that these measures may have a relatively rapid impact by lowering barriers to IPR trading (licensing) and lowering related transaction costs.[45] However, the Commission SWD does not offer a single specific suggestion about how to implement any of them. Besides, although the Commission is right about the significance of licensing for achieving interoperability, it fails to take into account the bigger problem of the legal nature of software agreements themselves. That is, determining the legal nature of software agreements has always been a great challenge for legal researchers and

---

(ed.), *Microsoft on Trial. Legal and economic analysis of a transatlantic antitrust case*, Edward Elgar, Cheltenham, 2010, p. 278; G. Surblytė, *The Refusal to Disclose,* op. cit., pp. 138–139.

[44] Commission SWD, op. cit., p. 3.

[45] Commission SWD, op. cit., p. 1 and 15.

practitioners. Moreover, there is no jurisdiction where software agreements would explicitly be included in the catalogue of contracts within codified civil law.[46] Consequently, proposing a variety of non-legislative measures aimed at facilitating access to interoperability information that will bring more problems than solutions does not look like very feasible.

Yet, bearing in mind the business practices used by major market players to enable or to restrain interoperability, what is the motivation to make use of these measures? Their main point is to better facilitate access, an act which is mainly controlled by copyright law in the field of software. In this regard, cases such as the *UsedSoft* decision,[47] although it does not relate to interoperability itself, should remind us not only of the great impact of copyright protection over software and over its uses, but also that copyright has further effects on the contractual framework that have, until now, been overlooked.

Therefore, in order to make non-legislative measures work in a field where the legal regime supports business practices which do not invite parties to negotiate, it will first be necessary to change that legal regime. It is indispensable to review its potential mismatches. The legislative measures explored in the Commission SWD address the three main intellectual property rights over computer programs: patents, trade secrets and copyright.

A. Potential Legislative Measures on Patents

Before exploring the proposed measures on patents, it is essential to recall how patent protects software interfaces (the specific part of the program where the interoperability information lies). Under the European Patent Convention (EPC), a computer program "as such" is not patentable subject matter.[48] Patents are not granted for program listings, which, as such, are protected by copyright.[49] To be sure, the application of

[46] R.M. Hilty, K. Köklü, and F. Hafenbrädl, "Software Agreements: Stocking and Outlook – lessons from the UsedSoft v Oracle case from a Comparative Law Perspective", IIC, Vol. 44, No. 3, 2013, p. 263; N. Shemtov, *The Legal Regulation of Decompilation of Computer Programs: Excessive, unjustified and in need of reform*, Unpublished Ph.D. Thesis, Queen Mary University of London [online], 2012, pp. 203–236. Available at: https://qmro.qmul.ac.uk/xmlui/handle/123456789/3132 (Accessed November 2013).

[47] ECJ Case C-128/11 – *UsedSoft v Oracle* (22 September 2012) OJ C 287, pp. 10–11.

[48] Article 52(2)(c) and (3) EPC.

[49] European Patent Office, "Patent for software? European law and practice" [online] 2013. Available at: http://www.epo.org/news-issues/issues/computers/

software architecture to a specific technical invention, of a technical character, may be protectable as part of a bigger patentable concept, but the scope of protection is limited to this specific application.[50] Hence, when access to the information contained in the interfaces does not imply the "making" or the "using" of the patented invention, there is no patent infringement. Besides, even if a patentee manages to obtain a patent on an architectural aspect of software, they must provide a disclosure that is detailed enough to enable a skilled person to understand the invention.[51] Therefore, current patent protection over software interoperability information should not present major obstacles to vibrant competition in practice.

Bearing this in mind and returning to the legislative measures proposed for inducing significant market players to license their patents on computer-implemented inventions, the Commission proposes: (1) the generalisation of licence of right (LOR) regimes in the European Union, creating at the same time a compulsory and automatic LOR for interfaces; and (2) an *ex novo* exception for interoperability in the Unitary Patent Regulation, inspired by the reverse engineering copyright exceptions in the Software Directive.[52]

As to the first proposal, LORs currently exist only in Germany and the UK.[53] Without considering the pros and cons of this type of legal tool for the patent licence system in general,[54] it does not seem very efficient or

---

software.html (Accessed November 2013). However, it is worth recalling the opinion of industry, such as in the case of Mr Marshall Phelps (former Corporate VP, IP Policy & Strategy, Microsoft, and VP, IP & Licensing, IBM) stating: "[The EPO] cannot distinguish between hardware and software so the patents get issued anyway". *See*: http://techrights.org/2012/07/30/tax-on-algorithms-in-europe/ (Accessed November 2013).

[50] See EPO Decision T 208/84 (Vicom / Computer related invention) EPOR 74.

[51] Article 83 EPC.

[52] Article 11.3 of the Regulation (EU) No 1257/2012 of the European Parliament and the Council of 17 December 2012 implementing enhanced cooperation in the area of the creation of unitary patent protection, OJ L 361, p. 1; Article 27(k) of the Council Agreement on a Unified Patent Court, 2013/C 175/01, OJ C 175, p. 1; Articles 5.3 and 6 of the Directive 2009/24/EC of the European Parliament and of the Council of 23 April 2009 on the legal protection of computer programs (codified version), OJ L 111 p. 16.

[53] §23 of the German Patent Act and Section 46 of the UK Patent Act.

[54] For a study on the License of Rights, *see*: I. Rudyck, "The License of Rights: Compulsory licensing and the value of exclusivity", SFB/TR 15 Discussion Paper No. 415, GESY, University of Munich, December 2012 [online]. Available at: http://epub.ub.uni-muenchen.de/17240/ (Accessed November 2013).

practical to force all European member states to adopt this tool only for better interoperability. On the matter of compulsory licensing, I have already noted that this does not amount to a balanced solution. Nevertheless, one statement in the working document on how compulsory licences will apply to patents raises some concern. The document states that "mandatory licences of right for interfaces would only apply to patent claims that cover interoperability information, not to all patents".[55] If the information of the interfaces is contained in the claims, and therefore shall be publicly disclosed, where is the need for compulsion? Although a computer-implemented invention (CII) is one that involves the use of a computer, computer network or other programmable apparatus, where one or more features are realized wholly or partly by means of a computer program, and among these features one can find parts of a computer program containing interoperability information. If a licence were needed to use interoperability information, would not this be a tacit admission that computer programs "as such" could be within the scope of the patent?

Finally, a proposal for an interoperability exception is contained in the Agreement on a Unified Patent Court.[56] This is not the place to offer an opinion on the Unitary Patent Package,[57] but the provision's text contains the exception for "the acts and the use of the obtained information as allowed under Articles 5 and 6 of the Directive 2009/24/EC, in particular, by its provisions on decompilation and interoperability". The use of the term "as allowed" again brings us back to the field of copyright, and the efficiency of these exceptions. As noted above in this chapter, this was found to be very low. Thus, how might the same exception in the field of patent be more efficient?

B. Potential Measures on Trade Secrets

Trade secret protection cannot be invoked against the use of interoperability information obtained through lawful reverse engineering techniques. This guarantees a certain degree of access to this type of

---

[55] Commission SWD, op. cit., p. 11.

[56] Article 27(k) of the Council Agreement on a Unified Patent Court, 2013/C 175/01, OJ C 175, p. 1.

[57] About the potential problems of the Unitary Patent Package, *see*: R. Hilty et al., "The Unitary Patent Package: Twelve reasons for concern", MPI Research Paper Series No. 12-12, October 2012. Available at: http://ssrn.com/abstract=2169254 (Accessed November 2013).

information when it is covered by trade secrets.[58] However, reverse engineering is a difficult and expensive process, and its current regulation, through copyright, does not leave room or legal certainty to really know when it is lawful.[59] Therefore, in many cases it does not adequately motivate the opening up of interoperability information.

A Directive for Interoperability inspired by the legal framework of the telecommunications sector (the Access Directives[60]) is the legislative measure that may help to facilitate licensing of interoperability information to significant market players. Specifically, Article 8.2 of the Directive 2002/21/EC addresses the issue of imposing certain obligations (transparency, non-discrimination, accounting separation, *access to, and use of, specific network facilities*, price control and cost accounting) on operators with significant market power.[61]

The basis is, once again, compulsion. The problems, besides those brought about by the compulsory approach itself, are also recognised by the Commission and lie in the potential breach of the EU principle of proportionality,[62] given the high implementation costs of such a Directive and in the huge difficulties in defining and identifying *ex ante* significant market power and the significant market players in the ICT sector.[63] If this were a realistic task, the whole interoperability problem would disappear without further ado. However, the inertia of the ICT sector, as already shown, does not allow for this type of approach.

---

58 Commission SWD, op. cit., p. 12.

59 As explained in the first part of this chapter. *See*: B. Gonzalez Otero, "Compelling …", op. cit., pp. 8–9.

60 Directive 2002/19/EC of the European Parliament and of the Council of 7 March 2002 on access to, and interconnection of, electronic communications networks and associated facilities (Access Directive), OJ L 108, p. 7; Directive 2009/140/EC of the European Parliament and of the Council of 25 November 2009 amending Directives 2002/21/EC on a common regulatory framework for electronic communications networks and services, 2002/19/EC on access to, and interconnection of, electronic communications networks and associated facilities, and 2002/20/EC on the authorisation of electronic communications networks and services, OJ L 337, p. 37.

61 Article 8.2: "Where an operator is designated as having significant market power on a specific market as a result of a market analysis carried out in accordance with Article 16 of Directive 2002/21/EC (Framework Directive), national regulatory authorities shall impose the obligations set out in Articles 9 to 13 of this Directive as appropriate."

62 Article 5.4 TFEU.

63 Commission SWD, op. cit., p. 15.

C. Potential Measures in Copyright

The analysis made by the Commission of potential copyright measures to facilitate licensing of interoperability information to significant market players can be summarised in one sentence: copyright does not offer control over the information embodied in work per se, and it is more likely to be used in combination with trade secrets.[64] According to the Commission, the alternatives provided by the Software Directive in obtaining interoperability information are the exceptions contained in its Articles 5.3 and 6 and they seem to be working perfectly, as no measure is proposed. As to provide an additional reason for not taking copyright into account, the document remarks on the uselessness of decompilation since there are tools and techniques to obfuscate executable code.[65]

Hence, although copyright does not offer control over the information embodied per se in work in general, it should also be stated that this proposition faces some problems when asserted regarding computer programs. That is, when going to the very basics of this intellectual property right, what copyright protects is the original expression of an idea, not the idea itself. In the case of software, as it has been internationally agreed upon, the form of expression, both object and source code, is protected as a literary work.[66] Considering the object code as a form of expression in literary work, it shows that software is, by nature, functional and technological work without any communicative purpose. This has paramount consequences over controlling the information contained in a program:

1. Since a computer program's form of expression is functional, variations of its expression will not matter because these possible variations come from utility reasons and not the "aesthetic freedom" or whim of its developer. Therefore, expression and function merge.[67] As a result, control over the interface specifications (the interoperability information) will depend upon: firstly, whether this interoperability information is considered an idea or an expression, and, secondly, if it is considered an expression, whether this information is considered an original expression of the work. The

---

[64] Commission SWD, op. cit., pp. 8 and 14.

[65] Commission SWD, op. cit., p. 14.

[66] Article 10 TRIPS and Article 4 WCT.

[67] G. Ghidini, *Innovation, Competition and Consumer Welfare in Intellectual Property Law*, Edward Elgar Publishing, Cheltenham, 2010, p. 133.

copyright regime established by the Software Directive provides control over the information embodied in the work per se.

2. The absence of a communicative purpose is reflected by the fact that object code is treated as a protected form of expression and restricts public access to the program's idea when software is solely distributed in object code.[68]
3. The fact that the object code is not the expression of an original idea but a functional expression brings it closer to a technical rule (an invention). The developer's originality lies in the source code, but copyright-holders of computer programs keep this as a trade secret, since it is not mandatory to disclose it in order to obtain copyright protection. This business practice, supported by the copyright regime, severely restricts competition from developing in interoperable programs because both know-how and software of interoperability information is within the source code.[69]

In addition to the above, access and use conditions of interoperability information do not really work in line with fostering innovation under the copyright reverse engineering exceptions. Even more, Article 6 presents a restriction not conceived by the general copyright paradigm. First, Article 5.3 permits observation, study and testing of the functioning of the program in order to determine the underlying ideas and principles. Although "black box analysis" proves very important in the process of establishing interoperability, it does not necessarily result in a comprehensive list of the information required for full interoperability. To determine all the relevant information, it may be necessary to analyse the source code or formula of the program so as to establish how it works internally, that is, to decompile the program, which could only be done without constituting a copyright infringement if the decompiler complies with the conditions established in Article 6. If Article 6 indeed reflects a pro-interoperability policy[70] by allowing access via decompilation of program's code to study its internal structure and other expressive aspects

---

[68] J. Drexl, *What is Protected in a Computer Program? Copyright protection in the United States and Europe,* IIC Studies, Vol. 15, VCH, Weinheim, 1994, p. 11.

[69] J. Gibson, "Once and Future Copyright", Notre Dame Law Review, Vol. 81, 2005, p. 190; J. Bartmann, *Grezen der Monopolisierung …* , op. cit., p. 122; J.K. Jeong, "Comparative Study on Legal Protection in the USA, EU, Japan and Korea for Computer Programs: Focus on program reverse engineering", IIP Bulletin, Vol. 17, 2006, p. 141.

[70] See Proposal for a Council Directive … , op.cit., p. 16.

of program text when this process is indispensable to achieving interoperability, it would make no sense to establish a right to access program internals, and then to condemn the reuse of interface information discerned in this process as infringing when it is necessary to achieve interoperability.[71] However, the garbled wording of its conditions, in particular the requirement regarding information not previously having been made "readily available" (could this be understood as refusal to license coming before the act of decompilation?) and the portion of the code that can be decompiled ("only those necessary for interoperability", but how to know the correct location "ex ante"?), together with the lack of jurisprudential interpretative criteria, have made this limitation unclear in terms of what interoperability information can be lawfully accessed.

Therefore, with the control copyright provides over the computer program, the only lawful way to access and use interoperability information, with a refusal to a licence, appears to be competition law,[72] but this is again an *ex post* and very exceptional measure (which is how it should remain to not trespass the principle of proportionality contained in Article 5.4 TEU[73]).

4. CONCLUDING REMARKS

Firstly, while it is too simple to say that high levels of interoperability per se lead to innovation and competition in the ICT sector, in most circumstances, and if implemented properly, ensuring interoperability is a sound public policy that contributes to innovation and enhances competition in the ICT space and consequently will lead to economic growth. However, Europe has not yet reaped the maximum benefit from software interoperability. How do we incentivise the disclosure of interoperability information? How do we encourage significant market players possessed of interoperability information to allow access to it on reasonable terms? There is not a single answer to these questions. A multidisciplinary

---

71 See, e.g., T. Dreier, "Rechtsschutz von Computerprogrammen: Die Richtlinie des Rates der EG vom 14. Mai 1991", Computer und Recht 7, 1991, p. 583; S. Lai, *The Copyright Protection of Computer Software in the United Kingdom*, Hart Publishing, Oxford, 2000, p. 98.

72 *See* Communication from the Commission – Guidance on the Commission's enforcement priorities in applying Article 82 of the EC Treaty to abusive exclusionary conduct by dominant undertakings, OJ C 45, 24/0272009.

73 Article 5(4) TEU: "Under the principle of proportionality, the content and form of Union action shall not exceed what is necessary to achieve the objectives of the Treaties".

approach, a combination of the different legal regimes that affect access and use of interoperability information, is therefore needed.

Secondly, we should not overlook the fact that legal protection regimes are normally the manifestation of the industries and cultures for which they have been articulated more than a neutral tool to regulate a legal situation.[74] Thus, makers of public and private policy would be well advised not only to work towards higher levels of ICT interoperability, but also to aim for less fragmentation among legal norms and policies applicable to information society phenomena. Such an approach requires a deeper understanding of the multifaceted interplay between law and interoperability.

Yet intellectual property law is a key enabler of greater innovation and enhanced interoperability in the ICT marketplace. Therefore, if there is a general agreement upon the role of the public authorities when promoting private sector *ex ante* solutions and to intervene only in appropriate cases when markets fail in certain ways,[75] copyright protection on software should not be taken too lightly. A complete revision of the Software Directive, with special focus on the object of protection and the reverse engineering exceptions, could help to restore balance to a field where the computer program's copyright-holder has been overprotected.

But the establishment of strong yet flexible intellectual property incentive systems and intellectual property protection frameworks needs to be done both within and outside of the standards-setting process. Consequently, in order to foster *ex ante* sharing of software interoperability information between all market players, standards need to be a special part of this multidisciplinary approach. However, the simplistic and erroneous view that the best way to effect interoperability is a public policy whereby government mandates technical standards should be avoided. Such attempts, preferring a certain technology or particular business or licensing model over others, can actually undermine the benefits of interoperability by limiting user options and impairing innovation and local economic development opportunities

[74] S. von Lewinski, *International Copyright Law and Policy,* Oxford University Press, Oxford, 2008, pp. 33–34.

[75] S.A. Baird, "Government role and the interoperability ecosystem", in L. Rubini (ed.), *Microsoft on Trial. Legal and Economic Analysis of a Transatlantic Antitrust Case*, Edward Elgar, Cheltenham, 2009, p. 248; U. Gasser and J. Palfrey, "Breaking down digital barriers: when and how ICT interoperability drives innovation", Berkman Publication Series, November 2007, p. 8; DAE, Action 25.

Finally, it should be borne in mind that in the new world of open innovation, the *ius prohibendi* granted by intellectual property rights is being replaced by the opportunity to build a collaborative bridge, to include partners instead of excluding competitors.[76] Therefore, it is equally important that decision-makers and industries recognise that a definition of an open standard that embraces the inclusion of, and fair, reasonable and non-discriminatory licensing for, IP-protected software technology actually enhances the open standards process and the resulting technological solutions.[77] Interoperability driven by open standards increases competition, drives down prices and provides more options for consumers.

In a nutshell, there is not an obvious set of guidelines that connects a means of achieving interoperability and specific outcomes. Further research, keeping a multidisciplinary approach, is needed. Nonetheless, the search for feasible measures should share the same underlying idea: having a "standard" that only one party can fully implement will not lead to software interoperability. The more open, inclusive processes of accomplishing software interoperability, once established, are more difficult to disrupt than those processes managed by a single firm.

---

[76] About the inclusivity trend, *see*: S. Dusollier, "The commons as a reverse intellectual property – from exclusivity to inclusivity", in H. Howe and J. Griffiths (eds.), *Concepts of Property in Intellectual Property Law*, Cambridge Intellectual Property and Information Law No. 21, Cambridge University Press, Cambridge, 2013, p. 258.

[77] N.L. Tsilas, "Open Innovation and Interoperability", in L. DeNardis (ed.), *Opening Standards: The global politics of interoperability*, MIT Press, Cambridge, Massachusetts, 2011, p. 98.

5. Is IP law a *lex specialis*? A dual test

Gustavo Ghidini

The question of whether intellectual property law is a *lex specialis* compels us to rethink intellectual property (IP) law in terms of systemic coherence. And consequently it also encourages an in-depth reconstruction of existing rules as well as the formulation of appropriate proposals for reforms thereof.

This proposition needs elaboration (in several ways):[1] first, on the precise meaning in relation to IP of *lex specialis* (or the concept of an 'exceptional' law). As concerns the field of IP, by *lex specialis* I mean a norm (including the interpretation of a norm) that, in regulating the conflicts of interests at stake, derogates from either or both of the following systemic tenets:

(a) first, the *coherence*[2] with the goals and purposes set by overarching principles of a (formally or substantially) constitutional nature, which should guide both legislators and interpreters in the sector of IP as well as in any other sector of ordinary law;
(b) second, the internal *consistency*[3] of IP law, reconstructed as a harmonized system of rules and principles, where any application of whatever rule to a case shall never contradict and/or bypass the relevant background principles of the IP system itself.

---

1 As a 'follower' of Humpty Dumpty, I feel obliged to clarify as exactly as I can the meaning I attribute to the terms of my discourse.

2 *Coherence* is a substantial requirement that imposes on interpreters and legislators the duty to provide decisions and laws that fit well with the overall principles of the legal system itself, while *consistency* is a formal requirement implied by the principle of non-contradiction and so it consists in avoiding contradictions with other existing rules. On this distinction see N. MacCormick, *Coherence in Legal Justification*, in A. Peczenik, L. Lindhal, B. van Roermund (eds), *Theory of Legal Science*, Reidel, Dordrecht, 1984, 235–251.

3 *Ibid.*

I call this the dual test. The second tenet above simply reflects the need for 'internal consistency' (that is, non-contradiction) of IP law that pertains to every system of rules. The first highlights the historical foundation of intellectual property rights (IPRs) as private endowments granted *instrumentally* – that is, as a *means to an end* – to satisfy such collective interests as the enhancement and circulation of innovation and culture ('science and the useful arts', in the words of Article 1, Section 8, clause 8 of the US Constitution), and, as concerns trademarks, the preservation of market transparency.[4]

Let me now anticipate a few examples reflecting the criteria I will articulate for checking the correspondence of features of IP law with the two aforesaid benchmarks of systemic coherence and consistency. These examples show that specific IP rules, or sets of rules, may contradict one or both of these principles.

In Italy, a recent legislative reform, deviating from the traditional (and TRIPS abiding[5]) perspective of protection under unfair competition rules, has substantially (albeit not formally) upgraded the regime of industrial and commercial confidential information to the rank of IPRs. Moreover, it has done so (obviously) with no time limitations.[6] This self-evidently

---

[4] In such functional perspective, it is worth recalling that the famous definition given by Le Chapelier (in introducing the first French post-revolutionary law on *droit d'auteur*, 1791) of intellectual property as '*la plus sacrée*' of all properties – a definition on which IP hardliners often speculate – was in fact intended to support the newly instituted regime of individual rights of freedom of expression (of course including authorship and publishing) stemming from the repeal of administrative censorship and corporations' and guilds' constraints on free initiative, and the consequent transformation of 'privileges' into 'equal rights'. In truth, that quotation was drawn (without citing) from the Turgot Edict of 1786, where the 'ownership of one's work' was upheld in order that each worker might get rid of all restrictions imposed by the corporatist order. In short: the very expression 'IP' was conceived as functional to, and coherent with, the new perspective of citizens' fundamental freedoms of both economic initiative and expression, inaugurated by the 'dual revolution' that crowned the Age of the Enlightenment.

[5] See TRIPS, Art. 39.

[6] See Articles 98–99 of Italian Code of Industrial Property. The prohibition of (unauthorized and) "abusive" acquisition, use, communication of confidential information is established "unfair competition rules *excepted*" (art.99 cit.; emphasis added). Thus, in such normative context: a) that prohibition cannot be qualified as an expression/application of aforesaid rules pursuant to Art. 39 TRIPS; (hence) b) that "abusive"' must systemically be read in the meaning of "not legally permitted", i.e falling outside the cases, e.g., of non-commercial uses authorized under either the research exception in patent law or "exceptions

discourages patenting, thus pre-empting both a basic positive effect of the patent regime (that is, the denial of exclusive protection to 'non-inventive' technical data) and also the public disclosure of new results of R&D. Obviously, in cases like this, even the reluctant jurist must *de lege lata* 'surrender' and entrust to a future reform their criticism of the *lex specialis.*

The anti-competitive effects of the upgrading of trade secrets to the rank of IPR is an example of a 'speciality' exhibiting the double defects of coherence and inconsistency at once: the *lex specialis* deviates from both the background principles of IP law and the recognized general principles of the legal system as a whole.[7]

The *lex specialis* approach is also seen in Article 5 of Directive 2009/24/EC, which, in applying copyright protection to software, forbids the development of improved programs, thus restricting the user to activities that do not go beyond that of ensuring interoperability between different programs. This is a rule that self-evidently derogates from the general principle of copyright law that grants full copyrights on derivative works, and only requests the consent of the right-holder of the original work for economically exploiting, through publication, the derivative work itself.[8]

Thus, it is the derogation from the above stated principle of coherence, rather than from that of consistency, that, in my opinion, sets the difference between a *lex specialis* and a law that we might label *specifica* (in the Latin meaning of *specificatio*), consisting of rules that 'adapt' to any particular IP-related subject matter – inventions, distinctive signs, industrial design, copyrighted works, and so on – both the principle of

and limitations" in copyright law. Cases (exceptions) whose provision obviously fits with an IPR perspective. And indeed same Code, Art.1, expressely lists "confidential business information" in the category of "proprietà intellettuale".

7 However, *coherence* and *consistency* are independent features: an IP law rule can be consistent in relation to the IP rules of reference, but not coherent with the overarching constitutional principles, and vice versa. For instance, the different regimes of translations under copyright law, as historically following one another (see below, text at fn 13), are a good evidence of such independence.

8 A good example indeed of what Hugh Laddie famously labelled as copyright's 'medieval chains … reinforced with late twentieth century steel' (The Hon. Mr Justice Laddie, *Copyright: Over-Strength, Overregulated, Over-Rated?*, [1996] *EIPR*, 1996, 253).

non-contradiction and the constitutional principles referable to the type of interests (private and collective) involved in IP-related conflicts.[9]

Of course, a legislative evolution (involution, in this case) may turn a *lex specifica* into one *specialis*. A significant example is offered by the recent repeal of what was Section 52 (headed 'effect of exploitation of design derived from artistic work') of the UK Copyright, Designs and Patents Act 1988 by the 2013 Enterprise and Regulatory Reform Act, Part 6, Clause 74(2).[10] Section 52 provided for a regime coherent with both the test of non-contradiction and the principle of freedom of competition, since it forbade that, for design works made 'by an industrial process', copyright protection might be sought after the expiry of the 25-year term of the protection of registered designs envisaged by EU Directive 71/98. Now, and putting aside the transitional regime that will be instituted,[11] the repeal of Section 52 will allow an all-too-easy straight, 'sequential' cumulation. That is to say, there will be overlapping of registered protection with copyright protection, and hence the institution of an extremely long, strongly anti-competitive (nay, rent-seeking) exclusive protection for producers of goods of utilitarian fruition.[12] This will encompass private consumption *and* industrial goods – the latter also increasingly the object of design-attentive manufacture. Cumulation with copyright exacerbates the pro-monopolistic perspective as concerns 'follow-on' design works realized by independent designers, and hence ultimately by competing producers. Indeed, such works might well be labelled as 'derivative' works, subject to the control and authorization (for production and trade) by the right-holder of the original work (typically, the corporate employer of, or transferee or licensee from, the original designer). In other words, modifications of the original design might be barred from entering the market as 'derivative' lookalikes.

---

[9] The main corollary of the distinction is that the interpreter can apply extensively, even by analogy, *lex specifica*, whereas *lex specialis* is subject to 'strict interpretation'.

[10] On this 'reform' see L. Bently's comment to the Bill as introduced: *The Return of Industrial Copyright?*, in 34 *EIPR* 654-672 (2012).

[11] A 'Call for evidence' has been launched by the British Government soliciting proposals for the establishment of a transitional regime. See: http://www.ipo.gov.uk/pro-policy/consult/consult/consult-live/consult-2013-s52.htm

[12] Overlapping, as well known, is a typical proxy for over-protectionist interpretations. As concerns products' shapes, in particular, see *ex multis* A. Kur, *Cumulation of IP Rights Pertaining to Product Shapes – An 'Illegitimate Offspring' of IP Law?*, in *Intellectual Property and Market Power*, ATRIP Papers, 2006–2007, Buenos Aires, 2008, 613 ff.

The proposed dual test should be applied also to assess the systemic coherence of situations of seeming 'non-intervention', that is, 'silence' of IP law *vis-à-vis* emerging substantive conflicts of interests. I describe these as 'seeming', since in truth the legal order has no gaps: when it does not expressly intervene to regulate conflicts, it 'leaves' the solution thereof to the relation of power (often, via 'free negotiation') between the parties in conflict. In other words, the law's silence is always apparent – and golden, usually, for the stronger party.

Take for example the case of a publisher who, having acquired the right to publish a book, chooses to print only a luxury edition at a very high price, thus reducing the overall readership, at the same time rejecting proposals from another publisher of popular, albeit highly reputed, editions (for example, Penguin) to publish much more widely accessible editions. The present copyright regime that (in the absence of illegal ad hoc pacts) allows such unbridled refusal, even when objectively wholly unjustified, runs counter both to the author's interest and to the collective interests of promotion and dissemination of culture. A proportionate and constitutionally coherent solution could well be found in granting a licence to the second publisher, under duty of a fair compensation to the first publisher – this, of course, in the absence of a serious justification for refusing (for example, the poor reputation of the second publisher).

Or take the case – even more important for the international circulation of culture – of the regime of translations. Since Berne's revision in 1908 in Berlin, copyright law has been fully 'levelled', even as concerns the duration of the exclusive regime, and as between reproduction and translation rights that authors transfer to publishers. Accordingly, the latter can at their full discretion refuse consent to a foreign publisher willing to have the work translated (without any duty to justify their choice, nor even to consult the author). This absolute discretion means that such refusal might be based upon an anti-competitive hostility toward the foreign publisher, or for 'ideological' motives, and so on. Recall that the original Berne Convention's text (Article 5), as well several national legislations of the nineteenth century, even prior to Berne, provided for the expiration of the exclusive right after some years (10, in Berne) from the publication of the original work.[13] Thus, the

[13] In Berne's 1896 Revision, the extension of exclusive protection throughout the entire general term of copyright was granted *upon condition* that an authorized translation had been diffused within 10 years from the first publication of the original work. It was in 1908 that the full extension was unconditionally granted. The more 'open' regime provided by Article V of the Universal

contemporary legal regime runs counter both to the (economic *and* 'moral') interest of the author to see their work diffused internationally and to the public interest in circulation of culture on an international basis.

Articulating specific examples – as I will do again below – does not exempt us from articulating the criteria or method for checking coherence and consistency with regard to the system of IP law and/or to the entire legal system. However, in pursuing this task, little or no theoretical difficulty is posed by the criterion of 'internal consistency' of this or that rule or set of rules with(in) the system of IP law, as expression of the principle of non-contradiction between rules addressing the same substantive subject matter. As shown by the examples above, respectively as concerns the regimes of industrial design and of software, this criterion calls for a 'comparative insight' at two levels of analysis: into the spectrum of the different IPR paradigms (for example copyright and 'registered designs') and 'inside' each single paradigm (for example the special software regime within copyright law).

The articulation of the criterion of 'constitutional coherence' is more complex.

Rather self-evidently, the overarching principles to which I am referring are primarily those enhancing freedom of competition, freedom and circulation of research and innovation, freedom and circulation of culture and information.[14]

Particular attention, in relation to IPRs' regime(s), should be devoted to the coherence with the principle of freedom of competition.[15] Such coherence requires, first of all, abiding by two corollaries of the principle itself:

Convention on Copyright, Geneva 1952, revised in Paris in 1971 (compulsory licence after seven years of inertia from original publication) unfortunately does not apply, because of the general principle of prevalence of Berne Convention, as set by paragraph (b) of the Declaration attached to Article XVII of same Geneva Act of the UCC.

[14] In more recent times, the panoply has been extended to such 'human rights' as health and environment. However, in this chapter I will not deal with these latter constitutional references, since I am (so far) inclined to think that the fulfilment of the public interests they protect is primarily to be entrusted to ad hoc public regulations and, to the enforcement of abuses.

[15] Rather obviously, the interpretative guideline just highlighted with reference to the principle of freedom of competition applies as well *vis-à-vis* the interpretative (and beforehand, legislative) 'alternatives' in copyright law. In particular, it would favour 'non *specialis*' constructions that – while respecting the right-holders' faculty to exclude economically significant free-riders – would

1. Respect the rule of *numerus clausus*, according to which IPRs are strictly defined by law in number and kind. IPRs grant powers in restraint of competition and are therefore to be qualified as *exceptions* to the constitutional principle at stake. Thus, for example, an interpretation of copyright law as covering genetic discoveries would *per se* be tantamount to introducing a *specialis* rule.
2. Favour a pro-competitive construction of IP law, even when the wording might in itself allow (allow, that is, not 'impose') a different interpretation. More specifically, while always respecting the IPRs' inherent function (protecting innovators against free riding, or firms' and products' identity and renown against misrepresentation), the rule(s) must be construed – to the extent that the wording allows – *in a manner that defends and promotes rather than erodes* the economic freedom of third parties, as well as the market's competitive fabric. It is in compliance with this guideline, for instance, that patent law has been construed so as to limit the patent's scope to the particular technical field and technical solution that the inventor has specifically claimed in the patent application.[16]

I have previously written about specific criteria for assessing the constitutional coherence of IP law.[17] But let me briefly recall two basic suggestions.

First, the hierarchy of constitutionally ranking interests, whereby some enjoy a wider scope of protection and accordingly must be privileged (also) by interpreters in addressing IP-related conflicts of interests, must be taken into account. This is the case, for example, in balancing the freedom of expression *vis-à-vis* freedom of enterprise, as highlighted by the regime of political speech versus advertising in European constitutional contexts.[18]

---

enhance freedom of expression and information. Or an approach that, in trademark law, would preserve, rather than restrict, the 'need to keep free' the use of descriptive signs, for example.

[16] See Rules 42 and 43, 'Content of the description' and 'Form and content of claims' of the 'Implementing Regulations' of the European Patent Convention and Article 5(3) of the European 'Biotech' Directive 98/44 EC.

[17] Gustavo Ghidini, *Exclusion and access in copyright law: The unbalanced features of the InfoSoc Directive*, in Graeme Dinwoodie (ed.), *Methods and Perspectives in Intellectual Property*, Edward Elgar, Cheltenham, 2013.

[18] And indeed, would 'freedom of expression' encompass advertising, it would be illegitimate to enforce misleading messages. See *e.g.* ECHR, Colman, June 28, 1993; European Commission on Human Rights' Report, October 1992; M. Birnhack, *Copyrighting Speech: A Trans-Atlantic View*, in Torremans (ed.),

Reference to such a 'hierarchy' (whose specific expression can vary from one constitutional order to another) is specifically suggested by the fact that *both* the rights of IPR holders and those of third parties seeking lawful access to the enjoyment of the protected goods (be they competitors, or non-competing subjects such as researchers) *all* enjoy in principle a constitutional rank: either that of freedom of enterprise and competition, or that of freedom of research and information.[19]

The concept of constitutional hierarchy encompasses the *convergence* of different constitutionally protected interests: in particular, those of (directly) individual and those of (directly) collective character. In other words, there are cases when the clash between different economic interests could be sorted out by considering, in the light of the constitutional framework, the further *societal effects* that the satisfaction of one interest could have in comparison with that of the other. While some economic interests merely belong and enhance the private sphere, others – even though belonging to the private sphere themselves – also enhance the satisfaction of the collective. (Just think, as in the example above, about the conflicting interests of two publishers in the translation of an important scientific work.) In such cases, it is constitutionally legitimate, and appropriate, to mandate such convergence.

Second, focus, in parallel, on the need to preserve the essential core of the protected conflicting interests at stake.[20] This need, which lies at the

---

Copyright and Human Rights – Freedom of Expression – Intellectual Property – Privacy, Kluwer Law International, The Hague, 2004, 37, 42. Of course, this only applies to commercial advertising, that is, promotion of sales of firms' products or services. But if a firm, even by advertisements, joins a debate on certain issues of public interest, its statements obviously enjoy full protection under the principle of freedom of expression. It's not the material medium that counts, but rather the function of the speech.

[19] See Charter of Fundamental Rights of the European Union, Art. 17(2), and corresponding official explanation. As concerns *individuals*, authors and inventors' IPRs enjoy even a 'human right' status: see Art. 27(2) Universal Declaration of Human Rights. On this perspective see, *ex multis*, P. Torremans, *Copyright and Human Rights*, The Hague, 2004; P. Yu, *Intellectual Property and Human Rights in the Nonmultilateral Era*, 64 Fla. L. Rev., 1045, 2012.

[20] As concerns IPRs, by 'essential core' I mean the protective function IPRs perform *per se* (essential = *ex se*), putting aside other functions – anti-competitive functions, in particular – that their exercise might perform in this or that market and/or regulatory context. Thus, in my view, said 'essential' function is simply and straightforwardly that of granting legal protection against the risk of losses from free-riding activities: more precisely, *those* free-riding activities capable (unlike those of mere researchers) of frustrating the owners' interest to recoup investment and obtain a *fair* compensation (fair, that is, 'appropriate', not

core of the principle of 'proportionality',[21] is satisfied, for instance, by Article 31(1) of TRIPS, which while granting a compulsory licence to the author of a high-profile improvement of a previous patented invention, 'compensates' the original patentee with a counterpart right to a licence on the improvement. Moreover, this well-balanced solution of an inter-individual conflict of interest is also and self-evidently coherent with the collective interests, acknowledged even at a constitutional level, in enhancement of R&D, competition and consumer welfare.

Thus, although Article 31(1) of TRIPS expresses a derogation from the general exclusionary power of the patentee, its intrinsic functionality to the enhancement of dynamic competition – the ultimate constitutional goal of patent regime – makes it a *specifica*, not a *specialis*, rule.

To the contrary, we should label as *lex specialis* the rule stated in Article 5 of the Information Society Directive whereby Member States *may*, at their discretion (Art. 5.2, 5.3), permit certain 'fair uses', whereas the same States *shall* enforce copyrights and related (neighbouring) rights, including those conferred in the application of encrypting software, so-called technological protection measures (TPMs) (Articles 2.1, 3.1, 4.1).

Other examples could be added to those already discussed. They would confirm what is hinted at in the title of this chapter: that is, that the assessment of IP law rules as *lex specialis* according to the criteria above gives different results *vis-à-vis* this or that IPR paradigm – and within each paradigm, *vis-à-vis* this or that norm or set of norms.

CONCLUSION

From the viewpoint of the dual test of systemic coherence and consistency, intellectual property law can be assimilated to a cathedral originally

---

'maximized', as the ECJ stressed in *Premier League et al v. QC Leisure et al* (C-403/08) from the exploitation of their work. (In this sense, and *only* in this sense, it can be said that IPRs provide an 'incentive' to invest.) Needless to say, the faculty to exclude free-riders interplays, as in the *verso* of a money bill, with the exercise of the contractual freedom to *include* chosen third parties in the access to the IPR (for purposes of cooperation in research/production/distribution), as it grants an *erga omnes* protection against any violation of the 'owned' IPRs.

[21] See for a critical overview, N. Reich, *How proportionate is the proportionality principle? Some critical remarks on the use and methodology of the proportionality principle in the internal market case law of the ECJ*, in *The European Court of Justice*, Intersentia, 25-10-2011, 83 ff.

designed by teams of independent architects in the Gothic style so poignantly and passionately evoked by John Ruskin.[22] But in the progressive course of construction, baroque features were substituted and/or added by new architects – 'court architects' (baroque is the privileged style of absolutist regimes). Thus it happened that certain façades of the cathedral present more, others less, baroque 'additions/substitutions'. The façade of patents less, that of trademarks more, that of copyright even more.

Such a conclusion, far from discouraging the partisans of a deep rebalancing of intellectual property law in favour of collective interests, should stimulate the many of us who are deeply concerned with the multifaceted over-protectionist, lobbyist-driven revision that the IP regime has progressively undergone, to react and unite in order to fine-tune and intensify our efforts to restore the cathedral: façade by façade.

---

[22] The reference is of course to *The nature of Gothic*, in *The Stones of Venice* [1851–1853], vol. II.

6. Inclusivity in intellectual property

Séverine Dusollier

Exclusivity has always been considered as the end and means of property, both in legal thinking and in economic analysis. The right to exclude is deemed to be a core element and a defining feature of a property right.[1] Exclusivity generates two outcomes: (1) *exclusion:* a right to exclude others from the use of the owned thing; and (2) *individuality:* a right held generally by one person only.

This focus on exclusivity in tangible property resonates too in intellectual property and has been reinforced by a critical view of situations devoid of exclusivity. In 'The Tragedy of the Commons',[2] Hardin argues against the commons on the ground that the simultaneous use of resources by many individuals acting independently and according to one's self-interest would necessarily lead to overuse and depletion. A similar story goes for intellectual property: creation and innovation cannot be depleted or overused, but leaving those in the commons where free-riding is easy due to the lack of exclusivity might lead to under production. The grant of exclusive rights is hence justified to incentivise innovation and enable creators to reap the value of their creation.[3]

Yet, contempt for lack of exclusivity and commons has started to change in recent years. In scholarship, the traditional view that commons lead to a tragedy has been challenged[4] and the positive role of commons has been highlighted, some describing situations of non-property where

---

[1] H. Smith, 'Property as the Law of Things', 125 *Harv. L. Rev*. 1691 (2012).

[2] T. Hardin, 'The tragedy of the commons' (1968) 162 *Science* 1243.

[3] For two classical analyses, H. Demsetz, 'Towards a theory of property rights', *The American Economic Review*, 1967, Vol. 57, pp. 347–359; W. Landes & R. Posner, 'An Economic Analysis of Copyright Law', *Journal of Legal Studies*, 1989, Vol. 28, p. 326.

[4] M. Heller, 'The Tragedy of the Anticommons: Property in the Transition from Marx to Markets' (1989) 111 *Harv. L. Rev.* 621–688.

commons can result in comedy,[5] others investigating situations of commons where an informal organisation leads to wealth maximisation and sustainability.[6] The commons scholarship, which emerged first around tangible resources, has spilled over to knowledge and information[7] and commons are now used as a critique against exclusionary and expansionist intellectual property[8] or are promoted as wealth-producing factors.[9] Commons cover situations with no property at all, which one can call 'open commons',[10] or where property rights are exercised to share and collectively use the resource, which have been described in economic literature as 'commons-property regimes'.[11]

Examples of resources held in common and governed by a regime of non-exclusivity are increasing, which has resulted in a renewed interest in scholarship for commons. In property, environmental concerns have prompted a look at the commons as a way to manage and preserve natural elements lacking any property rights.[12] Exclusive rights of property can be exercised in common when sharing a resource is needed to better preserve it,[13] exploit it (exchanges of microbial and genetic

---

[5] C. Rose, 'The Comedy of the Commons: Custom, Commerce, and Inherently Public Property' (1986) 53 *University of Chicago Law Review*, 711–781.

[6] E. Ostrom, *Governing the Commons: The Evolution of Institutions for Collective Action* (Cambridge University Press, 1990).

[7] R. Merges, 'Property Rights Theory and the Commons: The Case of Scientific Research' (1996) 13 *Social Philosophy and Policy* 145; Ch. Hess and E. Ostrom, 'Ideas, Artifacts and Facilities: Information as a Common Pool Resource', (2003) 66 *Law & Contemporary Problems* 111; M. Madison, M. Brett, B. Frischmann & K. Strandburg, 'Constructing Commons in the Cultural Environment' (2010), 95 *Cornell L. Rev.* 657; C. Rose, 'Ostrom and the lawyers: the impact of Governing the Commons on the American legal academy', *International Journal of the Commons* 5 (2011).

[8] L. Lessig, *The Future of Ideas: The Fate of the Commons in a Connected World* (Random House, 2001).

[9] Y. Benkler, *The Wealth of Networks: How Social Production Transforms Markets and Freedom* (Yale University Press, 2006).

[10] Y. Benkler, 'Between Spanish Huertas and the Open Road: A Tale of Two Commons?', *Convening Cultural Commons* conference, NYU, 2011, available at http://www.law.nyu.edu/sites/default/files/ECM_PRO_069712.pdf.

[11] E. Ostrom, *supra* note 6.

[12] A.-M. Chardeaux, *Les Choses Communes* (LGDJ, 2006); P. David, 'The Commons and the Climate – Dynamising the one to stabilise the other', *1st Global Thematic IASC Conference on the Knowledge Commons,* 2012.

[13] J. Acheson, *The Lobster Gangs of Maine* (Univ. Press of New England, 1988); E. Ostrom, *supra* note 6.

resources[14]) or use it with a sense of community (for example co-housing, communal gardens, shared vehicles). In intellectual property, commons range from a complete absence of exclusivity (public domain in copyright or patent), unenforceable exclusive rights (IP exceptions and limitations) to constructed commons[15] resulting from the very exercise of exclusive rights (copyleft licensing[16] such as open source software or Creative Commons) or the exercise of exclusivity in common (patent pools). Successful business models (for example Google Books based on public domain) or public initiatives (for example the digital library Europeana) further prove that economic or social wealth can be created out of non-exclusivity.

These examples show a greater subtlety in the models of (intellectual) property where property and commons are no longer antinomic but more interlaced and situated along a continuum. This chapter aims to describe discrete cases of non-exclusivity in intellectual property to demonstrate that a more complex picture, intertwining exclusivity and non-exclusivity, is developing and requires us to change our view of intellectual property.

Part I defines the notion of non-exclusivity used in this chapter, which will be covered by the terminology of 'inclusivity' to convey that some cases of non-exclusivity are not characterised by a lack of something or a default but are full of something else, of inclusive entitlements.

Part II distinguishes between different cases of non-exclusivity in intellectual property, highlighting in each category what makes them enter in inclusivity.

As a conclusion, I will urge the development of a regime covering inclusive situations in intellectual property to provide for preservation and sustainability, moving towards another regime of intellectual property, which could be a hybridisation of exclusive and inclusive entitlements.

---

[14] T. Dedeurwaerdere, 'The role of law, institutions and governance processes in facilitating access to genomics research', in van Overwalle (ed.), *Gene Patents and Clearing Models. From Concepts to Cases* (Cambridge Univ. Press, 2009).

[15] J. Reichman & T. Uhlir, 'A contractually reconstructed research commons for scientific data in a highly protectionist intellectual property environment', 66 *Law & Contemp. Probs* 315 (2003); Madison et al., *supra* note 7.

[16] S. Dusollier, 'Sharing Access to Intellectual Property through Private Ordering', 82 *Chicago-Kent L. Rev.* 1391–1435 (2003).

I. FROM NON-EXCLUSIVITY TO INCLUSIVITY

The commons that have been studied, in property and intellectual property, are characterised by the lack of exclusivity. They are not the opposite of property as commons can also be owned by someone, but they are characterised by the non-exclusive use of a resource.

There could be two different approaches to spaces of non-exclusivity in intellectual property. One could say that exclusivity is receding in intellectual property and that it leaves deserted spaces devoid of any rights. Another perspective would be to say that non-exclusivity is moving forward, opening new spaces for shared use. By comparison, scientists have realised that saying that the desert advances is not the same thing and does not have the same consequences as saying that the forest is withdrawing. The two faces of the same coin do not have the same value.

Similarly, non-exclusivity could be a simple negative: there is non-exclusivity where exclusivity is lacking. Non-exclusivity can also refer not to a *default* but to a *reverse* of exclusivity: non-exclusivity characterises situations where the use of a resource is marked by collectiveness and sharing. Here the absence of exclusivity is seen positively, as creating some collective space in the hollow left by the retreat of exclusivity. To describe such reversed exclusivity, I would opt for the terminology of 'inclusivity', which gives it a positive meaning that is better at conveying the meaning of commons in intellectual property. 'Inclusivity' and 'inclusive' could hence refer to the convex side of non-property, leaving the 'non-exclusivity' and 'non-exclusive' for its concave side.[17]

Whereas exclusivity of property has been defined by *exclusion* ('only me and not you') and *individuality* ('solely me'), inclusivity can be described by two characteristics: (1) the absence of a power to exclude others, which leads to inclusion of others in the use ('me *and* others') and (2) the collectiveness of uses, as opposed to the individuality of exclusive rights ('me *with* others').

In the following cases of non-exclusivity, the inclusive dimension of the entitlements that users thereby enjoy in the intellectual resource will be systematically described. Such entitlements would normally be equal and symmetric. The inclusivity could be the transverse characteristic of

---

[17] That might not always be the case as sometimes the lack of an exclusive right of the IP owner will not create an inclusive entitlement to a number of users. For instance, a patent holder forced to grant a compulsory licence loses his exclusive right but only to the benefit of the person requesting the licence and not to undifferentiated users.

commons, as it would grant, as Benkler said, "a freedom to operate under symmetric constraints" at the opposite of an exclusive property, based on an asymmetric power.[18]

II. THE MANY CASES OF INCLUSIVITY IN INTELLECTUAL PROPERTY

Inclusivity might result from discrete mechanisms of intellectual property. It can be created by law or by the IP owner, by contract or by unilateral decision. In each case, it flows from exclusivity that can be (1) absent, (2) reversed or (3) denied.

1. The Absence of Exclusivity

A. Public domain

The public domain in intellectual property is composed of intellectual assets that are not protected by a copyright or a patent,[19] or are no longer because of the expiration of the term of protection. In copyright, the public domain encompasses ideas, unprotected by the key principle of idea/expression dichotomy, unoriginal works, excluded works (which could be official texts and governmental works, works lacking fixation) and works whose protection term has lapsed. The public domain in patent includes abstract ideas, discoveries, unpatentable inventions, inventions lacking novelty, inventiveness or industrial application, expired patents, as well as patentable inventions that have not been subject to registration (voluntarily or not).

The public domain has always existed in intellectual property for it is the automatic counterpart of private property, which results from the selective conditions for protection and from the limited duration of the right. Historically, it had been rather neglected in the intellectual property regime and discourse. Being only the negative of the exclusive right, it

---

[18] Y. Benkler, *supra* note 10.

[19] The notion of public domain in trademark is less relevant as a trademark right only grants a relative protection to a sign in relation to determined products or services. What is not protected by a specific trademark can be protected by another one for different products or services. The reverse of the scope of protection of a trademark does not hence create a public domain.

has no intrinsic consistence or dedicated protection.[20] The public domain can be freely used indeed, but solely because no exclusivity vests in the work or invention. Such free use hence occupies this very absence, which also creates the legal limbo characterising the public domain: no legal protection or norms guarantee such freedom of use. It does not have its own consistence or body, but is only the spectre of the property right. Such absence draws some empty space, empty of any exclusivity, but also empty of any protection of that very freedom to use. More than a no-rights land, it is a wasteland, a fallow land. Calling it a domain seems preposterous and qualifying it as public only hints at its pretension to ensure public access and use to its resources, with no guarantee.[21]

Despite this lack of protection, discussion of the public domain has gained some momentum in the IP discourse in recent years. Scholars are increasingly interested in it, pleading for its defence,[22] and even WIPO devotes some normative efforts to it, notably in the Agenda Development, of which two Recommendations address the need to identify, preserve and protect the public domain in intellectual property.[23]

Public domain is created by the absence of exclusivity, as no one can claim exclusive rights in works or inventions contained therein.[24] Freedoms of use of public domain flow from that very absence of exclusive

---

[20] For an analysis of this lack of protection regime in copyright, see V.-L. Benabou & S. Dusollier, 'Draw me a public domain', in P. Torremans (ed.), *Copyright Law: A Handbook of Contemporary Research* (Edward Elgar, 2007), at 161.

[21] S. Dusollier, 'The public domain in Intellectual Property: Beyond the metaphor of a domain' in *Intellectual Property and Public Domain*, P.L. Jayanthi Reddy (ed.), (Icfai University Press, 2009) 31–69, available at: http://works.bepress.com/severine_dusollier/4.

[22] J. Boyle, *The public domain – Enclosing the Commons of the Mind* (Yale University Press, 2008); Y. Benkler, 'Free as the Air to Common Use: First Amendment Constraints on Enclosure of the Public Domain', 74 *N.Y.U.L.R.* 354 (1999); L. Guibault & B. Hugenholtz (eds.), *The Future of the Public Domain – Identifying the Commons in Information Law* (Kluwer Law International, 2006), and particularly J. Cohen, 'Copyright, Commodification, and Culture: Locating the Public Domain', at 121 or M. Birnhack, 'More or Better? Shaping the Public domain', at 60.

[23] See Recommendations 16 & 20. WIPO has also launched a series of studies on the public domain in all IP rights. See http://www.wipo.int/ip-development/en/agenda/projects.html

[24] At least by copyright or patent as the public domain, as it is organised in current regimes of intellectual property do not prevent the recapture of exclusivity by another IP right (for example a trademark on a public domain work) or by

rights. On that ground, public domain is sometimes qualified of *res communes*, which are defined in article 714 of the French civil code as resources that are not owned by anyone and whose use is common to all.[25] Such qualification could vest the public domain with some normative value as the common use is a defining feature of the notion along the lack of property.

Insisting on the notion of *res communes* highlights the collectiveness, hence the inclusivity, of the entitlements to use the public domain. By definition, the public domain is not only what is not protected anymore, but what can be used by anyone without infringing copyright or patent (held by no one). It thus creates equal and symmetric entitlements in all users.

This positive approach is so far only a matter of discourse. It insists on the inherent value of the public domain as providing raw material for further creation and innovation and begs for some legal regime enabling its preservation and sustainability.[26]

B. Exceptions and limitations

Exceptions to intellectual property also create spaces of non-exclusivity in a twofold way. On the one hand, the exclusive right cannot be enforced against a use covered by such exceptions. On the other hand, beneficiaries of the exception enjoy a non-exclusive privilege to use the work or invention. For example, the entitlement to make a private copy does not prevent anyone, who complies with the conditions of the exception, from also making a copy. The beneficiary of the exception cannot exclude anyone else from the same use. Such absence of exclusivity is precisely what makes me reluctant to consider the copyright exception as a genuine

---

another right or means of control (for example by property right in the embodiment of the work, contract, technological measure).

[25] S. Choisy, *Le domaine public en droit d'auteur* (Litec, 2002); A.-M. Chardeaux, *supra* note 12, § 230. See also S. Dusollier, *Scoping Study on public domain in copyright*, May 2010, WIPO, CDIP/7/INF/2, available at http://www.wipo.int/ipdevelopment/en/ agenda/pdf/scoping_study_cr.pdf. Outside of civil law regimes, some authors have also referred to the notion of *res communes* in Roman law. See C. Rose, 'Romans, Roads, and Romantic Creators: Traditions of Public Property in the Information Age', 66 *Law & Contemp. Probs.* 89 (2003).

[26] M. Birnhack, *supra* note 22, p. 60; V.-L. Benabou & S. Dusollier, *supra* note 20; D. Lange, 'Recognizing the Public Domain', 44 *Law & Contemp. Probs.*, 147 (1981).

subjective right, at least in civil law,[27] for the benefit of an exception is not exclusive but is granted in an equal and symmetric way to all eligible users, at the contrary of an exclusive right.

It should be noted that compulsory licences in patent, albeit being limitations to patent, are not comprised in our catalogue of inclusivity. The exclusivity of the patent owner is limited or paralysed by the grant of the compulsory licence but that does not create an equal right to all potential users of the invention, but only to the user requesting the licence and proving that they meet the requirements. The entitlement benefiting that licensee is hence non-symmetric or inclusive.

As for the public domain, exceptions have also taken a more central place in copyright legislation. Legislative or discussion documents are increasingly tackling the issue of exceptions, from the EC Communication on Copyright in the Knowledge Economy[28] – a rather unfit title for a discussion on the need to enlarge exceptions or make them more effective – to the Communication on the Internal Market for Intellectual Property.[29] The case of the Marrakesh Conference, which was the first diplomatic meeting dedicated only to an exception in copyright, proves the new importance of copyright limitations.[30]

Many of those documents insist on the role of the exceptions, as vectors of creation, innovation or transmission of knowledge – all roles traditionally attached to exclusive intellectual property rights.

2. The Reversion of Exclusivity

Owners of exclusive rights conferred by intellectual property sometimes decline to exercise such exclusivity in order to grant others large freedoms of use. Two cases could be distinguished: free licences, from software to patent, and the relinquishments of rights.

---

[27] Civil law recognises three forms of legal entitlements: subjective right (marked by enforceability and asymmetry as it is granted discriminately to some individuals), freedom (which are normally equally enjoyed by all individuals) and legitimate interest to which law can grant some protection.

[28] Communication of the European Commission, *Copyright in the Knowledge Economy*, 19 October 2009, COM(2009) 532 final.

[29] Communication of the European Commission, *The internal market of intellectual property*, COM (2011)287 final, 24 May 2011, §3.3.3.

[30] Marrakesh Treaty to Facilitate Access to Published Works for Persons Who Are Blind, Visually Impaired, or Otherwise Print Disabled, 31 July 2013.

A. Free or copyleft licences

Free licensing had its birth with the open source software movement. The inventors of free software exercised their copyright in the program to grant more freedoms than restrictions and share their exclusivity with any potential user. Therefore, the open source software has dug a hole of non-exclusivity within the very fabric of intellectual property. Eventually, from open source licences pertaining to software, similar principles have been applied to all types of protected works (Creative Commons[31]) and even to patented inventions (open source patenting).[32]

The term 'copyleft' that is sometimes attached to those licences is not only anecdotal. Beyond being a play on words between copy-*right* and copy-*left* when right is moved to the left, it also conveys the idea that the right is reversed to leave the use to the public.[33] The licences leverage the intellectual property right to impose freedoms of use, copying, distribution and modification (and in the case of software, the publication of source code) and even further to prohibit licensees from restricting the freedoms they themselves received.

Whatever the subject matter governed by the licence, work or invention, free licences create a double absence of exclusivity. Firstly, the copyright or patent-owners deprives themselves of the exclusivity of their rights to include others in the use (and, should the licence be viral,[34] prevents any reconstitution of exclusivity on creations derived from theirs). That engenders, in a second step, a non-exclusive entitlement to use the work or invention for all licensees (who are all potential users as the licence can be said to run with the software or work[35]). To that extent, licensees share inclusive entitlements as to the work or invention governed by the free licence.

---

[31] See L. Lessig, *Free Culture: How Big Media Uses Technology and the Law to Lock Down Culture and Control Creativity* (2004), at 183–200.

[32] S. Boettiger & D. Burk, 'Open Source Patenting', *Journal of International Biotechnology Law* 221 (2004); J. Hope, 'Open Source Genetics: A Conceptual Framework', in G. Van Overwalle (ed.), *Gene Patents and Collaborative Licensing Models. Patent Pools, Clearinghouses, Open Source Models and Liability Regimes* (Cambridge University Press, 2009), at 171–193; A. Rai, 'Open and Collaborative Research: A New Model for Biomedicine', in R. Hahn (ed.), *Intellectual Property Rights in Frontier Industries: Software and Biotechnology*, (AEI Press, 2005) at 131.

[33] S. Dusollier, *supra* note 16.

[34] A licence is said to be viral when it applies automatically – along the chain of distribution – to each new copy or derivative version of a work.

[35] M.J. Radin, 'Human, Computers, and Binding Commitment', 75 *Ind. L.J.* 1125, 1132 (2000).

Copyleft licences create non-exclusivity by exercising exclusivity, in a subversive move. This is not the law that declares the absence of exclusivity as is the case with public domain and intellectual property exceptions. The assertion of the exclusive right is paradoxically the founding rule of the licensing process and the strategy to trump the void of the public domain. Copyleft licences retain the control on the creation and condition the granting of freedoms to some obligations, including the further prohibition to prohibit. Conversely, when a creation is in the public domain, the complete absence of exclusivity makes it impossible to restrain its free use and prevent reconstitution of exclusivity on derivative work or invention.[36] Some authors have described such a method by explaining that free licences create "a self-binding commons rather than an unrestricted public domain".[37]

The "subversion" of exclusivity is "very much a modernist kind of property"[38] and has been criticised precisely for its recourse to private ordering tools (the contract) that does not completely renounce to the proprietary logic of intellectual rights.[39] The non-exclusive rights created to the benefit of the user of the work or invention are only enforceable against the licensor (and not *erga omnes* or against the world), which weakens the process of freedom-granting.[40] Yet, this relative enforceability is strengthened by the specific mechanics of contract (its acceptance being based on the use of the work) that results in the contract being more attached to the work or invention than to the contracting parties.[41]

The copyleft trick is a hybrid tool relying on exclusivity to refuse it, and relying on contract, thus on a relationship between parties, to grant an absolute status to the very thing governed by the contract.

Another example of a reversed exclusivity lies in the 'licences of right' created by article 8 of the EU Regulation on unitary patent protection

---

[36] This explains the strategy of the copyleft licensing instead of a relinquishment of copyright. However, copyleft movements have also developed licences formalising the relinquishment of a work into the public domain. See for instance the Creative Commons licence CC0.

[37] A. Kapczynski, S. Chaifetz, Z. Katz & Y. Benkler, 'Addressing Global Health Inequities: An Open Licensing Approach for University Innovations', 20 *Berkeley Technology Law Journal* 1072 (2005).

[38] C. Rose, *supra* note 7.

[39] N. Elkin-Koren, 'What Contracts Cannot Do: The Limits of Private Ordering in Facilitating a Creative Commons', 74 *Fordham Law Review* 398 (2005).

[40] S. Dusollier, *supra* note 16.

[41] Which is not specific to open source licence though, see M. Radin, *supra* note 35.

(inspired by the patent law of some Member States).[42] It provides that the proprietor of a European patent with unitary effect may file a statement with the EPO to allow any person to use the invention against some remuneration. It differs from the traditional exclusive power of a patent-owner to grant a licence, to the extent that such statement offers a licence to anyone under the condition of an appropriate remuneration. As in copyleft licensing, the patent-holder leverages its exclusive right to create licences that are not free as in open source software or Creative Commons, but that could be defined as inclusive as they do not exclude.

In both cases, the voluntary withdrawal of exclusivity engenders non-exclusivity and inclusion of users concerned by the licence.

B. The relinquishment of intellectual property

The free licences movement has sometimes gone a step further by developing licences relinquishing all intellectual property rights altogether. For instance, the Creative Commons CC0 enables authors to renounce their copyright in a work. This could be defined as a consented or voluntary public domain.[43] The exclusivity enjoyed by the creator is, as for classical free licences, subverted to forsake it and produce instead an absence of exclusivity. Works are here dedicated to the public domain with no subsistence of control or rights.

This is a radical move which raises serious questions of validity:[44] is the exclusivity conferred by law to the creator so exclusive that it can be surrendered?

Once that question is solved (which I will not do here), that consented public domain is subject to the developments made above for public domain.

---

[42] Regulation (EU) No 1257/2012 of the European Parliament and of the Council of 17 December 2012 implementing enhanced cooperation in the area of the creation of unitary patent protection, art. 8 [OJ L 361, 31.12.2012].

[43] The expression is taken from M. Clément-Fontaine, *Les œuvres libres*, Thèse de l'université de Montpellier, 2006, at 281.

[44] P. Samuelson, 'Challenges in the mapping of the public domain', in L. Guibault and B. Hugenholtz (eds.), *supra* note 22, at 9; R. Burrell & E. Hudson, 'Property Concepts in European Copyright Law: the Case of Abandonment', in H. Howe & J. Griffiths (eds.), *Property Concepts in Intellectual Property* (Cambridge University Press, 2013).

3. The Denial of Exclusivity

In some cases, the exercise of the exclusivity of intellectual property is paralysed in favour of a collectivisation of the use of works or inventions. What distinguishes those hypotheses from legal or compulsory licences that also operate a certain 'socialisation' of copyright or patent,[45] is that they do not state an exception to the exercise of the intellectual property right for a precise use that the lawmaker wishes to privilege, but on the ground of the status of the work or invention itself. Two cases can be cited: orphan works in copyright and standard-essential patents.

A. Orphan works

The European Directive of October 2012[46] allows libraries and archives to make available works that will be declared orphan after a diligent search. This creates a new exception to copyright for libraries, extending exempted uses to the act of public communication, but only for a certain category of works. Once a work has been considered as being an orphan, the exclusivity vested by copyright in such work will be frozen. To some extent, the non-exercise of the exclusive rights becomes a disabled exclusivity. The absence of the author or copyright-owner, whether voluntary or not, forces them to accept their rights to be coated with non-exclusivity, for libraries can use orphan work with no authorisation.

Whatever the need to solve a situation that does not benefit copyrighted works in any way, as the copyright is not enforced and no exploitation can take place, the solution of the orphan works directive discriminates between works as to their exclusivity. The parents, who disappear or are not known, lose the custody of their children. Even when they reappear, they will only get some compensation for past uses, under conditions determined by Member States.[47] One recital implies that the 'return' of copyright owners will integrally restore their rights: the use by libraries could then only be continued with their consent and under their conditions.[48]

---

[45] A. Strowel, 'Licences non-volontaires et socialisation du droit d'auteur: un danger ou une nécessité?', *Cahiers de Propriété Intellectuelle*, Jan. 1991, at 161–183.

[46] Directive 2012/28/EU of the European Parliament and of the Council of 25 October 2012 on certain permitted uses of orphan works. [OJ L 299, 27.10.2012]

[47] Article 6(5) of the orphan works directive.

[48] See recital 17 in fine of the orphan works directive.

The status of orphan work, once acknowledged in one country, is attached to the work and is made public through dedicated databases. Their amputated exclusivity is applicable and enforceable in all Member States, the libraries hence benefiting from an inclusive privilege to make that work available to the public. The orphan work lies to some extent in a middle territory between the full protection of copyright and the public domain. It is still protected by copyright but some freedom of use is granted to defined users; the exclusive rights still exist in theory but are disabled in practice, by default of someone to claim them.

A recent French law has similarly reduced the exclusive rights of authors, not only for orphan works but also for out-of-print works.[49] Works (the law mainly applies to books and published literary works) that would not be commercially available anymore are put on a list of 'unavailable books' (*livres indisponibles*). The publisher and author can take the work out of that list by declaring they intend to resume its exploitation. If they do not opt out their works from that list within a determined time, the exploitation of the right in the work will be entrusted to mandatory collective management that could license the work to other publishers for a new exploitation.

The copyright-owner (mainly the publisher, with the author benefiting from more possibilities to recover their rights) is thus obliged to effectively give a new commercial (and digital) life to the work, to exercise their exclusivity at the risk of losing it altogether.

Many critiques have been formulated against this peculiar solution that will create non-exclusivity on the sole ground of lack of exploitation (voluntarily or not) and only justified by some sort of digital agenda. A principle of 'opt-out', an *ex post* opposition, substitutes the normal principle of an explicit and *ex ante* authorisation ('opt-in'). In the US *Google Books* case, such tampering with the normal rule of copyright had been denounced by the Court[50] (with the relief at the time of the French Government and rights-owners).

In both cases (orphan works and out-of-print books), the retreat of exclusivity is justified by the need to foster the digital dissemination and

---

[49] Article L-134-1 of the Code de Propriété Intellectuelle, introduced by the law of 1st March 2012.

[50] *Authors Guild v. Google, Inc.*, 770 F. Supp. 2d 666 (S.D.N.Y., 22 March 2011) («A copyright owner's right to exclude others from using his property is fundamental and beyond dispute. (…) Under the [settlement], however, if copyright owners sit back and do nothing, they lose their rights. Absent class members who fail to opt out will be deemed to have released their rights even as to future infringing conduct»).

availability of works, by libraries or even by commercial publishers, countering the tradition of copyright as the very rule enhancing such dissemination by the grant of exclusivity. This is a radical move.

In orphan works, or the French *oeuvres indisponibles*, the exclusivity is denied or mitigated by law to enhance the dissemination of works, countering the normally preferred option of exclusive right. As in the case of copyright exceptions, the potential user of the work (the library for the orphan works and any publisher for out-of-print works) enjoys from inclusive and equal entitlements to use the work. This inclusivity occupies the place left by the exclusivity that has been taken away by law.

B. Standards-essential patents and FRAND licensing

The imperative of digital development also strikes in patents to curb the exclusivity of the property right. Competition law has indeed forced the exercise of patent in technologies essential to standards to adopt a more inclusive way. Standards are deemed to be an essential brick in the construction of networked technologies and interoperability, whether in telecommunications, mobile phones, digital formats or web communications.[51]

As a result, the exclusivity of patents when they pertain to standards has been restrained to some extent. The case of patent hold-up or patent ambush, where the patent-owner hides the existence of their patent or asks for excessive royalties when revealed, has first triggered some reaction of competition authorities.[52] The situation of such patent-owners is considerably advantageous as the users have no other choice but to implement the standardised technology and then to get a licence. In order to mitigate or counter possible abuse by patent-owners, the standard-setting organisations now impose on IP-owners the obligation to grant licences in their standard-essential patents (SEPs) under FRAND conditions (meaning on fair, reasonable and non-discriminatory terms). Whatever their legitimacy or necessity, it could be said that such imposed licence conditions curtail the exclusivity that vests in patent rights, since they reduce the power of the right-holder to set the amount of royalties or different conditions to distinct licensees.

The European Commission supports the imposition of FRAND conditions by exempting the standardisation agreement that would include

[51] F. Levêque & Y. Ménière, 'Technology Standards, Patents and Antitrust', 9 *Competition and Regulation in Network Industries* (2008).

[52] EU Commission, 15 January 2010, Rejection decision and Commitments decision, 9 December 2009, *Rambus*, COMP/38.636.

such a rule from the application of article 101 of the TFEU.[53] The question of whether an injunction, which is an important remedy to protect exclusivity, could be secured against an unauthorised user of standard-essential patent, who is willing to accept a FRAND licensing, is also challenged by the European Commission[54] and this question has been referred to the European Court of Justice.[55] The advocate general concluded in November 2014 that a prohibitory injunction by such a patent holder constitutes an abuse of its dominant position under Article 102 TFEU "where it is shown that the SEP-holder has not honoured its commitment even though the infringer has shown itself to be objectively ready, willing and able to conclude such a licensing agreement".[56]

What distinguishes that imposed FRAND licensing from refusal to license competition cases is the inclusivity characterising the former. IP owners have sometimes been forced to grant a licence in the latter case when their refusal was considered abusive under exceptional circumstances,[57] but the licence then benefited the user that could prove it met the conditions required by those circumstances, and not to any user. In standard-essential patent cases, the very exclusivity of the patent rights is eroded as the patent-owner is deprived of the power to agree to license or negotiate its conditions with any potential user. The competition authorities have substituted the exclusivity of the intellectual property right by an inclusive entitlement shared by all users of the technology. Any company that wishes to use a standardised technology enjoys an equal and symmetric right to the patented elements thereof.

---

[53] Communication of the Commission, Guidelines on the applicability of Article 101 of the Treaty on the Functioning of the European Union to horizontal co-operation agreements, OJ, 14 November 2011, C 11/1, §§ 257–335.

[54] Press release of the European Commission in the Samsung case, IP/12/1448, 21 December 2012; Press release of the European Commission on the Statement of Objections to Motorola Mobility on potential misuse of mobile phone standard-essential patents opening antitrust investigation against Motorola Mobility, 6 May 2013.

[55] Questions referred to the CJEU, Case C-170/13, *Huawei Technologies Co. Ltd v ZTE Corp., ZTE Deutschland GmbH.*

[56] Opinion of Advocate General Wathelet, 20 November 2014, C-170/13.

[57] ECJ, 6 April 1995. *Radio Telefis Eireann (RTE) & Independent Television Publications Ltd (ITP) v European Commission*, C-241/91 & C-242/91; ECJ, 29 April 2004, *IMS Health GmbH & Co. OHG & NDC Health GmbH & Co. KG*, C-418/01; Court of first instance, 17 September 2007, *Microsoft,* T-201/04.

III. TOWARDS SOME ORGANISATION OF INCLUSIVITY IN INTELLECTUAL PROPERTY

In the traditional discourse of property, exclusivity is considered as a means to reap the value of ownership (tangible property) or to incentivise creation and innovation (intellectual property). The lack of exclusivity is only seen as a default position, not requiring any legal organisation. The denomination of 'inclusivity' is not merely a semantic trick to reverse exclusivity. It could also bring about some normative changes in intellectual property law.

Departing from a negative appellation, the non-exclusive, which satisfies itself with no specific protection, could lead to the building of a legal regime protecting the value and sustainability of inclusive entitlements. For example, the touchstone of the definition of public domain in IP is the lack of protection; therefore the public does not benefit from any rights or secured legal entitlements in its contents.[58] Being a default position, the lack of exclusivity and enforceable legal entitlements in public domain content does not help resist attempts to recover private and exclusive rights in the resource.

Conversely, if we think of the public domain as an inclusive space, creating inclusive privileges to use, and not as a negative image of exclusivity, we can start to protect the public domain and preserve it from regained exclusivity and encroachments. It would not be appropriate to say, as the US Supreme Court did in the *Golan* case, that copyright can be vested in public domain works. Whereas one court of appeal had qualified the public domain as a "bedrock principle of copyright law" with the consequence that "what is in the public domain should remain there",[59] the Supreme Court held that "Neither the Copyright and Patent Clause nor the First Amendment makes the public domain, in any and all cases, a territory that works may never exit".[60]

One French court had also tried to give more strength to the public domain.[61] Two authors had restored and added a contemporary work of art in a public and historical square, the Place des Terreaux in Lyon. They sued a company having reproduced the square in a postcard that included both the public domain buildings and the pavement, which was a

---

[58] S. Dusollier, *supra* note 25; J. Cahir, The public domain: right or liberty?, in Waelde & MacQueen (eds.), *Intellectual Property – The Many Faces of the Public Domain* (Edward Elgar, 2007).

[59] *Golan v. Gonzales,* 501 F.3d 1179 (10th Cir. Colo., Sept. 4, 2007).

[60] U.S. Supreme Court, *Golan v. Holder*, 132 S.Ct, 873 (2012).

[61] TGI Lyon, 4 April 2001, *RIDA*, October 2001, note S. Choisy.

protected work. The key argument of the decision was that the public domain status of the buildings necessarily constrains and limits the exercise of copyright held by the authors of a derivative work to the extent required by the free reproduction of the public domain. Otherwise, a copyright would be indirectly restored in the public domain work for the benefit of the authors of its restoration or modification. The decision was upheld on appeal, mainly on different grounds, even though the Court of Appeal stated that "the protection granted to the authors of the new design of the square should not prejudice the common enjoyment",[62] which still recognises a positive protection of the public domain and of its inherent collective use. The Court de Cassation set aside any reference to the public domain and opted to allow the reproduction on the ground of the exception for ancillary reproduction of a work.[63]

Another example is copyright exceptions. Considered as mere defences to infringement actions, exceptions cannot grant users a genuine right to use the work that would be enforceable against contracts or technological measures of protection. But as inclusive privileges and with a proper status to that inclusivity, exceptions could gain a restored position in copyright law.

Inclusivity could also renew our thinking about what intellectual property is, particularly when we seek to apply it to traditional knowledge and folklore. An intellectual property right that could be able to grant inclusive rights would better pay tribute to the collective and shared use. In consequence, maybe traditional knowledge could enrich our notion of intellectual property, without being trapped by it?

Such examples would be testimonies of regimes where exclusivity intermingles with inclusivity to create a renovated form of property. They prove wrong the essentiality of exclusivity in intellectual property, for many cases cited here show that the purpose of creation and innovation can equally be achieved by granting spaces of non-exclusivity. The increasing recourse to non-exclusivity and the increasing attention paid by lawmakers to public domain, orphan works, limitations or FRAND licensing also reveals that IP-making is nowadays about regulating the relationship to creation and innovation, relying both on exclusive rights

[62] Lyon, 20 March 2003, *Communications – Commerce Electronique*, September 2003, note C. Caron. The Court of Cassation has confirmed the ruling on a very different justification, not making any mention of the public domain status of the underlying work. See Cass., 15 March 2005, available on <http://www.courdecassation.fr/jurisprudence_2/premiere_chambre_civile_568/arret_no_632.html>.

[63] Cour de Cassation, Arrêt n° 567 du 15 mars 2005.

and on spaces where collectiveness and non-exclusivity are organising the relationships to works and inventions.

As Julie Cohen pleaded for copyright, it might be necessary "to complicate [intellectual property], replacing its foundational private/public dichotomy with a more complex and fertile mix of rights and privileges".[64] One key challenge would be to effectively estimate the spaces of non-exclusivity in intellectual property, no longer as a backward process, but as forward progress that could deepen our organisation of protection and enhancement of creation and innovation.

---

64 J. Cohen, *supra* note 22, at 165.

7. Private ordering and consumers' rights in copyright law: A view of Japanese consumers

Branislav Hazucha, Hsiao-Chien Liu and Toshihide Watabe

INTRODUCTION

Once persons purchase something, they can conventionally do with their acquisition anything they want within the limits of the law. They can use it for their personal purposes. They can read their books, can listen to their music CDs and can watch their movie DVDs whenever, wherever and however they want, unless such uses interfere with the copyright holder's exclusive rights granted by copyright law. They can lend any of those things to their friends. They can make MP3 files from their music CDs in order to listen to those sound recordings on their MP3 file players. They can make back-up copies of their computer programs for cases of emergency where the original CD-ROMs or DVDs containing the computer programs are damaged. They can destroy or sell their tangible things to other persons in a garage sale or online auction.

This freedom has traditionally been reflected in copyright law by limiting the scope of exclusive rights granted to copyright holders so that an adequate and proper balance is struck between the private interests of copyright holders on the one side and the interests of the public and consumers of copyrighted works on the other. Many of those limits on the scope of copyright have, however, been challenged lately by copyright holders' licensing practices and use of technological protection measures, which prevent users from making back-up or other types of private copies, from lending their videogames to friends or from reselling their downloaded music tracks, movies or e-books to third parties. This practice has been buttressed, to a certain degree, by statutory changes in copyright law and by court rulings in several jurisdictions. They recognize that the embodiments of copyrighted works are different from other tangible things and the copyright holders are allowed to control how the consumers use their copyrighted works.

The recent trends in allowing copyright holders contractually to get rid of the statutory restrictions on the scope of their exclusive rights have caused a number of conflicts between norms belonging to different branches of law, especially to copyright law, contract law and property law. First, freedom of contract allows contractual parties to determine the terms and conditions of their contractual relationship within the limits of the law. Copyright holders commonly argue that this enables them freely to set the terms and conditions under which consumers are permitted to use their copyrighted works. Second, copyright law imposes several limitations on the copyright holders' exclusive rights. The copyright limitations and restrictions are habitually understood as the result of a bargain between the copyright holders' interest in the protection of legitimate interests in their copyrighted works and the public interest in accessibility and dissemination of those copyrighted works. Nonetheless, the copyright laws are rarely explicit on the character of those limitations. Some scholars and courts consider the copyright limitations and restrictions as mandatory provisions; others see them only as default rules which can be modified through contractual arrangements. Finally, contractual restrictions on the use of copyrighted works significantly impede the consumers' property rights in lawfully acquired embodiments of copyrighted works, especially their right to traffic or trade in their chattels.

To cope with the conflicts of norms within domestic law, a so-called *lex specialis* rule provides that a special norm trumps the application of a general norm under specifically defined circumstances. Although the *lex specialis* rule is said to be very simple and easy to apply, its application can bring challenging questions and heated controversies,[1] especially in cases where a conflict between norms appears between two different branches of law and this has not been explicitly expected by the legislator or courts. The question then arises which norm should overrule the other.

This chapter examines several examples of such controversy between contract law, property law and copyright law, where the question arises as to which of those norms are *lex specialis* and which are *lex generalis*. Should the freedom of contract allow the copyright holders to override the statutory restrictions on the scope of copyright holders' exclusive

---

[1] *See, e.g.*, Silvia Zorzetto, "The *Lex Specialis* Principle and its Uses in Legal Argumentation: An Analytical Inquire" (2012) Eunomía: Revista en Cultura de la Legalidad 61.

rights as default rules or should the statutory provisions of copyright law as *lex specialis* trump the freedom of contract? Are there any consumers' rights under copyright law? If so, can they be restricted by licensing agreements?

The analysis is divided into four parts. Section 1 scrutinizes the recent case law on the abovementioned conflicts of norms in three jurisdictions – the United States, the European Union and Japan. As there are considerable differences between the studied jurisdictions in solving those conflicts of norms, Section 2 looks into the importance of consumers considering such non-negotiable contractual arrangements fair and just in order to achieve the high level of consumers' compliance with copyright law, as well as technological protection measures and licensing agreements through which the copyright holders habitually in practice exercise their exclusive rights granted and protected by copyright law. Section 3 then presents an empirical study which scrutinizes the level to which Japanese consumers accept or reject several major technological and other contractual restrictions on the uses of copyrighted works imposed by copyright holders at the moment in Japan. Finally, Section 4 examines whether and how the current practice with using technological and other contractual restrictions reflects the consumers' preferences on the importance of individual types of copyrighted works (*e.g.* sound recordings, television broadcast, movies, videogames and performances) and their uses (*e.g.* copying, recording on live concerts, and format-, time- and place-shifting), which are observed by our empirical study.

This chapter concludes that the technological or other contractual restrictions imposed by copyright holders work efficiently only when they restrict uses which are not considered by the consumers of copyrighted works as important for them. Conversely, any attempt of copyright holders to restrict a use which is deemed by the consumers as vital, has failed so far on the market.

1. CONFLICTS BETWEEN COPYRIGHTS AND CONSUMERS' RIGHTS IN PRIVATE ORDERING

Copyright holders have routinely tried to control the use of their works as much as possible, especially in cases where they perceive that certain types of uses can negatively affect the sales of those works. Their attempts have given rise to a number of clashes between the interests of several stakeholders, including copyright holders, various intermediaries, consumers and organizers of new emerging markets. The conflicts have traditionally been solved by limiting the copyright holders' exclusive rights through several mechanisms, such as the exhaustion-of-rights doctrine[2] and a range of copyright limitations and exceptions.[3] Many national copyright laws have either expressly incorporated these into their statutory laws[4] or have left it to the courts to construct and further develop them.[5] They have even been recognized by several international treaties in the field of copyright law.[6]

The following analysis scrutinizes attempts by copyright holders to broaden the scope of their exclusive rights by contractual arrangements that try to override the abovementioned copyright limitations and restrictions in a number of cases, such as fixing retail prices of copyrighted works, restricting the resale of used copies of copyrighted works, and eliminating possible post-sale uses of the copies of copyrighted works by

---

[2] *See, e.g.*, Paul Goldstein and Bernt Hugenholtz, *International Copyright: Principles, Law, and Practice* (3rd edn, Oxford: Oxford University Press 2013) 311–4.

[3] *See ibid.* at 371–403.

[4] *See, e.g.*, the U.S. Copyright Act of 1976, 17 U.S.C. §109 (first sale doctrine), and §§107-8 and 110-2 (copyright limitations); Japanese Copyright Act of 1970, Act No. 48, as amended, art. 26*bis*(2) (exhaustion of rights) and arts. 30–50 (copyright limitations); Directive 2001/29/EC of the European Parliament and of the Council of 22 May 2001 on the harmonisation of certain aspects of copyright and related rights in the information society, OJ L167, 22.6.2001, p. 10, art. 4(2) (exhaustion of rights) and art. 5 (exceptions and limitations).

[5] *See, e.g.*, Campbell v. Acuff-Rose Music, Inc., 510 U.S. 569, 577, 114 S. Ct. 1164, 1170 (U.S. Sup. Ct., 1994) (stating that Section 107 of the U.S. Copyright Act continues the common-law tradition of fair use adjudication and requires case-by-case analysis rather than bright-linc rules).

[6] *See, e.g.*, Berne Convention for the Protection of Artistic and Literary Works, 9 Sept. 1886, as revised at Paris on 24 Jul. 1971, 1161 UNTS 31 (containing several types of copyright limitations and exceptions); Agreement on Trade-Related Aspects of Intellectual Property Rights, 15 Apr. 1994, Marrakesh Agreement Establishing the World Trade Organization, Annex 1C (1994) 33 ILM 1125 (containing Art. 6, which recognizes the exhaustion of rights and leaves it to the national laws of WTO Members, and Art. 13, which sets up the limits on copyright limitations and exceptions); World Intellectual Property Organization Copyright Treaty (1996) 2186 UNTS 152, 36 ILM 65 [hereinafter "WCT"] (regulating the exhaustion of rights in Art. 6(2) and copyright limitations and exceptions in Art. 10); World Intellectual Property Organization Performances and Phonograms Treaty (1996) 2186 UNTS 245, 36 ILM 76 [hereinafter "WPPT"] (regulating the exhaustion of rights in Arts. 8(2) and 12(2), and limitations and exceptions in Art. 16).

employing technological protection measures and digital rights management systems.

1.1 Control over Retail Prices and Secondary Markets

Historically, copyright holders have repeatedly tried to restrict the resale of authorized copies of their copyrighted works or at least to control the conditions under which their copyrighted works are resold on the market. One type of those endeavors has sought to determine the minimal retail prices for which the copies of their copyrighted works are to be sold by bookstores and other retailers to final consumers. The U.S. Supreme Court dealt with this issue in *Bobbs-Merrill Co. v. Straus*,[7] where the copyright holder wanted to determine the minimal retail price of its books by printing the retail price conditions on sold copies of them. The copyright holder printed, under the copyright notice, an additional notice which demanded the dealers to sell its books for at least one dollar net per copy.[8] When a dealer failed to do so, the notice stated that the copyright holder considered such a sale as an infringement of its exclusive rights granted by U.S. copyright law.[9] The Supreme Court, however, came to the conclusion that the plaintiff's notice went beyond the scope of copyright law, which did not create the right to impose any price limitation through the notice. In the Supreme Court's opinion, "[t]he owner of the copyright in this case did sell copies of the book in quantities and at a price satisfactory to it"[10] and therefore "[i]t has exercised the right to vend."[11] The notice was thus not binding on third parties; it was "ineffectual as against one not bound by contract or license agreement."[12] A similar doctrine – the exhaustion of rights or first sale doctrine – can be found in many other jurisdictions.[13]

In addition to fixing retail prices, copyright holders have customarily been interested in restricting the resale of used copyrighted works, but have not achieved any significant success in persuading courts or

---

[7] Bobbs-Merrill Company v. Straus et al. doing business as R.H. Macy & Company, 210 U.S. 339, 28 S. Ct. 722, 52 L. Ed. 1086, 1908 U.S. LEXIS 1513, 6 Ohio L. Rep. 323 (U.S. Sup. Ct., 1908).

[8] *See ibid.* at 341.

[9] *Ibid.*

[10] *Ibid.* at 351.

[11] *Ibid.*

[12] *Ibid.* at 2.

[13] *See, e.g.*, Japanese Copyright Act, *supra* note 4, art. 26*bis*(2); Directive 2001/29/EC, *supra* note 4, art. 4(2).

legislatures to allow such restrictions with regard to the analogue copies of copyrighted works. This issue has re-emerged with the practice of selling computer programs accompanied with diverse forms of licensing agreements. The licensing agreements routinely state that the user is only a licensee who is licensed to use the copy of the copyrighted computer program and the copyright holder retains the title to that copy. As a sale-of-goods contract and a licensing agreement have completely different legal consequences, the classification of this relationship as a contract between a copyright holder and a user of a copy of copyrighted work can have a considerable impact on the rights and obligations of both parties.

There are two main approaches to this issue in the jurisdictions studied. The first approach is presented by case law developed by the U.S. federal courts which are quite open to a broad interpretation of the notion of "license". In *Vernor v. Autodesk, Inc.*,[14] which dealt with the resale of used computer programs in a garage sale and online auction, the Ninth Circuit Court of Appeals held that a license has to satisfy three main conditions in order to be distinct from a sale of goods contract. It has to clearly state that the user is granted only a license;[15] the mere designation of a contract as a licensing agreement is not enough.[16] A licensing agreement also has to satisfy the two remaining conditions regarding content; it has to restrict the users' ability to transfer the computer program and impose notable restrictions on its use.[17]

As it is not so difficult to comply with those two conditions on the content of a licensing agreement, several scholars and courts outside the United States have expressed their worries about the survival of the first sale doctrine in the digital age, where it is easy to design the marketing of copyrighted works as involving a license.[18] This was one of the main

---

14 621 F.3d 1102, 2010 U.S. App. LEXIS 18957 (9th Cir., 2010).

15 *See ibid.* at 1111.

16 *Ibid.* at 1109.

17 *Ibid.* at 1111.

18 *See, e.g.*, John A. Rothchild, "The Incredible Shrinking First-Sale Rule: Are Software Resale Limits Lawful?" (2004) 57 Rutgers L. Rev. 1; Brian W. Carver, "Why License Agreements Do Not Control Copy Ownership: First Sales and Essential Copies" (2010) 25 Berkeley Tech. L.J. 1887; Aaron Perzanowski and Jason Schultz, "Digital Exhaustion" (2011) 58 UCLA L. Rev. 889. *See also* UsedSoft GmbH v. Oracle International Corp, Case C-128/11, para. 49 (Court of Justice of the European Union (Grand Chamber), 3 Jul. 2012) ("the effectiveness of that provision would be undermined, since suppliers would merely have to call the contract a 'licence' rather than a 'sale' in order to circumvent the rule of exhaustion and divest it of all scope").

reasons why the Court of Justice of the European Union was reluctant to follow this line of reasoning in *UsedSoft GmbH v. Oracle International Corp.*[19]

The core issue before the Court of Justice was whether a first sale had occurred and whether the user of a computer program was thus the "lawful acquirer" of a copy of the computer program. Contrary to the U.S. courts, the Court of Justice refused to restrict the application of the first sale doctrine in cases of marketing computer programs. The Court of Justice warned that a narrow interpretation of the notion of "sale", which would allow the exclusion of contracts entitled "licences" by the right holders, would allow them "to circumvent the rule of exhaustion and divest it of all scope."[20] The crucial points for the Court of Justice were whether the user could use a copy of a copyrighted work for an unlimited period of time and whether the copyright holder was paid the full value for the copy. Under the contract in question, the copyright holder, according to the Court of Justice, intended the user to use a copy of its copyrighted computer program permanently in return for the payment of "a remuneration corresponding to the economic value of the copy".[21] The copyright holder therefore transferred ownership of the copy.[22] The Court of Justice emphasized that the transfer of a copy of a computer program, which is accompanied by a licensing agreement between the parties, is sufficient to constitute a first sale within the meaning of Art. 4(2) of the Computer Program Directive.[23]

Similar issues have also been raised before the Supreme Court of Japan in two cases dealing with the sale of used or second-hand videogames.[24] The Japanese copyright law traditionally distinguishes between cinematographic works and other copyrighted works with regard to regulating the distribution of the copies of copyrighted works. The reason is that the main use of cinematographic works (on movie reels) differs considerably from the principal use of other types of copyrighted works, such as books, magazines, journals and music media. While the former are

---

19 Case C-128/11.

20 *See ibid.*, para. 49.

21 *Ibid.*, para. 45.

22 *Ibid.*, para. 46.

23 *Ibid.*, para. 48. *Cf.* Directive 2009/24/EC of the European Parliament and of the Council of 23 April 2009 on the legal protection of computer programs, art. 4(2), OJ L111, 5.5.2009, p. 16.

24 2001 (Ju) No. 952, (2002) 56(4) Minshu 808 (Sup. Ct. of Japan, 25 Apr. 2002); 2001 (Ju) No. 898, (2002) 1785 The Hanreijiho 9 (Sup. Ct. of Japan, 25 Apr. 2002).

mainly consumed through public performances in movie theaters,[25] the consumption of the latter is based on the sale of copies to individual consumers. Accordingly, Japanese copyright law recognizes that the holders of copyright to cinematographic works can retain the title to movie reels and other similar media; can determine the conditions of their use; and can demand the return or destruction of the embodiments of their copyrighted works.[26] On the other hand, the copies of books, magazines, journals and music media are normally sold to their consumers and the consumers can freely dispose of those copies.[27] The consumers can keep them without any time restrictions, can destroy them and can give or resell them to third parties. The copyright holders are deemed to recoup enough revenues from their investments by selling those copies. It is seen as unfair to allow the copyright holders to control the movement of those copies or to ask for any further payment for their resale.[28]

A similar situation[29] existed in the United States before several major rulings in cases dealing with computer programs and databases in the early 1990s. Contrary to the U.S. federal courts, the Japanese courts have not restricted the application of the first sale doctrine in case of computer programs. Although the copyright holder in the used videogame case argued that the parts of videogames are also cinematographic works and therefore videogames should be treated similarly to cinematographic works, the Supreme Court of Japan was of a different opinion. The

---

[25] Although this assumption can be partially challenged by the fact that the holders of copyrights in cinematograph works obtain a lot of revenues from the sales of pre-recorded movie media, such as movie DVDs and Blu-ray Discs, the revenues received from public performances of cinematograph works in movie theatres still represent a significant portion of their total revenues.

[26] *See* (2002) 56(4) Minshu at 810–1, paras. 3 and 4; (2002) 1785 The Hanreijiho at 10–1.

[27] (2002) 56(4) Minshu at 812–3, para. 4; (2002) 1785 The Hanreijiho at 11, para. 3.

[28] (2002) 56(4) Minshu at 811–3, paras. 4 and 5; (2002) 1785 The Hanreijiho at 10–1, paras. 3 and 4.

[29] *Compare* Straus v. Victor Talking Machine Co., 243 U.S. 490, 500-501, 37 S. Ct. 412, 415, 61 L. Ed. 866, 871, 1917 U.S. LEXIS 2016 (U.S. Sup. Ct., 1917) ("Courts would be perversely blind if they failed to look through such an attempt as this 'License Notice' thus plainly is to sell property for a full price, and yet to place restraints upon its further alienation, such as have been hateful to the law from Lord Coke's day to ours, because obnoxious to the public interest.") *with* United States v. Wise, 550 F.2d 1180 (9th Cir., 1977) (license of movie reels) and Hampton v. Paramount Pictures Corp., 279 F.2d 100 (9th Cir., 1960) (same).

Supreme Court clearly distinguished reels of cinematographic works, which are consumed through public performances in movie theaters and similar venues, from other copies of cinematographic works, such as videocassettes and movie DVDs. In regard to reels, the distribution rights, which cover the acts of assigning and lending the copies of copyrighted works to the public,[30] are not exhausted; but with videocassettes and DVDs of movies, the copyright holders' rights to offer to the public for assigning the ownership to the copies of copyrighted works as an integral part of their distribution rights are exhausted by the first sale of copies to final consumers[31] with the copyright holders only retaining the lending rights to those copies.[32]

The Supreme Court even expressed its view that inhibiting the free distribution of products on the market can harm the legitimate interests of copyright holders, since it creates obstacles to the smooth distribution of copyrighted works and their copies.[33] This can impair the ultimate goal of copyright law, which is contributing to the development of culture by protecting authors' rights.[34]

---

[30] *See* Japanese Copyright Act, *supra* note 4, art. 2(1)(xix). The Japanese Copyright Act distinguishes between "distribution rights", "assignment rights" and "lending rights" with regard to distribution of the copies of copyrighted works. The distribution rights, which cover the acts of assigning as well as lending the copies of copyrighted works to the public, are granted only for cinematographic works. The assignment rights and lending rights are granted for other types of copyrighted works than cinematographic works. In case of assignment rights, the Copyright Act expressly states that these rights are limited by the exhaustion of rights, contrary to the distribution rights and lending rights where the Act is silent about any exhaustion of rights.

This division is the result of historical development of regulating the distribution of the copies of copyrighted works. The first recognized rights were the "distribution rights" for cinematographic works. When the drafters of the 1999 amendment to the Japanese Copyright Act conceived the broadening of the scope of distribution in the Japanese Copyright Act, they opted for the introduction of a new right, contrary to extending the distribution right to all types of copyrighted works. The reason is that they wanted to restrict the application of the exhaustion of right doctrine only to the cases where the transfer of ownership to a copy of copyrighted work occurs.

[31] *See* Japanese Copyright Act, *supra* note 4, art. 26*bis*(2).

[32] (2002) 56(4) Minshu at 813, para. 5; (2002) 1785 The Hanreijiho at 11, para. 4. *See also* Japanese Copyright Act, *supra* note 4, art. 26*ter*.

[33] (2002) 56(4) Minshu at 811, para. 4; (2002) 1785 The Hanreijiho at 10, para. 3.

[34] (2002) 56(4) Minshu at 811, para. 4; (2002) 1785 The Hanreijiho at 10, para. 3.

A note should be made here that the copyright holders in both cases did not base their claims on any specific licensing agreements before the Supreme Court of Japan. Their entire arguments were based on the assumption that videogames are cinematographic works: they argued that as the exhaustion of rights doctrine does not expressly apply to cinematographic works, it should not apply to videogames either. It is thus not clear what would have been the Supreme Court's ruling if the argument had been based on the enforcement of a licensing agreement. Nevertheless, several scholars and a few rulings of lower courts in the field of patent law suggest that the Japanese approach to this issue might be closer to the European solution than to the U.S. one.[35]

1.2 Computer Programs versus Other Types of Copyrighted Works

The courts in many jurisdictions have been traditionally reluctant to restrict the application of the first sale doctrine when copyright holders put any warnings or other similar notices on copies of their copyrighted works, such as books, magazines, journals, audiocassettes, music CDs or movie DVDs, in order to claim any proprietary rights beyond the recognized scope of copyright law. This issue has recently been re-examined with regard to types of copyrighted works other than computer programs in the United States by the Ninth Circuit after its abovementioned ruling in the *Vernor* case. *Universal Music Group v. Augusto* dealt with promotional music CDs, which contained a warning that the user was only a licensee and the right holder retained title to that CD.[36] The Ninth Circuit was, however, not very willing to extend the application of the case law it had developed with regard to computer programs to other types of copyrighted works. The Ninth Circuit expressly stated that computer programs arc different and should be treated differently.[37]

---

35 *See*, *e.g.*, Yoshiyuki Tamura, "Youjinriron to Houhoutokkyo heno Tekiyoukanousei ni tsuite" (2005) 39 Patent Studies 5, 9–10 (discussing the exhaustion of rights in patent law); Kazuyuki Tanikawa, "Digital Content no Chuukohanbai to Shoujin no Gensoku: Oubei no Kinji no Doukou", in Doshisha University Intellectual Property Law Study Group (ed.), *Chitekizaisanhou no Chousen* (Tokyo: Koubundou 2013) 420 (discussing the exhaustion of rights in copyright law).

36 UMG Recordings, Inc. v. Augusto, 628 F.3d 1175, 2011 U.S. App. LEXIS 52 (9th Cir., 4 Jan. 2011).

37 *See ibid.* at 1183.

In this case, the copyright holder distributed promotional music CDs to various entities, such as radio stations, music critics and the like. The CDs contained a warning that they were not for commercial use. In addition, the warning stated that the users were only granted a license. If the receivers did not agree with the license, they were asked to return the CD or to destroy it. The defendant bought several of those promotional music CDs from various sources and wanted to auction them on the eBay website.

The crucial aspect in the case was that the music CDs were sent to their receivers as unsolicited mail. Pursuant to a special federal law on unsolicited mail in the United States, the goods sent in unsolicited mail were considered a gift.[38] The law was designed to prevent unfair marketing practices of sending unsolicited commercial articles to the public and then demanding the payment of their price. As the copyright holder sent the promotional music CDs as unsolicited mail, the Ninth Circuit concluded that the transfer of title to the copies occurred in the form of donation.[39] Consequently, the first sale doctrine applied to this transfer of ownership.

The Ninth Circuit also examined whether any licensing agreement could have been concluded in the event that the special regulation on unsolicited mail had not applied. The Ninth Circuit rejected any conclusion of a licensing agreement even in such a case, because the silence or inaction of the recipient cannot be construed as acceptance of an offer to conclude a license.[40] If someone receives an offer from another party, they can just leave it on a shelf and wait until the offeror comes to take the offer back.[41] The inaction of the receiver of an offer cannot be construed as acceptance of that offer.

The question that still remains is what happens if a music CD is provided under a so-called shrink-wrap license, that is, in a special package which provides the recipient with terms and conditions of a license stating that the recipient, by opening the package, agrees with the license. Would the Ninth Circuit be more willing to accept that the license agreement was properly concluded if the recipient tore the package open? If so, what would happen if all books, journals, magazines, music CDs and movie DVDs were marketed in such packages? Would any second-hand resale of those copyrighted works be considered

[38] *Ibid.* at 1180–81.
[39] *Ibid.* at 1181.
[40] *Ibid.* at 1182–3.
[41] *Ibid.* at 1182 n.6.

copyright infringement? If this practice was allowed, would it mean that the first sale doctrine would become completely inapplicable?

This brings us to a similar set of questions regarding the current status of providing various types of copyrighted works online, such as e-books, sound recordings or movies. Most authorized online downloading services have their terms of use and end user licensing agreements designed so that their users are only granted a license to use downloaded content while the online service providers retain the titles to those copies. The issue concerning the resale of downloaded files containing copies of copyrighted works has recently been scrutinized by a U.S. federal district court.

In *Capitol Records, LLC v. ReDigi Inc.*,[42] the U.S. District Court for the Southern District of New York examined an online system, which allowed its users to trade music files downloaded from iTunes. The defendant's business model was based on the premise that the resale of authorized music files should be treated similarly to the resale of audiocassettes or music CDs.[43] Nonetheless, the District Court was not open to this legal construction and it found that ReDigi had infringed the plaintiff's reproduction and distribution rights.[44] Although the ruling is on appeal, there is not much chance that the appellate court will significantly reverse the District Court's ruling in favor of the defendant.

The District Court emphasized in its ruling that the term "reproduction" must be construed very broadly. It should cover any recreation of something even when the original is destroyed.[45] As the transfer of a file through the internet requires making and deleting copies of the music file, the final copy is different from the original copy. The court then had no doubt that the making of copies occurred during the transfer of a music file between a user and ReDigi's Cloud Locker.[46] The court also rejected ReDigi's fair use defense, because the copyrighted works were highly creative; the copies were exact copies; the entire activity was done for commercial purposes; and ReDigi's business activities had a negative impact on the market for the copyrighted works concerned.

---

[42] 934 F. Supp. 2d 640, 2013 U.S. Dist. LEXIS 48043, 106 U.S.P.Q.2D (BNA) 1449, Copy. L. Rep. (CCH) P30, 405 (S.D.N.Y., 30 Mar. 2013).

[43] *See ibid.* at 644.

[44] *Ibid.* at 651.

[45] *Ibid.* at 649–50.

[46] *Ibid.* at 650.

The District Court also found that the copyright holders' distribution rights were infringed because copies of copyrighted works were distributed between the users and ReDigi's Cloud Locker.[47] At the same time, the court came to the conclusion that the first sale doctrine applies only to the authorized copies of copyrighted works. In this particular case, only the music files directly downloaded from iTunes were considered by the District Court to be authorized copies.[48] The copies which were produced during the transfer of the music files between the users and ReDigi's Cloud Locker were found to be unauthorized and therefore the first sale doctrine defense was inapplicable to those copies according to the court.[49]

The finding of the U.S. District Court is completely opposite to the ruling of the Court of Justice of the European Union in the *UsedSoft* case, where the Court of Justice considered all copies made during the transfer of a computer program to be covered, as necessary for the use of the computer program, by Art. 5(1) of the Computer Program Directive.[50] Nevertheless, it is not clear what would be the position of the Court of Justice in the case of copyrighted works other than computer programs.

As the ruling of the Court of Justice in the *UsedSoft* case is restricted to the interpretation of the Computer Program Directive, its implications for other types of copyrighted works can be a bit limited, especially when we take into account Recitals 28 and 29 in the preamble to the Information Society Directive.[51] The European Commission argued before the Court of Justice in the *UsedSoft* case that the Information Society Directive limits the application of the exhaustion of rights and the first sale doctrine to tangible things. The Commission pointed out that Recital 29 expressly rejects the application of the exhaustion of rights doctrine in cases of services, including online ones.[52]

Nonetheless, the text of the individual provisions of the Information Society Directive is a bit more nuanced than the Commission suggested. Art. 3(3) of the Directive excludes the application of the exhaustion of rights doctrine to the right of communication to the public of a work and the right of making available to the public other protected subject matters. To put it more bluntly, a right holder uploading copies of

---

47 *Ibid.* at 651.

48 *Ibid.* at 655–6.

49 *Ibid.* at 655.

50 Case C-128/11, para. 81. *Cf.* Directive 2009/24/EC, *supra* note 23, art. 5(1).

51 Directive 2001/29/EC, *supra* note 4.

52 Case C-128/11, para. 54.

copyrighted works and other protected subject matters does not allow third parties to upload copies of those somewhere else on the internet. The Article does not, however, say anything about the limitation of the exhaustion of rights doctrine in cases of reselling lawfully downloaded copies.

In this regard, Art. 4(2) of the Directive allows right holders to retain the title to copies of their copyrighted works and other protected subject matters. When the right holder retains the title to copies, their distribution right is not exhausted within the European Union. The actual interpretation of this provision will thus depend on the construction of "transfer of ownership". The Court of Justice in the *UsedSoft* case considered the downloading of a copy with the right holder's consent to be a transfer of ownership, regardless of any additional contractual arrangement between the parties. At the same time, it should be noted that the Court of Justice heavily relied in its ruling on the provision of Art. 1(2) of the Computer Program Directive, which requires the protection provided by the Directive to be applied to any form of a computer program.[53] Therefore, the Court of Justice did not want to distinguish between the protection of a computer program on a CD-ROM or DVD-ROM on the one hand and of a downloaded computer program on the other. It is, however, not apparent what the position of the Court of Justice would be in cases of downloaded e-books[54] and music or movie files, especially when the terms and conditions used by their online providers often state that the users are only licensees and the online providers retain the titles to those copies.

Although the Japanese courts have not dealt with any similar case up to now, they are seldom keen to allow restrictions on the application of the exhaustion of rights doctrine by contractual arrangements with regard to other types of intellectual property rights, as presented above.[55] Nevertheless, it is not clear whether they would be willing to treat copies of copyrighted works on tangible media and downloaded ones in the same way, even if the full value of a copy was paid to the right holder by a consumer.

---

[53] *See ibid.*, paras. 57–9.

[54] *See, e.g.*, Tess Priester, "Dutch Court Refers Preliminary Questions on the Lending of e-Books to ECJ" (2014), available at http://www.futureofcopyright.com/home/blog-post/2014/09/04/dutch-court-refers-preliminary-questions-on-the-lending-of-e-books-to-ecj.html (visited 30 Nov. 2014).

[55] *See supra* text accompanying footnote 35.

1.3 Control over Post-sale Use of Copyrighted Works

Digital technologies have not only brought new threats to the legitimate interests of copyright holders, but they have also allowed those copyright holders to control how consumers use copies of their copyrighted works. In the analogue world, some types of private non-commercial uses, such as private copying, were tolerated to a certain degree by the law[56] as well as copyright holders in many jurisdictions, since it was difficult to enforce the copyright holders' exclusive rights against such uses of copyrighted works. Digital technologies have, however, permitted the copyright holders to enforce the restrictions on uses of copyrighted works against any user of their copies. Technological protection measures and digital rights management have brought new, inexpensive and very efficient ways of determining and implementing restrictions on the uses of copyrighted works.

Nonetheless, a major problem faced by technological protection measures and digital rights management systems is that they can always be circumvented. As the persons who circumvent them are rarely in any contractual relationship with the copyright holders, the provision of legal protection against their circumvention has come to be deemed essential.

---

56 *See*, *e.g.*, CBS Songs Ltd. v. Amstrad Consumer Electronics plc [1988] AC 1013, 1060–1, [1988] 2 All ER 484, 498 (HL), where Lord Templeman acknowledged it tersely as follows:

> In these proceedings the court is being asked to forbid the sale to the public of all or some selected types of tape recorder or to ensure that advertisements for tape recorders shall be censored by the court on behalf of copyright owners. The court has no power to make such orders and judges are not qualified to decide whether a restraint should be placed on the manufacture of electronic equipment or on the contents of advertising. No one is to blame for the present situation. Copyright law could not envisage and now cannot cope with mass-production techniques and inventions which create a vast market for the works of a copyright owner but also provide opportunities for his rights to be infringed.

See also, *e.g.*, P. Bernt Hugenholtz, "The Story of the Tape Recorder and the History of Copyright Levies", in Brad Sherman and Leanne Wiseman (eds.), *Copyright and the Challenge of the New* (Alphen aan den Rijn: Kluwer Law International 2012) 179 (discussing the history of introducing the private copying exception and copyright levies in Germany, *inter alia*, due to the difficulty and disproportionality of enforcing the copyright holders' exclusive rights against the users of reproduction technologies).

Accordingly, international copyright law[57] and national copyright laws have adopted such legal protections.[58]

Over the past few decades, copyright holders have extensively implemented a number of technological protection measures with regard to various technologies that allow for the consumption of copyrighted works, such as DVD and Blu-ray Disc technologies for audio-visual recordings, scrambling technologies for analogue and digital television broadcasting, and technological protection measures used by videogame consoles.[59] The circumventions of those technological protection measures have already been addressed by courts in a number of jurisdictions, and the results have largely favored copyright holders.[60]

In a recent U.S. case, *MDY Industries, LLC v. Blizzard Entertainment, Inc.*,[61] the Ninth Circuit even recognized that a game developer, Blizzard, was entitled to restrict its users to "create or use cheats, bots, 'mods,' and/or hacks, or any other third-party software designed to modify the World of Warcraft experience".[62] For the purpose of preventing the use of robots playing on behalf of individual players within its system, Blizzard developed the Warden technology, which scanned the operational memory of users' computers for any running robots. The Ninth Circuit acknowledged that the Warden technology was a technological protection measure which protected access to Blizzard's copyrighted work. Consequently, the use of the defendant's robot, called Glidder, was found to be a circumvention of that technological protection measure.[63]

At this point, it should be noted that technological protection measures rarely allow the consumer to make any private or back-up copies, or to use copyrighted works in ways permitted by other copyright exceptions and limitations incorporated into national copyright laws. This raises the question of whether the users can demand from the copyright holders that

---

57 *See, e.g.*, WCT, *supra* note 6, arts. 11 and 12; and WPPT, *supra* note 6, arts. 18 and 19.

58 *See, e.g.*, Digital Millennium Copyright Act (1998) Pub. L. No. 105-304, 112 Stat. 2860, §103; Directive 2001/29/EC, *supra* note 4, arts. 6 and 7; Act No. 33 (1999) (Japan); Act No. 77 (1999) (Japan); Act No. 43 (2012) (Japan).

59 *See, e.g.*, Branislav Hazucha, Hsiao-Chien Liu and Toshihide Watabe, "Copyright, Protection Measures and Their Acceptance by Consumers", in Katja Weckström (ed.), *Governing Innovation and Expression: New Regimes, Strategies and Techniques* (Turku: University of Turku Press 2013) 271, 281–8.

60 *See infra* text accompanying footnotes 72–4.

61 MDY Industries, LLC v. Blizzard Entertainment, Inc., 2011 U.S. App. LEXIS 3428 (9th Cir., 17 Feb. 2011).

62 *See ibid.* at 11.

63 *See ibid.* at 55–59.

the technological protection measures comply with those exceptions and limitations.

The approach towards individual copyright exceptions and limitations diverges considerably between individual countries. In some countries, the copyright law expressly states that all or some of the copyright exceptions and limitations are mandatory and therefore cannot be overridden by a contractual arrangement.[64] For instance, Art. 5(2) of the Computer Program Directive explicitly states that "[t]he making of a back-up copy by a person having a right to use the computer program may not be prevented by contract in so far as it is necessary for that use." This is, however, more the exception than the rule. The standard practice is for copyright laws to be silent on the character of their provisions on copyright exceptions and limitations. It is then often unclear whether these provisions are mandatory or only default rules which can be overridden by contractual arrangements buttressed by technological protection measures and digital rights management systems.

Several scholars have argued that we should view copyright law as a fair and just balance between the rights of authors, intermediaries and consumers.[65] Similarly, a few courts have even expressly recognized that copyright exceptions and limitations give the users of copyrighted works certain rights.[66] Nonetheless, the majority of courts have objected to the

---

64 *See, e.g.*, Directive 2009/24/EC, *supra* note 23, art. 5(2); Belgian Law of 30 June 1994 on Copyright and Neighbouring Rights, as amended, art. 23*bis* (providing that exceptions in Articles 21, 22, 22*bis* and 23(1) and (3) are mandatory provisions).

65 *See, e.g.*, L. Ray Patterson and Stanley W. Lindberg, *The Nature of Copyright: A Law of Users' Rights* (Athens, GA: University of Georgia Press 1991); Jane C. Ginsburg, "Authors and Users in Copyright" (1997) J. Copyright Soc'y U.S.A. 1; Joseph P. Liu, "Copyright Law's Theory of the Consumer" (2003) 44 B.C. L. Rev. 397; Guy Pessach, "Reverse Exclusion in Copyright Law: Reconfiguring Users' Rights" (2001) (unpublished manuscript), available at http://ssrn.com/abstract=1813082 (visited 30 Nov. 2014).

66 *See, e.g.*, CCH Canadian Ltd. v. Law Society of Upper Canada [2004] 1 S.C.R. 339, 2004 SCC 13, paras. 12 and 54 (Sup. Ct. of Canada, 4 Mar. 2004) (recognizing the users' rights as follows: "[t]he exceptions to copyright infringement, perhaps more properly understood as users' rights", and "these allowable purposes should not be given a restrictive interpretation or this could result in the undue restriction of users' rights"); Anthony G. v. Société Civile des Producteurs Phonographiques (S.C.P.P.), Case No. 0504090091 (TGI Paris, 8 December 2005) (recognizing the right to private copy in the case of peer-to-peer file sharing); Christophe R. and UFC Que choisir v. Warner Music France and FNAC, Case No. 03/08874 (TGI Paris, 10 January 2006) (recognizing the right to private copy in the case of music CDs).

recognition of any consumers' rights. They merely recognize that copyright exceptions and limitations provide the users of copyrighted works with defenses against copyright infringement claims with no independent rights which the consumers could assert before the courts.

In circumvention cases, the defendants frequently tend to rely on several types of defense in order to justify the development or marketing of devices allowing the circumvention of technological protection measures. The courts have, however, been very reluctant to accept any of them. They frequently reject the need to make private copies or back-up copies by the users as an acceptable defense for developing or marketing devices indispensable for circumventing technological protection measures. Some courts have even noted that while back-up copies were necessary when media were not so reliable, progress in the quality and reliability of new media has made back-up copies redundant.[67] In addition, they have expressed their view that the main aim of circumvention devices is to allow the playing of pirated and pornographic works on the circumvented devices.[68] The courts have thus repeatedly deemed it sufficient for copyright holders only to warn consumers on restrictions imposed by technological protection measures.[69]

Nevertheless, many consumers perceive this as unfair and unjust because such laws allow for the restriction of their legitimate interests and rights. This has led to many technological protection measures being quickly circumvented. If individuals perceive something as unfair and unjust, there is a high probability that they will not comply with such technological protection measures and contractual arrangements. Instead they will search for a way to circumvent them. It is therefore very difficult to prevent mass circumvention of technological protection measures and digital rights management systems by millions of consumers who want to make private copies of movie DVDs or Blu-ray Discs, to use cheats in videogames or to disable other restrictions on their videogame consoles, computers or mobile phones.

---

[67] *See, e.g.*, Sony Computer Entertainment v. Paul Owen and Others [2002] EWHC 45 (Ch), [2002] E.C.D.R. 27, 304.

[68] *See ibid.* at 301 and 304.

[69] *See, e.g.*, Studio Canal, Soc. Universal Pictures vidéo France and SEV v. S. Perquin, UFC Que choisir, Judgment No. 549 FS-P+B+R+I (Sup. Ct. of France, 28 Feb. 2006).

2. IMPORTANCE OF STUDYING CONSUMERS' ATTITUDES

Contemporary copyright law has to overcome a number of difficulties in its application and enforcement in the digital environment. The most challenging controversies in this field are represented by online piracy and mass disregard of copyright law by internet users on digital networks, such as peer-to-peer file sharing networks[70] or online services allowing the storage of large-size files.[71] Similar problems are faced by copyright holders in case of a mass circumvention of technological protection measures and digital rights management systems.

Although technological protection measures were initially seen as a solution against the mass copying of copyrighted works by the public in the digital environment, the experiences with their actual operation have, so far, brought mixed feelings. Most of the technological protection measures which have been introduced to the market have been quickly circumvented. Many lawsuits worldwide have aimed to prevent acts of circumventing technological protection measures, such as those used by the DVD and Blu-ray Disc technologies or by videogame consoles. This litigation has targeted individuals who cracked technological protection measures,[72] as well as those who uploaded the necessary circumvention applications online, linked to the places where such applications were

---

[70] *See, e.g.*, A&M Records, Inc. v. Napster, Inc., 114 F. Supp. 2d 896, 2000 U.S. Dist. LEXIS 11862 (N.D. Cal., 2000), aff'd, 239 F. 3d. 1004, 2001 U.S. Dist. LEXIS 5446 (9th Cir., 2001); In re Aimster Copyright Litigation, 252 F. Supp. 2d 634, 2002 U.S. Dist. LEXIS 17054 (N.D. Ill, 2002), aff'd, 334 F.3d 643 (7th Cir., 2003); MGM Studios v. Grokster, Ltd., 545 U.S. 913; 125 S. Ct. 2764 (U.S. Sup. Ct., 2005); Universal Music Australia Pty Ltd v. Shaman License Holdings Ltd [2005] FCA 1242; In re Winny, 65 Keishu 1380 (Sup. Ct. of Japan, 2011).

[71] *See, e.g.*, U.S. Department of Justice, "Justice Department Charges Leaders of Megaupload with Widespread Online Copyright Infringement" (2012), available at http://www.justice.gov/opa/pr/2012/January/12-crm-074.html (visited 30 Nov. 2014); Perfect 10, Inc. v. Rapidshare, 2010 U.S. Dist. LEXIS 146053 (S.D. Cal., 2010); Atari Europe v. RapidShare AG, I ZR 18/11 (BGH, 2012).

[72] *See, e.g.*, Thomas Rieber-Mohn, "Norway: Court of Appeal Decision in Norwegian DVD Case" (2004), available at http://merlin.obs.coe.int/iris/2004/3/article29.en.html (visited 30 Nov. 2013); 321 Studios v. Metro Goldwyn Mayer Studios, Inc., 307 F. Supp. 2d 1085 (N.D. Cal., 2004).

located,[73] or provided the necessary kits and modchips for the circumvention of technological protection measures.[74]

Right holders tend to win these lawsuits, but it seems that the mass disregard of copyright law by copyright users has not changed significantly over the last twenty years. The main cause of this situation is habitually explained by the idea that many individuals perceive there to be a low probability of being caught for copyright infringing activities in the digital environment. Even if such individuals are caught, they are said to believe that the potential punishment will not be very severe. Moreover, many of them think that such activities are normal and therefore they do not perceive any threat of possible legal sanctions for such unlawful activities. Consequently, a number of proposals on how to solve this negative situation in the enforcement of copyright law in the digital environment suggest increasing the probability of being caught and the severity of potential sanctions. Similarly, most of the recently adopted changes of national copyright laws in many developed countries have been based on the same philosophy.

All of these proposed or adopted solutions have one thing common. They mainly focus on the external factor of obeying the law; they attempt to force individuals to comply with the copyright law. They do so by increasing the probability of catching individual copyright infringers and the severity of punishment and other sanctions for copyright infringing activities. Some of those measures attempt to technically prevent individuals from committing particular copyright infringing or even non-infringing activities.

The main problem with these initiatives is that they ignore the fact that there are other reasons why individuals comply with or disregard legal rules. In general, the reasons for obeying the law can originate outside or inside individuals. Several scholars[75] thus distinguish between *internal*

---

[73] *See, e.g.*, Universal City Studios, Inc. v. Reimerdes, 111 F. Supp. 2d 294 (S.D.N.Y., 2000), aff'd sub nom. Universal City Studios, Inc. v. Corley, 273 F.3d 429 (2d Cir., 2001).

[74] *See, e.g.*, Sony Computer Entertainment America, Inc. v. GameMasters, Inc., 87 F. Supp. 2d 976 (N.D. Cal., 1999); Sony Computer Entertainment v. Paul Owen and Others [2002] EWHC 45 (Ch); Kabushiki Kaisha Sony Computer Entertainment Inc & Others v. Ball & Others [2004] EWHC 1738 (Ch); Stevens v. Kabushiki Kaisha Sony Computer Entertainment [2005] HCA 58, (2005) 221 ALR 448, (2005) 79 ALJR 1850; Nintendo Co. Ltd and Others v. PC Box Srl and 9Net Srl, Case C-355/12 (Court of Justice of the European Union (Fourth Chamber), 23 Jan. 2014).

[75] *See, e.g.*, Stephen R. Perry, "Interpretation and Methodology in Legal Theory", in Andrei Marmor (ed.), *Law and Interpretation: Essays in Legal*

and *external factors* which affect the obeying of the law by individuals.[76] These views on factors affecting compliance with legal norms stem from scholars such as Herbert L.A. Hart,[77] Oliver W. Holmes[78] and many others.[79]

The external factors often come in the form of sanctions or other external restrictions of human activities. Their aim is to force individuals to behave in a particular way. This can be done by threatening specific sanctions for breaching a norm of behavior demanded by a legal norm. It is expected that the higher the probability of catching an individual is and the more severe the sanction for breaching a particular norm is, the more the individual will obey such a norm.[80] Likewise, some activities can be made impossible physically or otherwise. For instance, various technological protection measures prevent individuals from accessing or using digital content in specific ways.[81]

Philosophy (Oxford: Oxford University Press 1995) 97; Robert Cooter, "The Intrinsic Value of Obeying a Law: Economic Analysis of the Internal Viewpoint" (2006) 75 Fordham L. Rev. 1275; Branislav Hazucha, "Tanin no Chosakukenshingai wo Tasukeru Gijutsu ni Taisuru Kiritsu no Arikata: Dual Use Gijutsu no Kisei ni okeru Shakaikihan no Yakuwari" (2009) Intell. Prop. L. & Pol'y J., No. 24, p. 25, 63–66 (Japanese translation by Yoshiyuki Tamura and Kazunari Tanzawa).

[76] *See* Lawrence Lessig, *Code: Version 2.0* (New York, NY: Basic Books 2006) at 340–45.

[77] *See* Herbert L.A. Hart, *The Concept of Law* (3rd edn, Oxford: Clarendon Press 2012) 90 ("What the external point of view, which limits itself to the observable regularities of behaviour, cannot reproduce is the way in which the rules function as rules in the lives of those who normally are the majority of society. These are the officials, lawyers, or private persons who use them, in one situation after another, as guides to the conduct of social life, as the basis for claims, demands, admissions, criticism, or punishment, viz., in all the familiar transactions of life according to rules.").

[78] *See* Oliver Wendell Holmes, Jr., "The Path of the Law" (1897) 10 Harv. L. Rev. 457, 459 ("If you want to know the law and nothing else, you must look at it as a bad man, who cares only for the material consequences which such knowledge enables him to predict, not as a good one, who finds his reasons for conduct, whether inside the law or outside of it, in the vaguer sanctions of conscience.").

[79] *See, e.g.*, Benjamin C. Zipursky, "The Internal Point of View in Law and Ethics: Introduction" (2006) 75 Fordham L. Rev. 1143; Hazucha, *supra* note 75, at 63–66.

[80] *See, e.g.*, Gary S. Becker, "Crime and Punishment: An Economic Approach" (1968) 76 J. Pol. Econ. 169.

[81] *See* Lessig, *supra* note 76, at 345.

On the other hand, there are factors which affect individuals' human behavior from inside. These come from the characteristics of individuals, such as their gender, age, level of socialization, internalization of social norms, and so on. Here, an important aspect is whether individuals take a particular norm as a reason for their behavior, that is, whether individuals have internalized a particular social or legal norm and therefore find such a norm to be a foundation of their behavior.[82] When individuals internalize a norm, they think that obeying the norm is the right thing to do. Those individuals do not obey a norm because they perceive a high probability of being caught or because the possible sanctions are quite severe. Rather they obey because they think that obeying the norm is proper and the only right way of human behavior under specific circumstances.

In human behavior, notions such as "justice" and "fairness" play an important role in this assessment. Norms which are regarded as just and fair are ordinarily obeyed by individuals. On the other hand, if a norm is perceived to be unjust and unfair, it is frequently disregarded and circumvented by targeted entities. What is considered to be just and fair is commonly expressed in social norms which are recognized and followed by individual social groups.

Social norms represent an important way of regulating human activities.[83] Laws which are consistent with social norms are often strictly obeyed by individuals. Conversely, laws that are contrary to social norms and try to change an important social norm are usually difficult to implement and enforce. Lawrence Lessig therefore identifies social norms as one of four *modalities of regulation* – in addition to law, market and technology – that is, factors which can affect human behavior and can be used for regulating human behavior in a socially desirable way.[84] He argues that when a society wants to restrict a certain activity of a targeted entity, the society can employ some or all of those factors in order to prevent certain harmful activities or to induce other activities which are deemed socially beneficial.[85]

As discussed in Section 1, recent changes in copyright law and attempts by copyright holders to broaden their control over using copies of their copyrighted works heavily rely on the combination of three of the abovementioned modalities of regulation, that is, law, market and technology. However, experiences with the operation of the measures adopted

---

82 *See ibid.* at 344–5.

83 *See ibid.*

84 *See ibid.* at 120–32.

85 *See ibid.* at 122–3.

to this point show that they rarely work as efficiently as initially expected.[86] Accordingly, the following analysis considers the attitude of consumers towards individual restrictions of their uses of copyrighted works and other protected subject matters. Do they perceive various technological and contractual restrictions on the uses of copyrighted works as fair and just? Do they think that they have any right to the uses of copyrighted works which are unfairly and unjustly restricted by copyright holders through various licenses or technological protection measures? Do they recognize the abovementioned differences in treating computer programs and other copyrighted works? Do they think that what they could do in the analogue world they should also be allowed to do in the digital environment?

3. CONSUMERS' ATTITUDES TOWARDS TECHNOLOGICAL AND OTHER PROTECTION MEASURES

In order to examine the efficiency of technological and other protection measures, which are often used by right holders, we studied the attitudes of Japanese consumers. We had several reasons for doing so. On average, Japanese individuals tend to follow the authorities and to comply with the laws and the norms recognized by their communities. From the perspective of copyright industries, the Japanese markets with standard types of copyrighted works are mature markets and the Japanese consumers spend considerable amounts of money on purchasing the authorized copies of copyrighted works, such as books, music CDs or movie DVDs. Accordingly, if the consumers of this kind find any problem with technological or other protection measures, something has to be wrong and improper with such measures.

To study the Japanese consumers' attitudes, we designed a questionnaire in which we asked our respondents to what extent they accept or reject individual restrictions on their consumption of selected copyrighted works and other protected subject matters, such as sound recordings, movies, broadcasted television programs, videogames and live public music performances. The questionnaire was based on one core premise. If consumers find a restriction imposed by a right holder on their use of

---

[86] *See*, *e.g.*, Pierre Lescure, "Mission 'Act II de l'exception culturelle': Contribution aux politiques culturelles à l'ère du numérique" (May, 2013), available at http://www.culturecommunication.gouv.fr/var/culture/storage/culture_mag/rapport_lescure/index.htm (visited 30 Nov. 2014).

a work as problematic for them in any regard, we presume that there will be a higher probability that they will search for a way of circumventing such a restriction. On the other hand, if consumers perceive no problem with a particular restriction and accept it, we presume that they will rarely try to find any way of circumventing it.

3.1 Questionnaires and Data Collection

For studying the attitudes of Japanese consumers towards technological and other protection measures currently used in Japan, we identified seven of the most common restrictions. Those restrictions have been or are still habitually imposed through various technological and other protection measures by major right holders in Japan. They prevent the following types of uses: (i) the copying of sound recordings on music CDs; (ii) the shifting of format from music CDs to MP3 or other music files in case of sound recordings (format-shifting); (iii) the recording of broadcasted television programs for watching them later at a convenient time for the audience (time-shifting); (iv) the streaming of television broadcast via the internet for private purposes (place-shifting), for example when someone travels abroad and is interested in watching her favorite drama while abroad; (v) the copying of pre-recorded movie DVDs or Blu-ray Discs; (vi) the copying of videogames; and (vii) finally the sound recording of live public performances during concerts of popular music. As is evident, everyone regularly comes into contact with some or many of those uses and their restrictions in her everyday life.

We also considered including several other restrictions, such as those on the use of e-books, music streaming and online video-on-demand or video rental services, but in the end we decided to exclude those types of protected subject matters and any restrictions on their use from the scope of our questionnaire. The main reason was that only a limited number of consumers have any experience with those types of protected subject matters or restrictions on their use, because the markets with those forms of entertainments are still in the early stages of their development in Japan. For instance, the market for e-books in Japan does not represent a significant share of the entire Japanese book market. In addition, the Japanese e-book market is dominated by manga, and the manga market has its own specific characteristics compared with other types of copyrighted works. Although the study of consumers' attitudes towards the restrictions on the use of e-books might be very interesting, it might be better to study them together with the study of the entire manga market and methods of manga distribution. Similar objections apply to the other abovementioned emerging forms of entertainment. Their inclusion would make our survey more complicated and therefore we decided to put them aside for future possible research.

Our questionnaire was composed of several groups and types of questions. The main group of questions measured the respondents' attitudes towards the abovementioned individual restrictions on using the types of subject matters protected by copyrights or neighboring rights in Japan. For measuring the respondents' attitudes, we used Likert-type five-grade scales. We provided our respondents with five possible answers ranging from complete acceptance to complete rejection of individual restrictions. The respondents could select their responses from the following options: 1 – "I have no problem with it at all"; 2 – "I have almost no problem with it"; 3 – "I have neither any problem nor no problem"; 4 – "Maybe, I have a problem"; and 5 – "I clearly have a problem". In addition, the respondents were offered an additional option "I don't know" for cases where they had a problem with responding to a particular question.

In addition to this main group of questions, our questionnaire contained several other groups of questions where we wanted to measure various possible factors which can affect the respondents' attitudes towards the restrictions being studied. The first group of questions was composed of demographic questions, which were designed to collect data on our respondents' gender, age, income, occupation, residence and the like. We also asked our respondents whether they have any knowledge of copyright law and how they became acquainted with copyright law. The second group of questions focused on respondents' consumption habits with regard to the individual types of protected subject matters being studied, for example whether they listen to music, watch movies, play videogames, attend live concerts of popular music and the like. In addition, we asked our respondents whether they purchase or rent the protected subject matters being studied, such as music CDs, movie DVDs or Blu-ray Discs and videogames. The third group of questions aimed at revealing the respondents' views on the level of justified use of the subject matters being studied and at their actual experiences with copying them. Accordingly, we asked our respondents to what extent they think that they should be allowed to use the subject matters being studied, and to what extent they actually copy sound recordings or movies and record broadcasted television programs. The second and third groups of questions were composed of questions employing Likert-type five-grade scales[87] for measuring the respondents' attitudes and habits.

---

[87] An exception was the question on justified uses of copyrighted works, where we used a Likert-type seven-grade scale.

Before starting to conduct our survey based on this questionnaire, we ran a pilot study amongst a small group of students at the Hokkaido University Graduate School of Law. The students were asked to answer the questionnaire and then we talked with individual students about their opinions on the questionnaire. The main reason for conducting this pilot was to examine whether our questionnaire worked properly; whether the respondents fully understood the questions and options provided; and whether they faced any problems with understanding and responding to our questionnaire.

After the pilot study, we conducted a survey on the streets of Sapporo, which is the fifth most populous city in Japan. The reason for selecting Sapporo was to choose a sample of the average Japanese population. We wanted to study one of the large metropolitan areas outside the areas around Tokyo and Osaka, and Sapporo presented one such area. Our target number in the survey was to collect 500 responses from people on the streets of Sapporo. In the end, we collected 531 partially or fully responded questionnaires in the central area of Sapporo city between 27 July and 10 August 2010.

After conducting this street survey, we wanted to examine whether its findings[88] were specific for Sapporo and people living in comparable metropolitan areas or if they also apply to the entire Japanese population. Accordingly, a second survey was conducted online and covered all of Japan. For the collection of data, we used an online service provided by MyVoice Communications, Inc. for conducting public opinion polls.[89] Through its system, we collected 1,252 fully or partially responded questionnaires between 3 and 8 October 2012. Our online survey targeted respondents between 15 and 59 years old from across the entire territory of Japan.

As pointed out above, the main aim in conducting the second survey was either to confirm our previous findings based on the Sapporo street survey or to identify factors which would cause any differences between the findings of both surveys. As the findings of both our studies are very similar and comparable, the following analysis deals mainly with the results of our 2012 online survey.

---

88 For more details, *see* Hazucha, Liu and Watabe, *supra* note 59.

89 For more details, *see* http://www.myvoice.co.jp.

3.2 Analysis of Collected Data

Based on the conventional view, habitually presented by copyright holders, on how the public treats copyrighted works and their uses,[90] we expected that most of our respondents would have severe problems with the various kinds of restrictions being studied. Another possible option might have been that the respondents would find no problem with those restrictions and they would fully comply with them. Although the copyright holders might be very happy with such an outcome of our study, it would have suggested a considerable bias in the responses of our respondents, especially when we take into consideration that a considerable number of copyright users regularly circumvent some of the restrictions being studied.[91] Such an outcome of our survey would therefore suggest that the respondents were not being very truthful toward our survey and they were not being very honest in responding to our questionnaire. A third possible outcome might have been somewhere between the two abovementioned extremes. This outcome would have shown that the respondents were not able to clearly say whether the studied restrictions caused them any or no problems. The restrictions would thus be seen by the respondents as causing them some obstacles, but not very burdensome ones.

However, the outcome of our surveys was a bit more nuanced than we expected. Both surveys showed that some ways of using protected subject matters are more important to consumers than others. When those important uses were restricted by technological or other protection measures adopted by right holders, the respondents found that those restrictions caused them considerable problems in the consumption of the affected protected subject matters. On the other hand, when a particular use was not very important to respondents, they found its restriction to be

[90] *See, e.g.*, U.S. House of Representatives, Committee on the Judiciary, Subcommittee on Courts, the Internet, and Intellectual Property, "Consumer Benefits of Today's Digital Rights Management (DRM) Solutions" (5 Jun. 2002) (presenting views of numerous copyright holders on the behavior of the consumers of copyrighted works and on the need for strong protection of technological protection measures and digital rights management systems); U.S. House of Representatives, Committee on the Judiciary, Subcommittee on Courts, the Internet, and Intellectual Property, "Hearing: Chapter 12 of Title 17" (17 Sept. 2014) (presenting diverse views on the operation of technological protection measures and digital rights management systems).

[91] As presented below, a considerable number of our respondents (27.82%; n=111) clearly acknowledged that they copied pre-recorded movie DVDs and Blu-ray Discs in some way.

non-problematic. Accordingly, the respondents found some restrictions to be more problematic and other restrictions to be less so.

The results of our online survey concerning the respondents' judgment on their acceptance of or objection to restrictions on using different types of protected subject matters by technological protection measures and digital right management regimes can be observed in Figure 7.1. The figure depicts the means of respondents' judgments, with 95% confidence intervals, on the Likert-type five-grade scale after eliminating the responses where the respondents refrained from making judgment. The actual distribution of responses made by all respondents is presented in Figure 7.2.

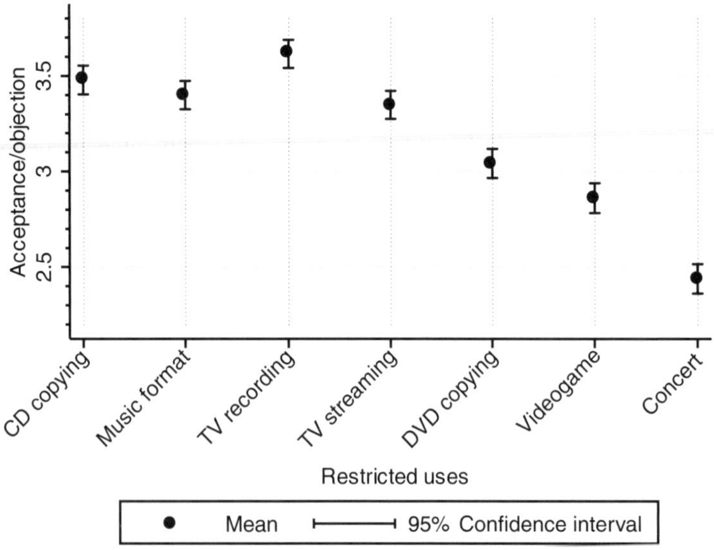

Figure 7.1 TPMs' acceptance/objection

A note should be made that the respondents refrained from answering (that is, they selected "I don't know") 8.73% of the time on average. The actual number of completed responses thus varies between individual restrictions. The respondents were more likely to answer with regard to uses with which they were more familiar, such as copying music CDs and pre-recorded movie DVDs or Blu-ray Discs, sound recording of live concerts, and recording broadcasted TV programs.[92] But more respondents refrained

[92] The respondents refrained from making their judgment as follows: copying music CDs (88 respondents; 7.03%) and pre-recorded movie DVDs or

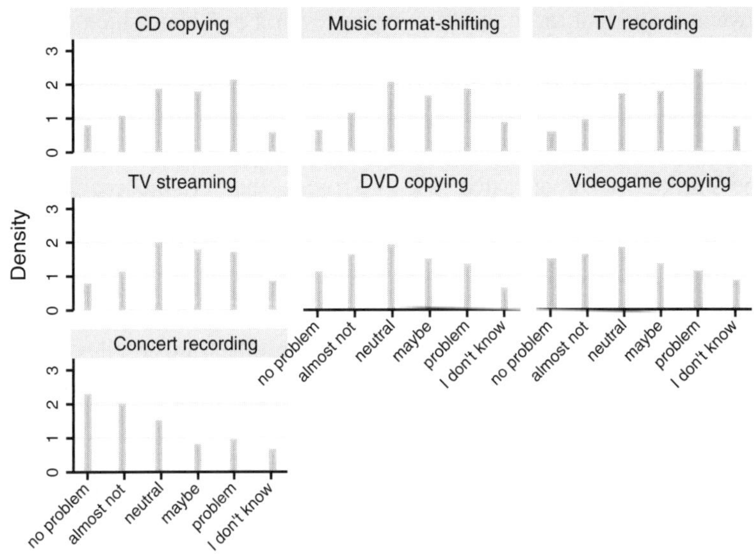

Figure 7.2 TPMs' acceptance/objection

from answering with regard to restricted uses that required advanced technical skills such as in the copying of videogames, private TV streaming and music format-shifting.[93] This confirms that our decision to exclude several new emerging types of entertainment, such as e-books, sound and video streaming and the like, from our survey was correct.

An alternative explanation might be that the survey participants refrained from responding more in those cases since it was difficult for them to make judgments on the different uses of the same or similar types of protected subject matters, which can be paired as follows: (a) the copying of music CDs and format-shifting from a music CD to an MP3 file; (b) the recording and streaming of TV programs; and (c) the copying of movie DVDs or Blu-ray Discs and the copying of videogames. However, it should be pointed out that the order in which the different restrictions on individual uses were presented was random and varied

Blu-ray Discs (94 respondents; 7.51%), sound recording on live concerts (95 respondents; 7.59%), and recording broadcasted TV programs (106 respondents; 8.47%).

[93] The respondents refrained from making their judgment as follows: copying videogames (123 respondents; 9.82%), private TV streaming (128 respondents; 10.22%) and music format-shifting (131 respondents; 10.46%).

between individual respondents in order to limit any bias which could be caused by the order of the restrictions in the questionnaire.

Turning back to the analysis of respondents' attitudes towards individual technological or other restrictions, the most problematic restriction in the eyes of our respondents was the restriction on the so-called time-shifting of broadcasted TV programs, that is, the recording of broadcasted TV programs in order to watch them later at a convenient time for an individual (mean=3.599±0.039, n=1,146).[94] The time-shifting of broadcasted TV programs was followed by restrictions on copying music CDs and other music media (mean=3.465±0.040, n=1,164),[95] format-shifting from music CDs to MP3 or other music files (mean= 3.384±0.039, n=1,121)[96] and the so-called place-shifting of broadcasted TV programs, that is, streaming a TV broadcast by the public via the internet for private purposes (mean=3.334±0.039, n=1,124).[97] The means of responses to individual restrictions differ statistically significantly from each other in *t*-test, with the exception of the last two mentioned restrictions.

On the other side of the spectrum was the restriction on sound recordings of live popular music concerts, which were found to be the least problematic for respondents of all the restrictions studied (mean= 2.455±0.41, n=1,157).[98] The acceptance of bans on sound recordings of

---

[94] The distribution of responses (n=1,146) between individual options on the 5-point Likert-type scale was as follows: 1 – absolutely not problematic (n1=87; 7.59%); 2 – almost not problematic (n2=144; 12.57%); 3 – neutral (n3=268; 23.39%), 4 – almost problematic (n4=272; 23.73%); and 5 – absolutely problematic (n5=375; 37.72%).

[95] The distribution of responses (n=1,164) between individual options on the 5-point Likert-type scale was as follows: 1 – absolutely not problematic (n1=116; 9.97%); 2 – almost not problematic (n2=157; 13.49%); 3 – neutral (n3=282; 24.23%), 4 – almost problematic (n4=272; 23.37%); and 5 – absolutely problematic (n5=337; 28.95%).

[96] The distribution of responses (n=1,121) between individual options on the 5-point Likert-type scale was as follows: 1 – absolutely not problematic (n1=99; 8.83%); 2 – almost not problematic (n2=171; 15.25%); 3 – neutral (n3=318; 28.37%), 4 – almost problematic (n4=249; 22.21%); and 5 – absolutely problematic (n5=284; 25.53%).

[97] The distribution of responses (n=1,124) between individual options on the 5-point Likert-type scale was as follows: 1 – absolutely not problematic (n1=113; 10.05%); 2 – almost not problematic (n2=171; 15.21%); 3 – neutral (n3=310; 27.58%), 4 – almost problematic (n4=272; 24.20%); and 5 – absolutely problematic (n5=258; 22.95%).

[98] The distribution of responses (n=1,157) between individual options on the 5-point Likert-type scale was as follows: 1 – absolutely not problematic (n1=363;

live concerts was followed by the restriction on copying videogames (mean=2.861±0.041, n=1,129).[99] Somewhere in the middle of our Likert-type five-grade scale was the respondents' position towards the restriction on copying movie DVDs and Blu-ray Discs (mean=3.030±0.040, n=1,158).[100]

3.3 Discussion

The findings of both of our surveys show that there are considerable differences in the importance of different types of copyrighted works (*i.e.* television programs, sound recordings, videogames, movie DVDs and live performances) and their particular uses (*i.e.* copying, recording on live concerts, and format-, time- and place-shifting) for consumers.

There are several possible explanations for these differences. One such explanation is that the respondents may have some tendencies in treating certain groups of individual restrictions in similar or comparable ways (*e.g.*, the time- and place-shifting of broadcasted television programs; the copying and format-shifting of music CDs; and so on), contrary to the way other groups of restrictions are treated (*e.g.*, the copying of music CDs contrary to the copying of movie DVDs and videogames). These tendencies can be explained by several possible factors.

First, the subject matter of the work at issue may matter; different uses of the same or similar subject matters are often treated similarly by respondents. For example, the respondents' attitudes towards the copying of music CDs and music format-shifting were very similar. Similar relationships were observed between the time- and place-shifting of broadcasted TV programs, and between the copying of movie DVDs or Blu-ray Discs and videogames.

31.37%); 2 – almost not problematic (n2=312; 26.97%); 3 – neutral (n3=231; 19.97%), 4 – almost problematic (n4=114; 9.85%); and 5 – absolutely problematic (n5=137; 11.84%).

[99] The distribution of responses (n=1,129) between individual options on the 5-point Likert-type scale was as follows: 1 – absolutely not problematic (n1=227; 20.11%); 2 – almost not problematic (n2=246; 21.79%); 3 – neutral (n3=280; 24.80%), 4 – almost problematic (n4=209; 18.51%); and 5 – absolutely problematic (n5=167; 14.79%).

[100] The distribution of responses (n=1,158) between individual options on the 5-point Likert-type scale was as follows: 1 – absolutely not problematic (n1=173; 14.94%); 2 – almost not problematic (n2=255; 22.02%); 3 – neutral (n3=291; 25.13%), 4 – almost problematic (n4=229; 19.78%); and 5 – absolutely problematic (n5=210; 18.13%).

Second, ongoing long-term practices may influence consumers. Some types of uses have already become normal activities amongst the public, while others are still new and emerging. The most common types (from the uses studied) were the copying of music CDs and the time-shifting of broadcasted TV programs. We observed that both types of uses were considered very important by our respondents, and therefore the majority of our respondents found restrictions on both types of these uses to be the most problematic for them.

Finally, technical and other obstacles and difficulties faced by consumers may matter to consumer perception. Restrictions on the copying of videogames and the sound recording of live concerts of popular music employ very advanced technical or physically intrusive protection measures. If anyone intends to circumvent technological protection measures used by most recent videogame consoles, they need to have advanced technical knowledge and skills. In addition, they need to have special devices to do so, such as kits or even modchips specially designed and manufactured for this purpose. Similarly, before being allowed to enter the venues where popular music concerts are held, the personal belongings of each attendant are searched by the organizers. If any sound or audiovisual recording device is found, the person is not allowed to enter the venue until she deposits that device in a locker prepared for such cases. Although these restrictions are quite restrictive and invasive, the respondents in our surveys did not find them to be problematic and they more or less accepted them.

A further possible explanation of the differences in treating the individual restrictions studied may be that the degree of acceptance or objection depends on the respondents' actual interest in a particular activity. For instance, when individuals have an interest in music and have no interest in videogames, they can find restrictions on copying music CDs to be problematic, but they can accept similar restrictions on copying videogames as being non-problematic. However, our survey does not support this explanation. The interests in the individual ways of using copyrighted and other protected works being studied had no or only a very weak correlation with the respondents' attitudes towards the restrictions on those uses.

On the other hand, we observed that the consumers' views on justified uses of copyrighted works and their actual copying habits were strongly correlated with their attitudes towards individual technological restriction measures restricting those uses. The respondents who think that no copy or only a single copy is sufficient tend to accept the restrictions of such uses more than those who think that copying within a family circle or even for any non-commercial use should be allowed.

In this regard, it should be noted that our respondents were not copyright pirates. They clearly recognized that there are some limits on their use of copyrighted works. Although they had little or almost no knowledge of copyright law, their judgment on the extent to which they should be allowed to use copyrighted works and other protected subject matters is very consistent with the current private copying exception under Article 30 of the Japanese Copyright Act.[101] Conversely, less than 21.48% of respondents thought that they should be allowed to upload the copyrighted and other protected works being studied online or to use them in any other non-commercial way.

There was also a difference in judging to what extent the consumers should be allowed to use individual types of copyrighted works. While the consumers' judgment on the level of justified use was very similar in the case of music CDs and broadcasted TV programs, the consumers recognized that they should be allowed to use pre-recorded movie DVDs in a narrower range of circumstances than in the case of the two other protected subject matters mentioned.[102]

In addition to consumers' views on justified uses of copyrighted works, we also observed that the consumers' actual copying habits matter. The consumers who do not indulge in copying activities tend to accept those restrictions more than the users who regularly make copies of copyrighted works. In this regard, it should be noted that there was no or only a very weak correlation between views on justified uses and copying activities. For instance, many users who thought that users should not be allowed to make any copies acknowledged that they make copies of the copyrighted works being studied. Conversely, some users who thought that they should be allowed to use studied copyrighted works in any non-commercial way did not make any copies.

---

[101] The respondents' views on justified uses of copyrighted works were consistent with Article 30 of Japanese Copyright Act as follows: in the case of time-shifting, 329 respondents (78.52%) from 419 respondents; in the case of copying music CDs, 343 respondents (79.03%) from 434 respondents; and in the case of copying movie DVDs or Blu-ray Discs, 346 respondents (86.72%) from 399 respondents.

[102] For instance, in the case of pre-recorded movie DVDs, 10.28% of our respondents (n=41) thought that they should not be allowed even to make any copies of them, contrary to 4.38% (n=19) and 3.34% (n=14) of respondents in the case of music CDs and TV programs, respectively.

4. CURRENT SITUATION WITH PRIVATE ORDERING AND THE INVISIBLE HAND OF THE MARKET

When we compared our results with the actual use of technological and other protection measures, we observed that the market significantly affected the ways in which technological and other protection measures are employed by right holders. Although numerous technological and other protection measures have been used by copyright and neighboring right holders over the last few decades, they are applied nowadays only on a very limited scale. They are mainly used in cases where the consumers are willing to buy such products. Accordingly, no restrictions are currently employed with sound recordings, be they music CDs or music files for downloading. In the late 1990s and early 2000s, the record labels attempted to impose various restrictions on the use of sound recordings, but all those efforts failed on the market.[103] Similarly, most authorized music downloading services do not restrict copying of downloaded music files by their consumers nowadays.[104] To prevent the mass use of downloaded authorized music files for peer-to-peer file sharing, some record labels require authorized online music downloading service providers to incorporate, into the provided music files, specific identifiers which can allow the original source of music files that have been leaked to be traced.[105] In such cases, the record labels are able to sue the consumer who downloaded the file and then made it available for mass sharing.

---

[103] *See*, *e.g.*, Deirdre K. Mulligan and Aaron Perzanowski, "The Magnificence of the Disaster: Reconstructing the Sony BMG Rootkit Incident" (2007) 22 Berkeley Tech. L.J. 1157. *See also* Bob Brown, "Sony BMG Rootkit Scandal: 5 Years Later" (2010) Network World, available at http://www.networkworld.com/news/2010/110110-sonybmg-rootkit-fsecure-drm.html (visited 30 Nov. 2014); Joris Evers, "Sony Halts Production of 'Rootkit' CDs" (2005) CNET News, available at http://news.cnet.com/Sony-halts-production-of-rootkit-CDs/2100-1029_3-5946825.html (visited 30 Nov. 2014).

[104] *See*, *e.g.*, Robbie Johnson, "Apple Drops DRM Copy Protection from Millions of iTunes Songs" (2009) The Guardian, available at http://www.theguardian.com/technology/2009/jan/06/apple-drops-itunes-copy-protection (visited 30 Nov. 2014); Bloomberg News, "Sony BMG Will Sell Music Without Copyright Protection" (2008) The New York Times, available at http://www.nytimes.com/2008/01/08/technology/08digital.html (visited 30 Nov. 2014).

[105] *See*, *e.g.*, Amazon.com, "Amazon Music Terms of Use" (2014), available at http://www.amazon.com/gp/help/customer/display.html?nodeId=201380010 (visited 30 Nov. 2014); Apple, "iTunes Store: Terms and Conditions" (2013), available at https://www.apple.com/legal/internet-services/itunes/us/terms.html (visited 30 Nov. 2013).

Likewise, in the early days of designing the technical standards for digital television broadcasting in Japan, the main proposal was to adopt a system which would be similar to the one used with regard to DVD technology, that is, to allow three options of no copying, allowing a single copy and allowing unrestricted copying.[106] However, the proposed regime was found to be too restrictive by many stakeholders. It brought opposition from the side of the associations representing the interests of consumers, which were also supported by the Japanese government. The outcome thus was that the originally planned regime of restrictions was watered down a bit and a new option was introduced.[107] This option allows the making of nine copies of recorded broadcasted television programs on one device. This is seen as the implementation of Article 30 of the Japanese Copyright Act, which allows the making of private copies within a limited circle. At the moment, all free-to-air channels use this option as the default for their TV broadcasting. Many TV broadcasters think that the use of more restrictive options would alienate their audience and therefore they refrain from such an approach towards the use of technological protection measures.[108]

In our survey, the copying of pre-recorded movie DVDs and Blu-ray Discs was located in the middle of the spectrum of consumers' attitudes towards restrictions on using copyrighted and other protected works. In practice, the technological protection measures are used with regard to DVD as well as Blu-ray Disc technology. As mentioned above, they allow three possible restrictions on copying pre-recorded audiovisual media. The options are as follows: no copy, single copy and no restriction. The pre-recorded movie DVDs and Blu-ray Discs, which are commercially marketed in Japan as well as in many developed countries,

---

[106] *See*, *e.g.*, Study Group on the Promotion of Digital Content Distribution, Telecommunications Policy Subcommittee, Telecommunications Council, "Summary of Minutes (3rd meeting)" (2006), available at http://www.soumu.go.jp/main_sosiki/joho_tsusin/eng/pdf/061024_1.pdf (visited 30 Nov. 2014).

[107] *See*, *e.g.*, Takeyoshi Yamada, "[Follow-up] Dubbing 10: Right Holders Compromise at Last Moment" (2008) Nikkei Technology Online, available at http://techon.nikkeibp.co.jp/english/NEWS_EN/20080625/153820/ (visited 30 Nov. 2014); Promotion for Content Distribution Division, Information and Communications Bureau, Ministry of Internal Affairs and Communications, "Council Recommendations on Measures for Promoting the Production and Distribution of Content, and Legal Systems for Increasing Competitiveness" (2013) 25(1) New Breeze 12–13, available at https://www.ituaj.jp/wp-content/uploads/2013/03/nb25-1_web-6.pdf (visited 30 Nov. 2014).

[108] This position was disclosed in the interviews of authors with several major TV broadcasting companies.

habitually employ the first option, that is, no copy. However, as our survey showed, a considerable number of our respondents (27.82%; n=111) clearly acknowledged that they copied pre-recorded movie DVDs and Blu-ray Discs in some way. As almost all pre-recorded commercial movie media available on the Japanese market do not allow making any copies, these respondents had to circumvent the respective technological protection measures to do so. Accordingly, although technological protection measures are used with regard to pre-recorded movie media by right holders, they are circumvented by a significant portion of the Japanese population. Many respondents accept these restrictions, but at the same time many others do not. In addition, it is not so difficult to search online for an application necessary for circumventing those technological protection measures. Although much litigation against entities uploading or linking to such applications has been won by the right holders all over the world, it seems that they have not achieved any considerable change in the availability and accessibility of such applications online.

On the other side of the spectrum of consumers' attitudes towards restrictions on using copyrighted and other protected works were located the restrictions on the copying of videogames for videogame consoles and on sound recordings of live concerts. In regard to these, strict technological and other protection measures have been adopted by copyright holders. Although they are circumvented by a few individuals, the outstanding majority of consumers accept these restrictions and the measures work quite well with them. Videogame consoles employ very advanced technological protection measures, which are regularly updated with each new generation of console. Similarly, the measures implemented at concert venues are quite strict. The concert attendants' belongings are searched for cameras and other recording devices. If any recording device is found, they are required to deposit it in lockers available at the venues. This situation may change due to use of smartphones, since it is physically impossible to ask all concert attendants to deposit their smartphones in lockers during a concert. Hence, we will see to what extent the use of smartphones will change the current practice with the bans on recording live concerts of popular music.

CONCLUSION

The analysis of the current situation in the three main jurisdictions showed that there are considerable differences amongst the countries studied in their approaches to solving conflicts of norms between copyright law, contract law and property law. Some courts deem copyright law as *lex specialis* to contract law or property law under specific conditions; others do not. While the freedom of contract often trumps the copyright law's exhaustion of rights doctrine in the United States, the courts in the European Union and Japan allow the exhaustion of rights doctrine and the consumers' freedom of traffic in chattels guaranteed by the property law to override and restrict the copyright holders' exclusive rights granted by copyright law and freedom of contract guaranteed by contract law. Similarly diverse approaches are to be found with the contractual restrictions on other copyright exceptions and limitations. Some countries consider copyright exceptions and limitations as mandatory provisions and therefore as *lex specialis* to freedom of contract, others take them only as default rules which can be freely curbed by contractual arrangements and technological protection measures.

This raises the question of how the consumers of copyrighted works, as the largest group of concerned stakeholders, perceive non-negotiable contractual arrangements that considerably alter the delicate balance between copyright holders' private interests and public interests in favor of the former. Although it might seem that consumers would categorically object to such private ordering, our empirical study on Japanese consumers' attitudes towards the main technological and other protection measures adopted by copyright holders shows that the actual situation might be a bit more nuanced than conventionally expected. Consumers find some types of copyrighted works and uses more important for them than others. If the uses of copyrighted works which are important for them are restricted by copyright holders, such restrictions are regularly perceived by consumers to be unjust and unfair and therefore they frequently disregard those restrictions and search for ways of circumventing them. On the other hand, if the uses of copyrighted works are less important for consumers, they habitually accept the restrictions, and the technological or other protective measures implementing those restrictions work very efficiently.

Our study also observed that even copyright holders, intentionally or unintentionally, take into account the consumers' preferences between individual types of copyrighted works and their uses. The most severe restrictions are often imposed only on uses which are not perceived by consumers to be very important for them. Conversely, the uses of copyrighted works which are very important for consumers are frequently either unrestricted or restricted merely to a limited degree. Any attempts to impose more comprehensive and invasive restrictions on them are destined from the beginning to be doomed.

8. Intellectual property protection for fame, luxury, wines and spirits: *Lex specialis* for a corporate "dolce vita" or a "good-quality life"?

Irene Calboli[*]

I. INTRODUCTION

In this chapter, I consider two exceptions to the general provisions (*leges generales*) of intellectual property law governing the protection of trademarks and geographical indications of origin (GIs). In particular, I consider the *leges speciales* that have been introduced with respect to two specific subject matters by the Agreement on Trade-Related Aspects of Intellectual Property Rights (TRIPS): anti-dilution protection for well-known marks, as provided in Article 16.3,[1] and anti-usurpation protection for GIs identifying wines and spirits, as provided in Article 23.[2] This latter protection could be extended to other GIs as part of the built-in

* Professor of Law, Marquette University Law School; Visiting Professor, Faculty of Law, National University of Singapore. The arguments presented in this chapter draw on my research on luxury trademarks and geographical indications of origin (GIs). In this chapter, I borrow the expression "dolce vita" ("sweet life") from the Italian actor and director Federico Fellini and his 1960 comedy-drama film "*La Dolce Vita*." I am grateful to Graeme Dinwoodie for his insightful comments on previous drafts of this chapter. I also thank Ashley Swick for research assistance.

[1] Art. 16.3, Agreement on Trade-Related Aspects of Intellectual Property Rights. *See* Agreement on Trade-Related Aspects of Intellectual Property Rights, 15 April, 1994, Marrakesh Agreement Establishing the World Trade Organization, Annex 1C, LEGAL INSTRUMENTS – RESULT OF THE URUGUAY ROUNDS [1994] vol. 31, 33 I.L.M. 81, http://www.wto.org/english/docs_e/legal_e/27-trips.pdf [hereinafter TRIPS].

[2] TRIPS, *supra*, note 1, Art. 23(1).

agenda also introduced by TRIPS.[3] In both cases, these *leges speciales* enhance the protection granted, respectively, to well-known marks and GIs identifying wines and spirits, beyond the protection granted to marks and GIs in general (which is limited to acts that could amount to confuse and mislead consumers in the marketplace).

Based upon this analysis, I explore whether these *leges speciales* should be viewed merely as an additional example of the growing pressure in favor of enhanced protection that has characterized intellectual property debate in the past decades, or whether Articles 16.3 and 23 of TRIPS could also be explained differently. In particular, I consider whether these *leges speciales* should be seen exclusively as tools promoting a corporate "dolce vita" (sweet life) (by allowing businesses to further exploit their well-known marks and GIs), or whether they could also be explained as the result of a *mentalité* that aims to protect values such as "tradition", "authenticity", and "high quality" as an important part of the general culture of the countries and the constituencies promoting the adoption of these provisions.[4] For example, in Italy and France (two countries supporting the adoption of these provisions) the *mentalité* of "high quality" constitutes an important societal value in most aspects of everyday life, including with respect to the quality of clothes, food, wine, spirits, and commercial products.

Generally, intellectual property scholars tend to look suspiciously at these types of social value- and culture-related arguments to justify intellectual property protection, especially enhanced protection such as that granted by the provisions at issue. Skepticism in this respect has been repeatedly expressed by academics in the Anglo-American world, who have traditionally preferred to rely on utilitarian theories based on law and economics, namely on economic incentives and market competition. In contrast, natural and moral rights traditions – the theories upon which enhanced intellectual property protection is often justified – have been more openly accepted in civil law countries, particularly by scholars in continental Europe.[5] Yet, despite the existing scholarly

---

[3] *Ibid.*, Art. 24(1).

[4] For a more detailed analysis, see Irene Calboli, *Of Markets, Culture, and* Terroir*: The Unique Economic and Culture-Related Benefits of Geographical Indications of Origin*, in RESEARCH HANDBOOK IN INTERNATIONAL INTELLECTUAL PROPERTY 433 (Daniel Gervais ed., 2015).

[5] The literature in this respect is extensive. For the purpose of this chapter, see in particular Barton Beebe, *Intellectual Property and the Sumptuary Code*, 123 HARV. L. REV. 809, 884–87 (2010) [hereinafter Beebe, *Sumptuary Code*] (positing the challenges facing a "philanthropic" use of intellectual property

skepticism on the part of (some) academics, social value- and culture-related arguments are certainly relevant in this context. Accordingly, a reading of the provisions at issue as the result also of a *mentalité* aiming at protecting a culture of "high quality" and a "good-quality life," including high-quality products, offers equally important insights for the debate in these areas.[6]

In particular, Articles 16.3 and 23 of TRIPS grant additional protection to signs (trademarks and GIs) that indicate the origin and quality of products that are frequently (albeit not always) known for their higher quality compared with the type-level products that are produced in the same market sectors. The histories of many of these products demonstrate how local artisans manufactured, or grew and processed the ingredients to produce, these products with high-quality materials, attention to details, and often in limited quantities (as opposite to mass produced products). Perhaps even more relevant, many of these producers met higher-quality standards not because the law imposed those standards upon them.[7] Instead, these producers generally considered, and in many instances continue to consider, high quality as the most important feature

---

law); Kal Raustiala & Stephen R. Munzer, *The Global Struggle Over Geographic Indications*, 18 EUR. J. INT'L L. 337, 359–360 (2007) (criticizing the anti-usurpation GI protection as anticompetitive). Some authors, however, have supported a reading of intellectual property law based on its social function. *See, e.g.*, MADHAVI SUNDER, FROM GOODS TO A GOOD LIFE: INTELLECTUAL PROPERTY AND GLOBAL JUSTICE 31 (2012) (suggesting that "intellectual property law must adopt broader social and cultural analysis"). Other authors have taken this alternative reading further, and compared the traditional cost-benefit utilitarian analysis with a different type of analysis, particularly turning to concepts such as "happiness" and "well-beingness" to assess the objectives of intellectual property law. *See, e.g.*, Estelle Derclaye, *What Can Intellectual Property Law Learn from Happiness Research?*, in METHODS AND PERSPECTIVES IN INTELLECTUAL PROPERTY 177 (Graeme B. Dinwoodie ed, 2013); John Bronsteen, Christopher Buccafusco, and Jonathan Masur, *Well-Being Analysis vs. Cost-Benefit Analysis*, 62 DUKE L. J. 1603 (2013).

6 For a comprehensive analysis and critique of the provisions on trademark dilution and on GIs, see Beebe, *Sumptuary Code*, *supra* note 5, at 885.

7 For example, trademark law cannot force trademark owners to retain superior product quality apart from the requirement that trademarks cannot be used misleadingly, lest trademark registrations can be cancelled. *See, e.g.* 15 U.S.C. § 1052(a) (2000) (prohibiting the registration of marks that are deceptive). Likewise, even though several authors have compared GIs to certification trademarks, the language of TRIPS only provides that GIs guarantee that the GI-denominated products derive their characteristics, qualities, or reputation from GI-denominated regions. In particular, the granting of GI status does not

of their products. Accordingly, they heavily invested (and often continue to invest) in the products' materials and manufacturing techniques in order to maintain a reputation of high quality as their distinguishing product feature. Thus, the *leges speciales* at issue are certainly derived also from the desire to protect the producers of these high-quality products against unfair competition and misappropriation, and in turn to safeguard this tradition of "high quality." This argument has been repeated by supporters of these provisions and remains important, particularly with respect to those producers who continue to invest in the high quality of their products.

My analysis in this chapter proceeds as follows. In Part II, I briefly recount the introduction into TRIPS of anti-dilution protection as the *lex specialis* for well-known marks beyond the traditional protection granted to trademarks based on a likelihood of consumer confusion. In Part III, I survey the TRIPS provisions on GIs and, specifically, the adoption of anti-usurpation protection as *lex specialis* for GIs identifying wines and spirits. Building upon the considerations in Parts II and III, in Part IV I offer some observations about the reasons behind the protection established in these provisions, including non-purely economic reasons such as a "good-quality life" *mentalité*. In this Part, I consider the potential benefits of a balanced application of these provisions. Notably, I argue that these provisions could promote a business model based on high(er) quality, including with respect to labor standards and respect for the environment. I conclude by noting that, by revisiting existing controversies in these areas from the angle of a "good-quality life" *mentalité*, we can better understand the origin and the scope of these *leges speciales*. And we can develop insights on the appropriate limits to the application of these provisions to the instances in which these provisions effectively promote a "good-quality life" for society as a whole and not solely a corporate "dolce vita."

---

per se require compliance with high-quality production techniques, such compliance remaining a discretionary choice for the national or regional authorities (e.g., the EU). *See* TRIPS, *supra* note 1, Art. 22.1. *See also* Daniel J. Gervais, *A Cognac After a Spanish Champagne? Geographical Indications as Certification Marks*, in INTELLECTUAL PROPERTY AT THE EDGE 130 (Rochelle C. Dreyfuss and Jane C. Ginsburg eds., 2014).

II. INTELLECTUAL PROPERTY PROTECTION FOR FAME AND LUXURY: ANTI-DILUTION PROTECTION AS *LEX SPECIALIS* IN TRADEMARK LAW

As is well recognized by trademark scholars, starting in the early twentieth century trademark protection has been justified primarily on theories of economic efficiency and consumer protection.[8] In particular, the traditional account recites that trademarks are protected as conveyers of commercial information to the public, and prohibit only improper use of signs identical or similar to the marks by unauthorized third parties that is likely to confuse the public about the origin of the marked products.[9] Under this account, consumer protection remains the primary focus, and trademark law protects business goodwill only as a secondary concern, not *per se*, but under the frameworks of unfair competition law or the law of passing-off.[10] These limits on trademark protection have been generally justified because of the social costs that trademarks represent for market competition and, in turn, for society. Trademarks grant their owners the right to exclude other parties from using identical or similar words or symbols to identify similar goods or services for a virtually unlimited time period. This, in turn, may lead to the risk of creating an undesirable monopoly on language and other forms of expression – such as color, shapes, even sounds and gestures – should trademark protection extend to trademarks as properties *per se* rather than be limited to the protection of trademarks' "distinctive" function, that is, the ability of trademarks to identify products in the marketplace and convey information about the origin and quality of the products.[11]

---

[8] *See* William M. Landes & Richard A. Posner, *Trademark Law: An Economic Perspective*, 30 J.L. & ECON. 265, 265–66 (1987) ("[T]rademark law … best can be explained on the hypothesis that the law is trying to promote economic efficiency."); *see also* Mark A. Lemley & Mark P. McKenna, *Owning Mark(et)s,* 109 MICH. L. REV. 137 (2010); William P. Kratzke, *Normative Economic Analysis of Trademark Law*, 21 MEMPHIS ST. U. L. REV. 199, 205 (1991).

[9] For background materials and references, see generally Irene Calboli, *The Case for a Limited Protection of Trademark Merchandising*, 2011 U. ILL. L. REV. 865, 875–76 (2011) [hereinafter Calboli, *Merchandising*].

[10] *Ibid. Cf.* Mark P. McKenna, *The Normative Foundations of Trademark Law*, 82 NOTRE DAME L. REV. 1839 (2007).

[11] *Ibid.*

Yet, despite this traditional account, the position that trademarks constitute important business assets – often the most relevant assets of a company – has always been a *leitmotif* in the business world. In particular, trademark owners have generally resisted the idea that trademarks should be protected only insofar as the unauthorized use of identical or similar signs can confuse the public, and have repeatedly argued that trademarks should be protected also against competitors' free riding and unauthorized uses by third parties that tarnish the goodwill and reputation of their marks.[12] Throughout the decades, part of the judiciary has also supported this position.[13] Notably, common law courts originally based their jurisdiction over trademark infringers on the invasion of the property in the marks – especially in marks that consisted of new and invented terms – without the need to prove any likelihood of consumer confusion.[14] Similarly, in some civil law countries, namely the Benelux countries, the traditional standard for trademark protection has never been a likelihood of confusion, but instead the association that could be created between the senior marks and the unauthorized identical or similar signs.[15]

---

[12] In this respect, *see* Frank I. Schechter, *The Rational Basis of Trademark Protection*, 40 HARV. L. REV. 813, 825. (1926–1927). Schechter promoted in the United States the idea initially developed in Germany that "[t]he true functions … are, then, to identify a product as satisfactory and thereby to stimulate further purchases by the consuming public." *Ibid.* at 818.

[13] For a detailed reconstruction of the decisions issued by early English and American courts, see McKenna, *supra* note 10, at 1850–1871. For a more recent position, see Frank H. Easterbrook, *Intellectual Property is Still Property*, 13 HARV. J. L. & PUB. POL'Y 108, 118 (1990). According to Judge Easterbrook, "we should treat intellectual and physical property identically in the law." *Ibid.*

[14] *See* Edward S. Rogers, *Comments on the Modern Law of Unfair Trade*, 3 U. ILL. L. REV. 551, 552–54 (1909) (offering a detailed analysis of relevant decisions until the early 1900s). In the *Trade-Mark Cases*, 100 U.S. 82 (1879), the Supreme Court also referred to the right to use a mark as "a property right." *Ibid.* at 92.

[15] The former Benelux Trade Mark Act of 1971 provided, in Article 13, that "the proprietor of a mark may, by virtue of his exclusive right, oppose" the following acts: "1. Any use made of the mark or of a like symbol for the goods or services in respect of which the mark is registered, or for similar goods or services" and "2. Any other use, in economic intercourse, of the mark or of a like symbol made without a valid reason under circumstances likely to be prejudicial to the proprietor of the mark." Benelux Trade Mark Act, Trb. 1962, 58 Art. 13-Al and 2.

Still, despite the early common law decisions and the Benelux approach, courts and legislators generally subscribed to a confusion-based framework for trademark protection in the majority of jurisdictions during the course of the twentieth century. Similarly, most national legislators wrote the requirement of "likelihood of confusion" into domestic trademark laws as the sine qua non for trademark protection. The Paris Convention for the Protection of Industrial Property, adopted in 1883 and revised several times between its adoption and the 1970s, included "confusion" as one of the conditions for protection against unfair competition in Article 10*bis*, and with respect to the protection of well-known marks in Article 6*bis*.[16] The adoption of TRIPS in 1994 ultimately confirmed "likelihood of confusion" as the general standard for trademark infringement for all member countries of the World Trade Organization (WTO) in Article 16.1.[17]

Regardless of the acceptance of "likelihood of confusion" as the legal standard for trademark protection, however, the pressure to directly protect trademarks *per se* never left trademark practice. Trademark owners continued to use marks as "things"[18] throughout the decades, either because of a "widespread ignorance" of the law or by "making the most of [its] exceptions."[19] In addition, in the early twentieth century, prominent practitioners started to support the position that the function of a trademark was not just that of distinguishing goods and services, but also to attract consumers by relying on the distinctiveness and uniqueness of a mark. In particular, in the United States, Frank Schechter elaborated the theory (imported and "adapted" from Germany) of trademark dilution. Under this theory, trademarks ought to be protected against the

---

16 *See* Article 10*bis* and Article 6*bis* of the Paris Convention for the Protection of Industrial Property, Mar. 20, 1883, 21 U.S.T. 1583, 828 U.N.T.S. 305, *available at* http://www.wipo.int/clea/docs/en/wo/wo020en.htm [hereinafter Paris Convention]. Still, the Paris Convention did not directly mention the wording "likelihood of confusion" as the general standard for trademark infringement for registered marks.

17 TRIPS, *supra* note 1, Art. 16.1. Article 16.1 recites that "[t]he owner of a registered trademark shall have the exclusive right to prevent all third parties not having the owner's consent from using in the course of trade identical or similar signs for goods or services which are identical or similar to those in respect of which the trademark is registered where such use would result in a likelihood of confusion." *Ibid.*

18 *See, e.g.,* Mark A. Lemley, *The Modern Lanham Act and the Death of Common Sense*, 108 YALE L.J. 1687, 1687–88 (1999).

19 Nathan Isaacs, *Traffic in Trade-Symbols*, 44 HARV. L. REV. 1210, 1210 (1931).

dilution, that is, the "whittling away," of their uniqueness and distinctiveness.[20] In this context, well-known marks were seen as the category of marks more vulnerable to suffer harm from the loss of their uniqueness and "attractive power," and thus deserving anti-dilution protection.

In 1925, the pressure for additional protection for well-known marks also brought the international community to accept the special status of well-known marks as part of the Hague Revision of the Paris Convention. In this forum, member countries of the Paris Convention adopted Article 6*bis*, which mandates that members should refuse or cancel the registration, or prohibit the use of any mark that "constitute[s] a reproduction, an imitation, or a translation, liable to create confusion, of a mark considered by the competent authority of the country of registration or use to be well-known in that country."[21] Certainly an important victory in favor of the recognition of a separate status for well-known marks, the adoption of Article 6*bis* nevertheless continued to be linked to the requirement of consumer confusion between the well-known marks and the infringing signs.

As a result, trademark owners continued to lobby for additional protection against the dilution of the distinctive power of their marks regardless of the existence of consumer confusion.[22] The legislative history of the 1946 United States Trademark Act (Lanham Act) shows, for example, that anti-dilution proposals were introduced in some of

---

[20] *See* Schechter, *supra* note 12, at 818. By importing into the United States an idea originally developed in Germany, Schechter developed the theory that "[t]he true functions of the trademark are… to identify a product as satisfactory and thereby to stimulate further purchases by the consuming public." *Id.* For critical overview of the origin of the anti-dilution theory, see Barton Beebe, *The Suppressed Misappropriation Origins of Trademark Antidilution Law: the Landgericht Elberfeld's Odol Opinion and Frank Schechter's* The Rational Basis of Trademark Protection, in INTELLECTUAL PROPERTY AT THE EDGE 59 (Rochelle C. Dreyfuss & Jane C. Ginsburg eds., 2014).

[21] Article 6*bis*, Paris Convention for the Protection of Industrial Property, Mar. 20, 1883, last revised at Stockholm July 14, 1967, 21 U.S.T. 1583, 828 U.N.T.S. 305 [hereinafter Paris Convention]. The provision was introduced during the Convention's revision at The Hague Conference on November 6, 1925. The request for cancellation was five years from the date of the registration, whereas no time limit applies in the cases in which the registration was filed, or the mark was used, in bad faith. *See* Marshall A. Leaffer, *Protection of Well-Known Marks: A Transnational Perspective*, in TRADEMARK PROTECTION AND TERRITORIALITY CHALLENGES 18 (Irene Calboli & Edward Lee eds. 2014).

[22] *See, e.g.* Schechter, *supra* note 12, at 825–26. *See also* Rudolph Callmann, *He Who Reaps Where He Has Not Sown: Unjust Enrichment in the Law of Unfair Competition*, 55 HARV. L. R. 595 (1942).

the drafts of the statute, but were ultimately rejected in the final version of the 1946 Act. Still, some U.S. states succumbed to the pressure of the business world and enacted state-wide variations of anti-dilution protection.[23] Trademark owners also continued to pressure lawmakers in the United States into recognizing anti-dilution protection at the federal level. The same was true in some European countries and at the international level. Throughout the decades, the pressure for enhanced trademark protection continued to grow, also due to economic changes in product manufacturing and distribution, a growing and interconnected international marketplace, the widespread use of licensing agreements, and the rise of trademark merchandising as an important vehicle for additional profits (royalties) for trademark owners.[24]

Eventually, in 1994, trademark owners succeeded in their plea with the adoption of Article 16.3 of TRIPS, which introduced anti-dilution protection at the international level.[25] In particular, the final language of Article 16.3 of TRIPS expanded the reach of Article 6*bis* of the Paris Convention beyond similar goods and services. More relevantly, the provision no longer required a likelihood of consumer confusion as the basis for trademark protection of well-known marks under the circumstances indicated under Article 16.3. Instead, the provision recites that protection for well-known marks now requires prohibiting the use or the registration of identical or similar signs with respect to any goods or services when such use or registration would indicate a connection with existing well-known marks and "provided that the interests of the owners of the registered trademark[s] are likely to be damaged by such use."[26] The

---

[23] *See* Walter J. Derenberg, *Dilution and the Antidilution Statutes*, 44 CALIF. L. REV. 439, 449 (1956). Schechter himself drafted one of the proposals, the Perkins Bill, in 1932, which included protecting "coined or invented or fanciful or arbitrary mark[s]" against uses that could "injure the good will, reputation, business, credit or securities of the owner of the previously used trademark[s]." *Ibid.* (citing H.R. 11592, 72d Cong. (1st Sess. 1932)).

[24] *See, e.g.*, Calboli, *Merchandising*, *supra* note 9, at 877–880.

[25] *See, e.g.*, DANIEL GERVAIS, THE TRIPS AGREEMENT: DRAFTING HISTORY AND ANALYSIS 108–111 (1998). Not all authors agree, however, that Article 16.3 of TRIPS mandates the introduction of anti-dilution protection as a requirement under TRIPS. *See* Paul J. Heald, *Trademarks and Geographical Indications: Exploring the Contours of the Trips Agreement*, 29 VAND. J. TRANSNAT'L L. 635 (1996) (stating that anti-dilution protection is not a requirement under Article 16.3 of TRIPs).

[26] TRIPS, *supra* note 1, Art. 16.3. In 1999, the World Intellectual Property Organization issued a *Joint Recommendation on the Protection of Well-Known Marks* in order to provide guidelines for the factors that should be taken into

adoption of Article 16.3 of TRIPS followed the introduction of a similar provision in the European Trademark Directive in 1988.[27] The European provision was derived from the trademark provisions in the Benelux and was largely implemented by the EU Member States (even though the implementation of the provision was optional).

As a result of Article 16.3 of TRIPS, most countries worldwide had now to implement anti-dilution protection as the *lex specialis* protecting well-known marks into their national laws[28] – including those countries that were not in favor of anti-dilution protection before the adoption of TRIPS. The adoption of the provision, and the resulting changes that had to be introduced into the national trademark laws, nonetheless met with criticisms.[29] Several scholars voiced their discontent with the new standard and emphasized that anti-dilution protection departs from the pro-consumer and pro-competitive objectives of trademark law in favor of protecting corporate interests directly.[30] Two decades after the adoption of TRIPS, the anti-dilution *lex specialis* for well-known marks

---

account when defining a mark as well-known. *See* World Intellectual Property Organization [WIPO], *Joint Recommendation Concerning Provisions on the Protection of Well-Known Marks*, WIPO Doc. 833(E) (Sept. 29, 1999), http://www.wipo.int/about-ip/en/development_iplaw/pub833.htm.

[27] Article 5(2), Council Directive 89/104, 1989 O.J. (L 40) 1 (EEC), now replaced by European Parliament and Council Directive 2008/95, 2008 O.J. (L 299) 25 (EC) [hereinafter EU Trademark Directive]. Article 5(2) is based on Article 13A(2) of the old Uniform Benelux Law. *See* Commission of the European Communities, *Memorandum on the Creation of an EEC Trade Mark*, SEC (76) 2462, BULLETIN OF THE EUROPEAN COMMUNITIES (July 6, 1976), *reprinted in* 7 INT'L REV. INTELL. PROP. & COMPETITION L. 367 (1976); *see also* Peter Prescott, *Has the Benelux Law Been Written into the Directive?,* 3 EUR. INTELL. PROP. REV. 99 (1997).

[28] *See generally* FREDERICK W. MOSTERT, FAMOUS AND WELL-KNOWN MARKS: AN INTERNATIONAL ANALYSIS (1997).

[29] *See* Kenneth L. Port, *The "Unnatural" Expansion of Trademark Rights: Is a Federal Dilution Statute Necessary?*, 85 TRADEMARK REP. 525, 552–59 (1995). For an overview of the criticisms in the United States, see the various contributions published in 24/3 SANTA CLARA COMPUTER & HIGH TECH. L.J. (2007); *see also generally* ILANAH SIMON FHIMA, TRADE MARK DILUTION IN THE UNITED STATES AND EUROPEAN UNION (Oxford Univ. Press 2011).

[30] Some authors compared the adoption of trademark dilution with the introduction of an unwanted and unnecessary "moral" right into trademark law. *See, e.g.*, Sandra L. Rierson, *The Myth and Reality of Dilution*, 11 DUKE L. & TECH. REV. 212 (2012); Laura Bradford, *Emotion, Dilution, and the Trademark Consumer*, 23 BERKELEY TECH. L.J. 1227 (2008).

continues to be controversial.[31] In Part IV, I acknowledge that several of the arguments that have been raised against anti-dilution protection are well founded. However, I also consider the role of the above mentioned "high-quality" *mentalité*, and posit whether this protection could be justified, in some cases, as a tool to prevent the misappropriation of marks identifying products of high quality, and thus as a tool to promote a culture of high quality in manufacturing in general.[32]

III. INTELLECTUAL PROPERTY PROTECTION FOR WINES AND SPIRITS: ANTI-USURPATION PROTECTION AS *LEX SPECIALIS* FOR GEOGRAPHICAL INDICATIONS OF ORIGIN

Another area in which enhanced protection is granted to commercial indicators via a *lex specialis* is the area of GIs – namely with respect to geographical terms that identify wines and spirits.[33] As I elaborate below, this *lex specialis* extends anti-usurpation protection to the GIs at issue regardless of the existence of any consumer confusion or unfair competition. Historically, this enhanced type of protection started as a limited affair under the auspices of the Madrid Agreement for the Repression of False and Deceptive Indications of Source on Goods (Madrid Agreement), which for the first time provided added protection to the indications of the geographical source for wines.[34] A similar type of protection was later introduced into TRIPS for GIs identifying wines and spirits.

The adoption of TRIPS marked a milestone in advancing the GI protection agenda. As parties to TRIPS and member countries of the WTO, the majority of countries worldwide had to implement the "legal means" to prevent the use of GIs that mislead "the public as to the

[31] The current controversies have primarily focused on the interpretation of the (statutory or judicial) factors to assess dilution and on the availability of defenses. Some authors, however, continue to question the acceptability of anti-dilution protection as an additional cause of action besides trademark infringement. *See, e.g.*, Barton Beebe, *The Continuing Debacle of U.S. Anti-dilution Law: Evidence from the First Year of Trademark Dilution Revision Act Case Law*, 24 SANTA CLARA COMPUTER & HIGH TECH. L.J. 449 (2008).

[32] *See* discussion *infra* Part IV.

[33] TRIPS, *supra* note 1, Art. 23(1).

[34] Article 4, Madrid Agreement for the Repression of False and Deceptive Indications of Source, Apr. 14, 1891, 828 U.N.T.S. 168, *available at* http://www.wipo.int/clea/docs/en/wo/wo032en.htm.

geographical origin of the goods," or that "constitute[] an act of unfair competition within the meaning of Article 10*bis* of the Paris Convention" under the rule of Article 22.[35] Article 22 also required that WTO member countries "refuse or invalidate the registration of a trademark which contains or consists of a geographical indication with respect to goods not originating in the territory indicated" when the use of the GI "is of such a nature as to mislead the public as to the true place of origin."[36]

Besides this general protection, WTO member countries agreed on enhanced protection, a *lex specialis* under Article 23, for GIs identifying wines and spirits. The fact that countries from both the "old world" and "new world" camps had, and have, considerable interests in the wine and spirits business undoubtedly contributed to the double standard created between general GIs and GIs related to wines and spirits under TRIPS.[37] In particular, Article 23 prohibits the use of terms that are similar or identical to GIs identifying wines and spirits when the products do not "originat[e] in the place indicated by the geographical indication," including when "the true origin of the goods is indicated or the [GI] is used in translation or accompanied by expression such as 'kind', 'type', 'style', 'imitation', or the like."[38] Article 23 additionally states that member countries may refuse or invalidate trademark registrations containing or consisting of GIs identifying wines or spirits.[39]

Despite this anti-usurpation protection, however, GIs identifying wines and spirits remain subject to the general exceptions provided under Article 24 of TRIPS. Specifically, Article 24 grandfathers existing trademark rights with names similar or identical to GIs that were in use, or had been registered in good faith before the date of the implementation of TRIPS in the member country where the mark was registered, or before the GI was protected in its country of origin.[40] In addition, member countries are not obliged to "prevent continued and similar use of a particular [GI] of another Member identifying wines or spirits in connection with goods and services"

---

[35] TRIPS, *supra* note 1, Art. 22.2(b).

[36] *Ibid.*, Art. 22.2(a). TRIPS did not mandate any specific means to implement GI protection, leaving TRIPS members free to adopt the means that best suited their respective legal systems. *See generally* Dev Gangjee, *Quibbling Siblings: Conflicts Between Trademarks and Geographic Indications,* 82 CHI.-KENT L. REV. 1253, 1256–9 (2007) (recounting the scholarly discussion over the possibility to protect GIs under trademark law).

[37] TRIPS, *supra* note 1, Art. 23.1.

[38] *Ibid.*

[39] *Ibid.*, Art. 23.2.

[40] *Ibid.*, Art. 24.5.

where the GI has been used "in a continued manner with the same or related goods or services" in the territory of that country for at least ten years prior to April 15, 1994 (the date of the adoption of TRIPS), or where this continuous use has been in good faith.[41] Finally, Article 24 provides that the terms that have become generic in a given TRIPS member country can continue to be used as such in the territory of that country.[42] The ongoing disputes over the use of terms like "champagne," "chablis," "cognac," and so forth between European and North American countries are relevant examples of the impact of this exception and likely the reason behind the adoption of this provision.

In addition to establishing anti-usurpation protection for GIs for wines and spirits, TRIPS provided a built-in agenda for future GI negotiations. Article 23 requires, in particular, that member countries agree to enter future negotiations in order to establish a multilateral system of notification and registration of GIs for wines and spirits, which would facilitate their enforcement and prevent their illegal use.[43] Similarly, beyond the domain of wines and spirits, Article 24 of TRIPS mandates that member countries agree to engage in future negotiations in order to extend the anti-usurpation protection granted to GIs for wines and spirits to all GIs.[44]

In an attempt to promote discussion on these topics, and advance the TRIPS built-in agenda, the debate on GIs protection was included in the list of issues to be addressed by the Doha Ministerial Declaration as part of the Doha "Development" Round of WTO negotiations in 2001.[45] In particular, the Doha mandate included creating a multilateral register for wines and spirits (and possibly for all GIs), and extending anti-usurpation protection beyond GIs for just wines and spirits.[46] Perhaps an overly ambitious objective, both issues were supposed to be debated, and resolved, by the end of 2003. But when national delegations met in Cancun in 2003, they could not reach an agreement.[47] Moreover, the

[41] *Ibid.*, Art. 24.4.

[42] TRIPS, *supra* note 1, Art. 24.6.

[43] *Ibid.*, Art. 23(4). *See also* Justin M. Waggoner, *Acquiring A European Taste for Geographical Indications*, 33 Brook. J. Int'l L. 569, 578 (2008).

[44] TRIPS, *supra* note 1, Art. 24(1).

[45] *See* Ministerial Declaration, WTO document WT/MIN(01)/DEC/1, adopted in Doha, Qatar, November 14, 2001 [hereinafter Doha Declaration]. *See also* the consolidated statement by Cristophe Geiger, Daniel J. Gervais, Nobert Olzak, Vincent Ruzek, *Towards a Flexible International Framework for the Protection of Geographical Indications*, 1 WIPO Journal 147, 157–58 (2010).

[46] Doha Declaration, *supra* note 45.

[47] Details about the WTO negotiations in Cancun are available at http://www.wto.org/english/ tratop_e/trips_e/gi_background_e.htm.

negotiations collapsed and no significant progress was made in order to pave the way for the multilateral registry and extending anti-usurpation protection beyond GIs for wines and spirits. As of today, this impasse continues at the multilateral level,[48] and countries have discussed issues related to GIs primarily within the framework of individual free trade agreements (FTAs).[49] In these fora, both camps have been able to reach some modest success in advancing a compromise position on GI protection, yet controversy has continued to dominate the debate.[50]

Not surprisingly, the recognition of GI protection and the adoption of a *lex specialis* anti-usurpation for GIs for wines and spirits were greeted with mixed reactions by member countries.[51] Supporters of GIs hailed the provisions as much-needed recognition of an important type of right that is necessary to protect and promote GI-denominated products. In this respect, they repeatedly highlighted the unique communicative function

---

[48] In 2011, the Director General of the World Trade Organization (WTO) reported that WTO Members' positions on GIs continued to diverge. *See* WTO, Document No. TN/C/W/61, 21 April 2011, *available at* http://www.wto.org/english/tratop_e/trips_e/ art27_3b_e.htm.

[49] *See* Intellectual Property Chapter of recently concluded FTA between the European Union (EU) and Singapore. Articles 11.16–11.23, DRAFT EU-Singapore FTA, September 2013, Chapter 11, Intellectual Property, http://trade.ec.europa.eu/doclib/docs/2013/september/tradoc_151761.pdf (providing extensive protection for GIs, including the creation of domestic registries in the members of the FTA). *Cf.* Articles QQ.D.1–13, Trans-Pacific Partnership, Intellectual Property [Rights] Chapter, Consolidated Text (May 16, 2014) https://www.wikileaks.org/tpp-ip2/. The TPP is currently being negotiated between Australia, Brunei Darussalam, Canada, Chile, Japan, Malaysia, Mexico, New Zealand, Peru, Singapore, Vietnam, and the United States.

[50] *See, e.g.*, the Agreement Between the United States and the European Community on Trade in Wine, U.S.–E.C., Mar. 10, 2006, http://www.ttb.gov/agreements/us_ec_wine_agreement.shtml (allowing the sale in the EU of wines produced in the US with methods not permitted otherwise in the EU in exchange to "seeking to change the legal status" of several quasi-generic wine-related indications). Art. 6.1 of the Agreements establishes the terms of the US commitment, which is detailed in Industry Circular No. 2006-1, M. 10, 2006, http://www.ttb.gov/industry_circulars/archives/2006/06-01.html. Similarly, in March 2014, as part of the ongoing trade negotiations between the United States and the EU, the EU requested that the US cease to use names of cheeses that are protected by GIs in Europe but are considered generic in the US. *See Europe Starts Food Fight with U.S. over Cheese Names*, L.A. TIMES, March 12, 2014, http://www.latimes.com/business/la-fi-eu-cheese-fight-20140312,0,1938455.story#axzz2wViO7JJK.

[51] For a detailed analysis of debate on GIs, see DEV GANGJEE, RELOCATING THE LAW OF GEOGRAPHICAL INDICATIONS (2012).

that GIs perform in the marketplace, and advocated the reopening of GI negotiations in order to adopt the multilateral registry mentioned in Article 23, and extend anti-usurpation protection for all GIs. Supporters of GIs also repeatedly stressed that GIs play a fundamental role as promoters and guarantees of the quality of the GI-denominated products because of the specific characteristics of the territory where the products are grown or manufactured, characteristics that, in their whole, cannot be replicated elsewhere.[52]

Against these arguments, however, opponents of GI protection repeated that GIs do not encourage and reward innovation, but instead promote tradition and conformity within a very specific geographical region; thus they are essentially an impediment to progress,[53] and are anti-competitive, particularly when they offer anti-usurpation protection beyond needed to avoid consumer confusion and deception.[54] Opponents of GIs also objected to international negotiations regarding the creation of a multinational register for wines and spirits and the possibility of expanding GI protection to the anti-usurpation level for all GIs.[55] In particular, they raised the argument – used also against anti-dilution protection in the domain of trademarks – that protection against consumer confusion, the current general standard under Article 22 of TRIPS, is sufficient and any added protection would simply become a subsidy and a marketing tool in favor of GI-denominated products and regions against other producers of the type-level products, and in turn against

---

52 *See, e.g.*, Michelle Agdomar, *Removing the Greek From Feta and Adding Korbel to Champagne: The Paradox of Geographical Indications in International Law*, 18 FORDHAM INTELL. PROP. MEDIA & ENT. L.J. 541 (2008). *See also* Irene Calboli, *Expanding the Protection of Geographical Indications of Origin Under TRIPS' "Old" Debate or "New" Opportunity?*, 10 MARQ. INTELL. PROP. L. REV. 181, 184 (2006) [hereinafter Calboli, *Expanding Protection*].

53 *See, e.g.*, Raustiala & Munzer, *supra* note 5, at 359–360. *Cf.* Dwijen Rangnekar, *The Socio-Economics of Geographical Indications: A Review of Empirical Evidence from Europe*, UNCTAD-ICTSD Project on IPRs and Sustainable Development, 15, May 2004, *available at* http://ictsd.org/i/publications/12218/?view=document [hereinafter Rangnekar, *Socio-Economics of GIs*].

54 *See* Raustiala & Munzer, *supra* note 5, at 352–59.

55 For an overview of these arguments, see Felix Addor & Alexandra Grazioli, *Geographical Indications Beyond Wines and Spirits – A Roadmap for a Better Protection for Geographical Indications in the WTO TRIPS Agreement*, 5 J. WORLD INTELL. PROP. 865, 867 (2002). *But see* Steven A. Bowers, *Location, Location, Location: The Case Against Extending Geographical Indication Protection Under the TRIPS Agreement*, 31 AIPLA Q.J. 129, 140 (2003).

market competition.[56] In Part IV, I agree with several of these criticisms. In particular, I criticize the definition of GIs offered by Article 22 of TRIPS, according to which GIs are "indications which identify a good as originating in [a] territory" in which "a given quality, reputation or other characteristic of the good is *essentially* [but not necessarily *exclusively*] attributable to its geographical origin."[57] Still, I support extending anti-usurpation protection to all GIs when GI-denominated products originate exclusively from the GI-denominated region. In these instances, this protection could benefit local and rural development as well as promote the conservation of local culture. Also in this area, understanding the role of the "high-quality" *mentalité*, according to which "good quality" products are an important societal value, is important to fully grasp the complexity of the GI debate and the related controversies.[58]

IV. INTELLECTUAL PROPERTY LAW AS *LEX SPECIALIS* FOR A CORPORATE "DOLCE VITA" OR FOR A "GOOD-QUALITY LIFE"?

As I mentioned above, the introduction of Articles 16.3 and 23 into the final text of TRIPS was met both with opposition and cheers by different constituencies. In general, I agree that the introduction of these provisions derived, to a large extent, from the pressure to extend exclusive rights in, respectively, well-known marks and GIs and to maximize their marketing value. The realization of this "corporate dolce vita," however, is not the only possible (full) justification for the provisions at issue. Instead, these provisions certainly also originate in a *mentalité* that values "high quality" as an important societal value – a value that, according to the supporters of this *mentalité*, should be defended with appropriate legal means, that is, with provisions like those analyzed in this chapter. Accordingly, in this Part, I suggest that the debate over anti-dilution

---

56 *See* Raustiala & Munzer, *supra* note 5, at 351. *But see* Marco Ricolfi, *Geographical Symbols in Intellectual Property Law*, *in* SCHUTZ VON KREATIVITÄT UND WETTBEWERB 242 (Reto M. Hilty, Josef Drexl & Wilhelm Nordemann eds., 2009).

57 TRIPS, *supra* note 1, Art. 22(1). Similarly, WIPO defines GIs as "sign[s] used on goods that have a specific geographical origin and possess qualities, reputation or characteristics that are essentially attributable to that origin." WIPO, *Overview of Geographical Indications*, http://www.wipo.int/geo_indications/en/ (last visited March 21, 2014).

58 *See* discussion *infra* Part IV.

protection for trademarks and anti-usurpation protection for GIs cannot be grasped in its entirety without considering this *mentalité*. Despite criticisms of it, acknowledging this *mentalité* remains crucial to fully understand, in the correct historical, social, and national context, the importance placed by the supporters of these enhanced protections on concepts such as "authenticity" and "tradition." In particular, these concepts embody equally important societal values that deserve to be considered as a matter of public policy, compared to concepts such as "innovation" and "competition," the value traditionally at the basis of the justification of intellectual property rights in the Anglo-American world.

Acknowledging this *mentalité* does not amount, however, to dismissing the criticism expressed with respect to the provisions at issue.

As I indicated above, several scholars have criticized the introduction of anti-dilution protection into trademark law, stressing that the justification for such protection rests on the assumption that trademarks deserve to be protected as business assets rather than as indicators of commercial origin and product quality.[59] In particular, these scholars have noted that anti-dilution protection was adopted in order to safeguard "the uniqueness or individuality of [famous] trademark[s],"[60] thus their "singularity,"[61] against the unauthorized use "upon either related or non-related goods."[62] Yet, well-known trademark owners frequently do not hesitate to "self-dilute" the uniqueness of their well-known trademarks with brand extensions on a large variety of (often unrelated and mass-marketed) products, from which they capture lucrative royalties.[63] Accordingly, these scholars have correctly pointed out that anti-dilution protection is no longer protecting trademark uniqueness, but rather the ability to extract value from the use of these marks on related or unrelated products.[64] Similarly, they have noted that anti-dilution protection is frequently used as a tool to protect well-known marks as symbols per se,

---

[59] *See*, e.g., Laura Bradford, *Emotion, Dilution, and the Trademark Consumer*, 23 BERKELEY TECH. L.J. 1227 (2008); Clarissa Long, *Dilution*, 106 COLUM. L. REV. 1029 (2006).

[60] Schechter, *supra* note 12, at 825. "[D]ilution is the 'destruction of the uniqueness of a mark by its use on other goods.'" *Ibid.* at 823.

[61] *Ibid.* at 831.

[62] *Ibid.*

[63] *See* Sara Stadler Nelson, *The Wages of Ubiquity in Trademark Law*, 88 IOWA L. REV. 731, 791–92, 798–99 (2003); Elizabeth C. Bannon, *The Growing Risk of Self-Dilution*, 82 TRADEMARK REP. 570 (1992).

[64] *Ibid.*

and in turn as symbols of (desired) social status and (presumed) wealth, a value that should not be protected as a matter of public policy.[65]

These criticisms are certainly on point with respect to many trademarks that are today used on every imaginable product – from smart phone covers, to key chains, sun glasses, and so forth. But not all well-known trademarks' owners engage in this type of "value extracting" brand extensions, and embrace a mentality in which more profits become an equally relevant, or even more relevant, factor than the high quality of their products. This mentality (pun intended) frequently dominates among large companies, multinational corporations, and investment funds, for which the most important business objective seems to have become high profits at all costs, and thus larger volumes of sales to often unknown consumers worldwide.[66] In contrast, some small, mid-size, and at times also larger businesses, continue to follow a tradition of high quality, perhaps less quantity, and personalized attention to consumers – the same tradition that made their products, and their marks, well-known in the first place.[67] In this respect, the argument could be made that anti-dilution protection could be justified in the instances where such

[65] This non-functional and status-signaling effect of trademarks has been generally explained by recalling people's desire to signal wealth and social status "by conspicuous consumption." This effect is traditionally called the "Veblen effect" after American economist and sociologist Thorstein Veblen. *See* THORSTEIN VEBLEN, THE THEORY OF THE LEISURE CLASS (Houghton Mifflin 1973) (1899). *See also generally* Laurie Simon Bagwell & B. Douglas Bernheim, *Veblen Effects in a Theory of Conspicuous Consumption*, 86 AM. ECON. REV. 349 (1996). For additional criticism, see Jeremy N. Sheff, *Veblen Brands*, 96 MINN. L. REV. 769, 794 (2012); Jeffrey L. Harrison, *Trademark Law and Status Signaling: Tattoos for the Privileged*, 58 FLA. L. REV. 195, 210–26 (2007); Glynn S. Lunney, Jr., *Trademark Monopolies*, 48 EMORY L.J. 367, 404–408 (1999).

[66] *See* Michael J. Silverstein & Neil Fiske, *Luxury for the Masses*, HARV. BUS. REV., Apr. 2003, at 48; *see also* Erin Shea, *54pc of Affluent Consumers Think Luxury Brands are Lowering Quality Standards: Ipsos*, LUXURY DAILY (May 2, 2013), http://www.luxurydaily.com/54pc-of-affluent-consumers-say-luxury-brands-lowered-quality-standards-ipsos/.

[67] Some of these companies are famous world-wide, such as Bruno Magli, a company known for the high quality of its footwear that are manufactured with meticulous detail and sold in company stores or in high-scale retailers. Others are niche-famous – like the luxury handbag designer Maddalena Marconi in my native Bologna. In general on the difference between mass-luxury and importance of high quality and uniqueness see Jean-Noël Kapferer, *Why Luxury Should not Delocalize: A Critique of a Growing Tendency*, March-April, EUROPEAN BUSINESS REVIEW 28 (2012); LUCIEN KARPIK, VALUING THE UNIQUE: THE

protection could promote the ability of these businesses to signal the higher quality of their products – in terms of materials, style, and techniques used in making these products.

In particular, should the owners of these well-known marks not be able to prevent free riders from making subpar, yet non-confusing, similar products or from using similar marks for unrelated products, these subpar or unrelated products could ultimately impact the ability of these producers to signal the higher-than-average quality of their products. In turn, this could deter these producers from investing in product quality, or could drive them out of the market, especially in the case of small businesses. In these instances, anti-dilution protection could fulfill a valuable social function as an incentive for these producers to maintain a high product quality, which could promote a culture of high product quality for competitors (in order to compete) and for the market in general – in other words, a race to the top in terms of high-quality products.[68] This race for high quality could have multiple positive effects for society, as products of high(er) quality are frequently made with higher health-, labor-, and environment-related standards compared to mass-produced lower quality products.[69] As a result, promoting and protecting high-quality products with anti-dilution provisions could bring

ECONOMICS OF SINGULARITIES (Princeton University Press, 2010, Nora Scoot translator).

[68] This argument has been highlighted by distinguished scholars. *See* Edward S. Rogers, *The Lanham Act and the Social Function of Trademarks*, 14 LAW & CONTEMP. PROBS. 173, 175 (1949) (arguing that without trademarks, "[t]here could be no pride of workmanship, no credit for good quality, no responsibility for bad."); WILLIAM M. LANDES & RICHARD A. POSNER, THE ECONOMIC STRUCTURE OF INTELLECTUAL PROPERTY LAW 168, 179 (2003) ("[A] firm with a valuable trademark will be reluctant to lower the quality of its brand because it would suffer a capital loss on its investment in the trademark. … [L]egal protection of trademarks encourages the production of higher-quality products.").

[69] In this respect, recent years have seen the arrival of, *inter alia*, the movement of "slow fashion" whose primary purpose is to raise awareness about the negative externalities of low quality products in the fashion industry. *See* ELIZABETH CLINE, OVERDRESSED: THE SHOCKINGLY HIGH COST OF CHEAP FASHION (2013); KATE FLETCHER & LYNDA GROSE, FASHION AND SUSTAINABILITY: DESIGN FOR CHANGE (2012). *See also* Jean-Noël Kapferer, *All That Glitters is Not Green: The Challenge of Sustainable Luxury,* Nov./Dec. EUR. BUS. REV. 40 (2010); Annamma Joy, John F. Sherry, Alladi Venkatesh, Jeff Wang & Ricky Chan, *Fast Fashion, Sustainability, and the Ethical Appeal of Luxury Brands*, 16 FASHION THEORY 273 (2012). "Luxury brands can become the leaders in sustainability because of their emphasis on artisanal quality." *Id.* at 291.

additional benefits in terms of incentivizing healthier and fairer production standards in general as a matter of public policy.[70]

A similar set of considerations applies to the debate on the *lex specialis* for GI protection. Criticisms similar to those against anti-dilution protection have been repeated, to a large extent, also with respect to anti-usurpation protection for GIs. In particular, opponents of this protection have argued that the overarching purpose of intellectual property rights is to incentivize innovation on a fixed term basis, which in turn cannot justify perpetual rewards for creation, such as the protection granted with GIs. Opponents have also repeated that protection against consumer confusion is adequate to provide sufficient market incentives to GI-denominated products – additional protection unnecessarily restricts market competition and ultimately is a subsidy and a tool to protect local markets.[71] As I indicated in Part III, this critique is particularly on point for GIs identifying products that are not exclusively made in the GI-denominated region.[72] Notably, as I have argued before, anti-usurpation protection (and GI protection in general), is certainly questionable when GI-denominated products do not effectively and exclusively derive from the GI-denominated regions. In these instances, GIs cannot fulfill their function of providing consumers accurate information regarding the GI-denominated products and can lead, in turn, to giving consumers misleading information about the actual origin of the products, or their ingredients.

Still, when products come from the GI-denominated territory, the criticism that anti-usurpation protection represents a subsidy, or marketing tool, for GI-denominated products is not so compelling. The argument could instead be made that anti-usurpation protection provides unique benefits in

---

[70] Should these marks not be protected against dilution, their function of signaling reliable positive messages about the health-, labor-, and environment-related standards that they use could be also impaired. *See* Stephanie Clifford, *Some Retailers Reveal Where And How That T-Shirt Is Made*, N.Y. TIMES, May 9, 2013, at A1; Annamma Joy et al., *Fast Fashion, Sustainability, and the Ethical Appeal of Luxury Brands*, 16 FASHION THEORY 273, 291 (2012) ("Luxury brands can become the leaders in sustainability because of their emphasis on artisanal quality."); Kirsi Niinimäki, *Eco-Clothing, Consumer Identity and Ideology*, 18 SUSTAINABLE DEVELOPMENT 150 (2010); Barbara Mihm, *Fast Fashion in a Flat World: Global Sourcing Strategies*, 9 INT'L BUS. & ECON. RES. J. 55 (2010); Donald N. Sull & Stefano Turconi, *Fast Fashion Lessons*, 19 BUS. STRAT. REV. 4 (Summer 2008). For a similar argument in the context of patent law, see Derclaye, *supra* note 5, at 194 (turning to "happiness" as a motivator to incentivize certain types of inventions versus others).

[71] *See* Raustiala & Munzer, *supra* note 5, at 351.

[72] *See* Calboli, *Expanding Protection*, *supra* note 52, at 200–203.

terms of economic incentives granted to local communities and the international community should consider extending this protection beyond GIs for wines and spirits, as indicated in Articles 23 and 24 of TRIPS. In particular, since GIs motivate regional producers to create and maintain social capital and value for the entire group operating within that region,[73] anti-usurpation protection may permit GI beneficiaries to prevent free-riders from capturing some of this value by producing similar, yet non-confusing but also non-authentic (and potentially tarnishing), versions of the authentic products.[74] As regional producers bear the cost of developing and maintaining the reputation of GI-denominated products, they are vulnerable to free riders who piggyback off of this reputation.[75] Should GI beneficiaries not be able to prevent free riders, free riders could make subpar products with little concern regarding the impact that lower standards could have on the reputation of the GI-denominated products in the long term.[76] This, in turn, could tarnish the reputation of the GI-denominated products and directly impact the market for these products.

Moreover, it is undeniable that, in many instances, GI-denominated products are of higher quality compared with the type-level generic products.[77] Accordingly, a system of enhanced GI protection, including the prohibition to produce subpar products, could result in motivating outside producers to invest more in product quality in order to match (and compete with) the quality of GI-denominated products. In other words, enhanced GI protection could stimulate a "race to the top" in terms of product quality – the arrival of Australian and California wines as serious competitors of European wines proves this point, and so does the growth of local food movements in several countries, including the United States. Equally important, GI producers are generally aware of the importance of maintaining the well-beingness of their regions and the

---

[73] *See* Rangnekar, *supra* note 53, at 15–16. *See also* Dev Gangjee, *Geographical Indications and Cultural Heritage*, 4 WIPO Journal 92, 94–5 (2012) [hereinafter Gangjee, *GIs and Cultural Heritage*] (noting that "[t]hese geographical signs exhibit features of club goods, whereby the right to exclude is enjoyed by all members of the club").

[74] Rangnekar, *supra* note 53, at 9–10; Agdomar, *supra* note 52, at 578–580. *But see* Raustiala & Munzer, *supra* note 5, at 352–354, 361–364.

[75] Margaret Ritzert, *Champagne is from Champagne: An Economic Justification for Extending Trademark-Level Protection to Wine-Related Geographical Indicators*, 37 AIPLA Q.J. 191, 212–220 (2009).

[76] *See* Agdomar, *supra* note 52, at 586–587.

[77] *See* Emily C. Creditt, *Terroir vs. Trademarks: The Debate over Geographical Indication and Expansions to the TRIPS Agreement*, 11 Vand. J. Ent. & Tech. L. 425, 427 (2009).

land. Thus, they frequently adopt high quality production practices not only to maintain the reputation of their products, but also to safeguard the health of their regions. This frequently translates to higher respect for the environment, attention to public health-related concerns, and investment in local labor, including high skilled labor both to safeguard the traditional manufacturing techniques of GI-denominated products as well as to promote innovative techniques compatible with these traditions.[78] In this context, anti-usurpation provisions could incentivize these good practices in producing and distributing the GI-denominated products.[79] In turn, this could motivate outside producers to match these good practices for their own products, thus establishing a culture of good practices that would benefit consumers, the environment, public health, and labor practices also beyond GI-denominated regions.

Of course, anti-dilution and anti-usurpation protections do not come without costs for competition, and the recognition of enhanced protection over signs and geographical names invariably raises concerns, both with respect to competition and expressive uses of these signs. Accordingly, these enhanced protections should be applied carefully. In particular, anti-dilution protection for trademarks should remain a rare finding, as the confusion-based standard for infringement is sufficient in most instances to protect well-known marks against subpar copies and threats to a mark's uniqueness.[80] Anti-dilution protection should also be balanced with permitting unauthorized descriptive, comparative, non-commercial, and parody or free-speech-related uses of these marks by third parties.[81] The same considerations apply to anti-usurpation protection for GIs, as such protection may

---

[78] Agdomar, *supra* note 52, at 586–587. The argument is that asymmetrical information places the consumer in a weaker position because the consumer cannot optimize their choices due to the lack of a full set of information. GIs can serve to improve communication: they signal quality and expertise and enable consumers to distinguish between premium-quality products and low-end products.

[79] Rangneckar, *supra* note 53, at 13–14.

[80] The notion of "likelihood of consumer confusion" has also undergone a considerable expansion in the past decades. Today, it includes confusion as to the "control," "sponsorship," "endorsement," or "affiliation/association" with the marked products. In the United States, this expansion started as a judicial doctrine and was later incorporated into the statutory language with the 1988 Trademark Revision Act. *See* Lanham Act § 43(a), 15 U.S.C. § 1125(a) (2000).

[81] On these aspects, see Lisa P. Ramsey, *Increasing First Amendment Scrutiny of Trademark Law*, 61 SMU L. REV. 381 (2008). See also 15 U.S.C. § 1125(c)(3) (2006) "Exclusions" (listing specific exclusion from anti-dilution protection, including relating to non-commercial or expressive uses of well-known marks). The provision was introduced into the original text of Section 43(c) of the Lanham Act

also chill speech, particularly non-misleading commercial speech such as comparative advertising and descriptive uses of GIs, in addition to increasing barriers to entry for competitors.[82] This is precisely why, even under a system of anti-usurpation protection, competitors should be free to turn to GI terms accompanied by the terms "style," "like," or "type" to describe their own products, as long as such use does not engender consumer confusion as to the fact that these products are not the authentic products. Even though TRIPS directly excludes the use of these comparative terms for GIs identifying wines and spirits in Article 23,[83] an amendment to these provisions could (or should) be considered while implementing a system of enhanced protections for all GIs. Such amendment would certainly be difficult to pursue in practice, yet it seems necessary for a balanced system of GI protection.

Still, when these *leges speciales* are well administered under a system that guarantees the functioning of a competitive marketplace and the unauthorized (non-confusing) use of well-known marks and GIs for expression related-purpose, the provisions under consideration in this chapter do not seem to represent the threat otherwise described by critics. Instead, these provisions could become vehicles to fulfill important societal objectives such as promoting higher-quality products and higher respect for the environment. This, in turn, can foster both local development and a more sustainable development for society as a whole.

V. CONCLUSION

Since the adoption of TRIPS in 1994, concerns and skepticism have been expressed with respect to the growing role played by intellectual property

---

as part of the adoption of the Trademark Dilution Revision Act (TDRA) of 2006, Pub. L. No. 109-312, §§ 2, 3(e), §§ 43, 45, 120 Stat. 1730, 1733 (codified as amended at 15 U.S.C. §§ 1125, 1127) (effective Oct. 6, 2006).

[82] *See* Harry N. Niska, *The European Union Trips Over the U.S. Constitution: Can the First Amendment Save the Bologna That Has a First Name?*, 13 MINN. J. GLOBAL TRADE 413, 440–441.

[83] TRIPS, *supra* note 1, Art. 23.1. For example, this prohibition could be abolished as part of a compromise that would permit the expansion of anti-usurpation protection beyond GIs for wines and spirits. *But see* Council Directive 97/55, Art. 3a(1), 1997 O.J. (L 290) 18, 21 (EC). Article 3(a)1 states that "[c]omparative advertising shall, as far as the comparison is concerned, be permitted when the following conditions are met … (f) for products with designation of origin it relates in each case to products with the same designation" (excluding the possibility of comparing GI-denominated products and non-GI-denominated products).

law as corporate subsidies, as well as guarantors of a modern "sumptuary code."[84] In particular, few developments in trademark law have been more fiercely criticized than the adoption of Article 16.3 of TRIPS, and in turn the introduction of anti-dilution protection for well-known marks. The protection of GIs, particularly anti-usurpation protection for GIs identifying wines and spirits under Article 23 of TRIPS, has also traditionally been criticized as one of the most prominent areas in which intellectual property law is artificially building scarcity in the absence of confusion or deception for the public. More specifically, anti-dilution protection for trademarks and anti-usurpation protection for GIs have both been criticized as types of rights falling outside the traditional incentive-driven justification for intellectual property because neither type of protection promotes "more" products, "more" competition, and "more" innovation, but instead represents a barrier to entry, an incentive to capture more value in tradition instead of innovation and, in turn, a subsidy for corporate or local interests against a competitive marketplace.[85]

In this chapter, however, I have highlighted that, while these criticisms are valid, they frequently do not consider an important aspect of the debate – the *mentalité* of "high quality" products and "good-quality life" that distinguishes the countries and many of the constituencies that supported, and continue to support, both anti-dilution protection for trademarks and anti-usurpation protection for GIs. This *mentalité* played an important role in the introduction of these provisions. As such, understanding this *mentalité* remains crucial to rebalance the debate in these areas, not only in order to justify the adoption of these provisions, but also to remind the supporters of these provisions about the rationale behind their adoption. Notably, anti-dilution law aims at protecting the uniqueness of well-known marks, not well-known marks per se as objects and status symbols. Likewise, anti-usurpation protection for GIs aims at fostering local development, not at protecting GIs as a marketing tool for products not entirely produced in the GI-denominated regions.

---

84 I borrow the expression "sumptuary code" from Barton Beebe. *See* Beebe, *Sumptuary Code*, *supra* note 5, at 878–884. In this chapter, I have adopted views that may seem in contrast with Professor Beebe's position. Yet, I consider my position not to be antithetical, but rather complementary. In particular, Professor Beebe and I are considering the same legal developments perhaps with different eyes, but we both advocate for better standards for consumers, and express, likely differently, the same concerns for the concentration of intellectual property rights in the hands of certain intellectual property owners, generally large and multinational corporations.

85 *See* discussion and references *supra* Parts II & III.

Yet, when well-administered and enforced under a system guaranteeing against overreaching rights, anti-dilution protection for well-known trademarks and anti-usurpation protection for GIs could play a positive role not only for their beneficiaries, but also for society as a whole. In this respect, both sets of protections could effectively help promote a culture of "high-quality" products compared with products of lesser quality, which could in turn result in incentivizing higher product standards, and thus perhaps a "good-quality life," for everyone. As distinguished scholars have noted in different contexts, these *leges speciales* could even contribute to build that "good life and the sort of society that would facilitate its widespread realization."[86] Accordingly, even though the terms "high quality" or "good life" remain difficult to pinpoint (and have different meanings to different audiences), it is important to acknowledge this *mentalité* as a legitimate component of the debates over the *leges speciales* at issue.

Against the arguments brought forward by the opponents of these provisions – generally based on a law and economic reading of intellectual property incentives as tools to foster "more" products, "more" competition, and "more" free-riding – "more" may not necessarily be a "better" option for society as a whole when it comes to defining what constitutes a "good-quality life." To the contrary, "more good-quality" products may be a more desirable choice for the public, even though this choice may imply "less quantity." Despite the skepticism of opponents of the provisions at issue, "high-quality" products are also often made with "more" attention to the manufacturing process – whether based on traditional or new techniques – including the ingredients and materials used, and often labor and environmental-related standards. In contrast, "more" products often implies lower quality products, with shorter product life. This generally results in faster production cycles, which almost invariably adopt questionable production standards (particularly in the absence of a culture of "more" in terms of stricter quality requirements, higher transparency in product labelling, etc.). In this respect, the provisions at issue favoring the protection and the promotion of "high-quality" products could offset some of the negative externalities brought forward by a commercial model based on "more" products and fast production cycles. Accordingly, considering the *mentalité* of "good-quality life" behind these provisions could contribute an important point of view to the debate over the values to be protected by intellectual property law.

---

86 William W. Fisher III, *Reconstructing the Fair Use Doctrine*, 101 HARV. L. REV. 1659, 1664 (1998) (*also cited* by Beebe, *Sumptuary Code*, *supra* note 5, at 887, n. 429).

9. Provocations and challenges concerning enforcement and civil procedure in IP

Kimberlee Weatherall*

1. INTRODUCTION

Prosaic as they may seem, the rules of evidence, standards and burdens of proof, and provisional remedies, as well as the rules which govern the progress of cases and the conduct of trials, could well have a very significant effect on how punitive IP is in practice.[1] These rules matter, both for the parties involved in litigation and for the health of the IP system as a whole. Well-designed litigation procedures can make the whole IP system work, but bad design can generate more litigation and costs, and undermine IP's positive effects. This chapter argues that important things are happening, both internationally and domestically, in civil and criminal procedure and remedies specifically relating to IP, and that IP scholars need to pay more attention to these developments.

More importantly, this volume addresses the question whether IP is a *lex specialis*: a specialised set of rules; a kind unto itself; separate to and different from other bodies of law. One purpose of asking this question is to explore whether doctrines and ideas from other bodies of scholarship can assist us to resolve problems and puzzles in IP. Developments in the civil procedure of IP law may be critiqued using implements from outside the usual IP toolbox. The requirement in international IP instruments that procedures for the enforcement of IP are 'fair and equitable'

* Associate Professor, Sydney Law School. The author acknowledges the able research assistance of Neha Kasbekar, comments from participants at the ATRIP Annual Congress of 2013 and David Starkoff, and the research support of the Legal Scholarship Support Fund at the University of Sydney.

[1] William R. Cornish, Josef Drexl, Reto Hilty and Annette Kur, 'Procedures and Remedies for enforcing IPRs: the European Commission's proposed Directive' (2003) 25 *EIPR* 447, 448.

provides a point of intersection between human rights law, civil procedure and IP, where thinking from outside IP scholarship can be used in ways that could be helpful.

2. DEVELOPMENTS IN CIVIL PROCEDURE IN IP AND THE NEED FOR OUTSIDE PERSPECTIVES

Enforcement procedures only really entered the international IP system 20 years ago, with the conclusion of the *Agreement on Trade-Related Aspects of Intellectual Property Rights* (TRIPS).[2] The Berne and Paris Conventions both leave general enforcement and remedial measures as matters for domestic law and policy,[3] with one important exception: requiring that member states give authorities the power to seize infringing copies.[4] Having 'debuted' in TRIPS, enforcement provisions have become more and more detailed in successive international instruments. In the early 2000s, a series of bilateral and regional preferential ('free') trade agreements, particularly those negotiated by the US and EU, contained a scattergun collection of specific provisions on enforcement beyond the rules found in TRIPS. The *Anti-Counterfeiting Trade Agreement* (ACTA), concluded in late 2010, is more systematic and comprehensive: it contains extensive provisions on matters of proof such as rights to information in the possession of infringers and intermediaries; provisional and border measures; final remedies; criminal liability; online enforcement and more. Despite (or rather because of) the less-than-enthusiastic reception of ACTA, the range of procedural innovations the US contemplated in early proposals for the Trans-Pacific Partnership

[2] Cf. the document produced by the Secretariat of the Negotiating Group on Trade-Related Aspects of Intellectual Property Rights, including Trade in Counterfeit Goods during the TRIPS negotiations, which purports to describe provisions of the international agreements on IP enforcement: Document MTN.GNMG/NG11/W/18 (10 February 1988). Closer reading reveals that most provisions summarised are better characterised as dealing with substantive rights (e.g., to control imports).

[3] *Berne Convention for the Protection of Literary and Artistic Works*, opened for signature 9 September 1886, 1161 UNTS 30 (entered into force 5 December 1887) ('Berne Convention') Art 5, Art 6*bis*(3) and 10*bis*(1); *Paris Convention for the Protection of Industrial Property*, signed on 20 March 1883, 828 UNTS 305 (Stockholm revision entered into force 26 March 1970) ('Paris Convention') (Paris is largely silent on enforcement in general).

[4] Berne Convention Arts 16(1) and (2); 13(3); Paris Convention Arts 10, 10*bis*, 10*ter*.

Agreement (TPP) was even more extensive.[5] These developments are unusual when compared with areas of commercial regulation outside IP. International treaties do not, in general, tell states how to run legal proceedings in corporate law, or tort, or real property; despite Article 41(5) of TRIPS, it seems that international IP treaties increasingly do intrude on these domestic concerns.

There have also been ongoing innovations in IP enforcement at a domestic level. Australia, for example, has in the last decade completely revised its criminal provisions in copyright and trade mark;[6] broadened the available presumptions for proving subsistence and ownership of IP;[7] and revised its border measures to allow for seizure and destruction of alleged infringing goods without consent and without any court process.[8] In 2011 the US *Stop Online Piracy Act* ('SOPA') proposed privatised enforcement procedures that would have seen more emphasis on privatised forms of online enforcement and less court involvement. Rules relating to IP litigation and enforcement procedure have become more specialised over time: many countries are not only developing distinct procedural rules for IP cases, but in some cases have created specialised courts and/or judicial officers.[9] Although this could also be said in other

---

[5] The Trans-Pacific Partnership Agreement is a proposed regional trade agreement between Australia, Brunei Darussalam, Canada, Chile, Malaysia, Mexico, New Zealand, Peru, Singapore, the United States, Japan and Vietnam. For an analysis of a (leaked) US proposal for the IP chapter, see Kimberlee Weatherall, *An Australian Analysis of the February 2011 Leaked US TPPA IP Chapter Text – Copyright and Enforcement* (July 2011) SelectedWorks <http://works.bepress.com/kimweatherall/22>; Sean Flynn et al., 'The US Proposal for an Intellectual Property Chapter in the Trans-Pacific Partnership Agreement' (2012) 28 *American University International Law Review* 105. For an analysis of the enforcement provisions of a later leaked draft IP chapter, see Kimberlee Weatherall, *TPP – Australian Section-by-Section Analysis of the Enforcement Provisions of the August Leaked Draft* (November 2013) SelectedWorks <http://works.bepress.com/kimweatherall/27>.

[6] *Copyright Amendment Act 2006* (Cth), Sch 1; *Intellectual Property Laws Amendment (Raising the Bar) Act 2012* (Cth) Sch 5.

[7] *Copyright Amendment Act 2006* (Cth) Sch 2.

[8] *Intellectual Property Laws Amendment (Raising the Bar) Act 2012* (Cth), Sch 5.

[9] See, e.g., Rochelle Dreyfuss, 'The Federal Circuit: A Case Study in Specialized Courts' (1989) 64 *New York University Law Review* 1; Rochelle Dreyfuss, 'Forums of the Future: The Role of Specialised Courts in Resolving Business Disputes' (1995) 61 *Brooklyn Law Review* 1; Rochelle Dreyfuss, 'The Federal Court: A Continuing Experiment in Specialization' (2004) 54 *Western Case Law Review* 769.

areas of law (many legal systems have specialised family law courts, or abbreviated procedures in certain kinds of disputes, for example in construction law), the shape of those specialised developments in IP and their intersection with international developments makes scrutiny worthwhile. Given continued policy attention to the challenges of enforcement, there is every reason to believe that developments in procedure and remedies in IP, both international and domestic, will continue.

IP scholars could safely leave matters procedural to scholars procedural if these developments were generalised across different areas of law or even across commercial areas of law. However, the regular appearance of extensive enforcement provisions in international IP negotiations requires certain domestic procedures *exclusively* in IP.[10] As such, these issues are at least partially the responsibility of IP scholars.

How, then, should we analyse these developments? Adopting an internal perspective, we could try using the analytical tools of IP scholarship: that is, looking at the impact of procedural innovations on whether the substantive goals of IP law are achieved.[11] Assuming that the substantive goal of IP law is utilitarian – that is, to provide incentives for investment in creation and distribution – we could assess the impact of procedures and remedies on those incentives. Or taking IP law's goal of protecting creators' personality interests, we could evaluate the accessibility of enforcement to individuals asserting personal connections with their creative output. We could consider procedural rules' effects on the diffusion of knowledge and innovation, or, perhaps, in the case of registered rights such as patents or trade marks, their impact on the accuracy and usefulness of the register.[12]

---

[10] Some recent international negotiations have also made considerable inroads into administrative procedure – e.g. the grant of patents and trade marks. These provisions are not addressed here.

[11] Another approach in the procedural justice literature seeks to assess whether procedure improves the accuracy of the application of the law (without looking to more general goals). As Bone points out, however, given that 100 per cent accuracy in the application of law is not possible, there will always be a trade-off between the costs of improving application and the benefits – meaning we always end up coming back to a need to assess how important the particular rules are – bringing us back to policies and not just black-letter law: Roger Bone, 'Procedure, Participation, Rights' (2010) 90 *Boston U L Rev* 1011.

[12] See, e.g., the literature on standards for assessing patents at examination and litigation stages, such as Mark Lemley, 'Rational Ignorance at the Patent Office' (2001) 95 *Northwestern University Law Review* 1495.

One problem with this approach is that IP scholars (and stakeholders) divide on the (relative) importance of these various theoretical justifications: we could easily end up going around in circles. Even if we could agree on theoretical justifications, and wanted to analyse the impact of enforcement procedures on those justifications, most of the questions raised are unanswerable. Only the utilitarian theory lends itself to any kind of quantitative measurement, and attempting to calculate the impact of any given procedural innovation *on incentives* to create, or even profits, is a complex task, because it is difficult to isolate that effect from other variables affecting creative businesses. The measurement problems here are *hard.* Even if we confine ourselves to asking whether the 'special' nature of IP justifies differential procedural treatment, there are problems. Although policy debates are filled with assertions from IP owners that IP is 'particularly difficult' to enforce, the accuracy of such assertions is an open question. We have never examined whether there are *more* difficulties with enforcement or *more* infringement of rights in IP than in other areas. How would you even measure whether there is more IP infringement than, say, commercial fraud, or use of illicit substances? One way to get at some of these questions might be to ask commercial firms where IP issues rank in their list of problems as compared with, say, navigating tax law or other areas of regulation: but little research of this kind has been done and it is hard to do well. The usual method is to survey businesses, but within any given firm, different people are likely to deal with these different legal and commercial issues and the answer you get on a survey will likely depend on who fills in the form.[13]

But there are deeper problems with relying on our traditional IP analytical tools to assess developments in enforcement. Naturally, the jurisprudence concerning justice in civil procedure has its own internal divides, but although some commentators accept accurate application of the substantive law and promotion of its values as the appropriate

[13] For an attempt of this kind, see A. Leahy, D. MacLaren, D. Morgan, K. Weatherall, E. Webster and J. Yong, 'In the Shadow of the China-Australia FTA Negotiations: What Australian Business Thinks about IP' (2008) 27 (1) *Economic Papers* 1. Another interesting attempt to get at the issues indirectly looks at whether infringement is seen as a significant investment risk: see Jonathan Band and Jonathan Gerafi, 'Infringement Risk in Copyright-Intensive Industries' (2014), available at http://infojustice.org/archives/31827.

measure of 'procedural justice',[14] there is a strong strain in the procedural literature contending that there are process values not reducible to the simple question, 'Is the law applied as written?' According to this strain in the literature, achieving substantive legal goals is not the only goal of procedure. These commentators contend that there are other important values that need to be incorporated into design of legal procedure. Such values include facilitating participation by plaintiffs *and* defendants, so that they are invested in the result even if adverse to their interests.[15]

The literature on procedure is notable for its recognition of the interests of *all* parties to legal proceedings. Defendants as well as plaintiffs have a stake in appropriate procedure, impartial treatment and the right to be involved in processes that affect their interests. By comparison, IP theory has little to say, in general, about the infringer or their concerns. Sometimes infringers' concerns may be important: when they are themselves a creator seeking to 'stand on the shoulders of giants', for example, or when they are a technology innovator (like the inventors or sellers of video recorders or online communication services) such that arguments about 'encouraging creativity' must acknowledge their position. But infringers as individuals with personhood interests of their own regardless of their creativity, or as companies with legitimate businesses to run, are largely invisible to most IP theory except as mere objects of regulation. At most they enter our frame at a larger, societal scale: as blips or datapoints within a global assessment of the IP system's costs and benefits. IP theory has little to say about justice to a particular defendant whose assets may have been confiscated or whose house might be sold to pay a damages claim, or who may be faced with a bewildering pile of paperwork to reclaim goods seized at the border, if the overall effect of such rules is to streamline or improve IP enforcement.

Perhaps this is why we need the tools of procedural thinkers: so as not to miss something important about the role, and individual personhood and interests, of the defendant and other parties affected by IP enforcement. If we focus only on a gross-level calculation of the 'IP costs and benefits' of stronger enforcement procedures (such as seizure of infringing copies or intrusive information-gathering exercises), we could end up

---

[14] See e.g. Roger Bone, 'Making Effective Rules: The Need for Procedure Theory' (2008) 61 *Oklahoma Law Review* 319; Bone, above n 11.

[15] R.S. Summers, 'Evaluating and Improving Legal Processes – A Plea for "Process Values"' (1974) 60 *Cornell Law Review* 1; Lawrence Solum, 'Procedural Justice' (2004) 78 *Southern California Law Review* 181.

justifying some very troubling procedural innovations and we risk treating defendants as mere means to an IP end.

Even leaving deep theoretical questions to one side, turning to jurisprudence in civil procedure and human rights has rhetorical advantages. Despite the obvious free speech and privacy issues that are raised in online copyright enforcement, it can sometimes be difficult to argue for the free speech or privacy interests of 'pirates'. As Horten has shown, in at least one regional dispute over copyright and telecommunications law reform that we know of, it was the right to a fair trial and due process which became central to the debate around the appropriate scope of copyright-owners' powers and tools for enforcement online.[16] It seems that a fair trial and due process are more obviously unqualified goods: even criminals should get due process.

A second advantage of turning to the tools developed by civil procedure scholars is that many recent international IP instruments require IP enforcement procedures to be 'fair and equitable'. Here the requirements of fair process may have a distinct advantage over other human rights as a tool for critique. Major human rights instruments embodying rights such as the right to freedom of expression or privacy tend not to be incorporated into trade agreements – but IP instruments are.[17] Reading procedural protections into trade agreements creates an opening for a country to complain of contraventions in the context of its trade relations and, at least in theory (and subject to discussion of the practicalities below), complain of violations using trade dispute settlement procedures.

---

[16] Monica Horten, *The Copyright Enforcement Enigma: Internet Politics and the 'Telecoms Package'* (Palgrave Macmillan 2012) chapter 12. Horten outlines how rights to due process and a fair trial moved to the centre of debates over proposals to impose enforcement obligations on telecommunications and internet access providers in a detailed history of EU directives concerning the revision of telecommunications regulation.

[17] Rights to privacy and data protection laws are sometimes mentioned: see e.g. ACTA Art 4. That article is, however, negatively expressed: ACTA does *not* require disclosure of information where such disclosure would be contrary to local law or international agreements. ACTA Art 27 is the strongest provision of this kind and is positively expressed, specifying that enforcement procedures relating to infringement of copyright over digital networks 'shall be implemented in a manner that … *consistent with that Party's law*, preserves fundamental principles such as freedom of expression, fair process, and privacy': Art 27(2). The reference to local law, however, means these values are not justiciable at an international level.

3. FAIR AND EQUITABLE PROCEDURES

3.1 The Legal Obligation to Enact 'Fair and Equitable' Procedures and its Interpretation

Recent IP treaties have included a requirement that enforcement procedures be 'fair and equitable' in addition to specific limitations embedded in text granting procedural rights.[18] The exact wording and context of this obligation varies from instrument to instrument. The key multilateral obligations are found in TRIPS Art 41(2), which requires member states to ensure that enforcement procedures are 'fair and equitable', followed by the more explicit requirement that procedures 'shall not be unnecessarily complicated or costly, or entail unreasonable time-limits or unwarranted delays'. Article 41 contains several more procedure-related provisions, including a preference for written decisions; a requirement that parties be heard on evidence used to make decisions; and opportunities for judicial review and appeal. Article 42, which bears the title 'fair and equitable procedures', requires that civil judicial procedures be available to right-holders to enforce any IP right, and then outlines a number of subsidiary requirements of fairness and equity during the pre-trial and trial phases of litigation: namely, the provision of timely and sufficiently detailed notice to the defendant; the availability of representation by independent legal counsel; the absence of 'overly-burdensome requirements' concerning mandatory personal appearances; the opportunity to substantiate claims and present all relevant evidence; and the institution of procedural safeguards to identify and protect confidential information. Notably, Art 41 applies to all parties involved in an IP enforcement dispute: it therefore applies to defendants, although claims within WTO processes under Art 41 to date have related to access to enforcement procedures for rights-holders.[19]

---

[18] For an example of more specific procedural rights included in IP treaties, see TRIPS Article 50(4), which requires notice without delay to parties affected by provisional measures adopted *inaudita altera parte*, and a right to review and to be heard on the application of such measures. Other similar 'embedded' limitations include TRIPS Art 50(6) (revocation of provisional measures on the request of the defendant); Art 51 (requiring the defendant to be notified immediately on suspension of goods by customs); and Art 55 (limiting the duration of suspension).

[19] Namely, the Havana Club case (*United States – Section 211 Omnibus Appropriations Act of 1998* – WTO document WT/DS176/AB/R); the complaint brought the US/Australia in *EC – Protection of Trademarks and GIs* WTO

Both the most recent plurilateral agreement negotiated on IP enforcement, ACTA, and the European Union's *Directive 2004/48/EC of the European Parliament and of the Council of 29 April 2004 on the enforcement of intellectual property rights*[20] ('IPRED I') in Arts 6(2) and 3(1) respectively, echo the TRIPS language that enforcement procedures must be fair and equitable and not be unnecessarily complicated or costly, or entail unreasonable time-limits or unwarranted delays without repeating all the specific requirements in TRIPS Arts 41 or 42.[21] ACTA and IPRED I both contain a further provision concerning proportionality, not found in TRIPS except in certain specific provisions.[22] ACTA articulates an additional requirement that procedures 'provide for the rights of all participants subject to such procedures to be appropriately protected' (without elaborating further on which rights might be relevant).

Not all international agreements dealing with IP enforcement include an obligation to ensure procedures are fair and equitable.[23] The IP

---

document WT/DS174/R and the complaints (settled during consultations) submitted by the US against Sweden (WT/DS86/1) and Argentina (WT/DS196) concerning the availability of provisional measures in civil enforcement cases.

[20] OJ L 194 02/06/2004 P.0016-0025 ('IPRED I').

[21] This obligation in Art 6(2) of ACTA is confined to the implementation of ACTA. The obligation in TRIPS is stated in more general terms, requiring that *any* procedures aimed at IP enforcement meet the standard of being 'fair and equitable'. In IPRED I, the obligation is general in the sense that parties are obliged under the directive to 'provide for the measures, procedures and remedies necessary to ensure the enforcement of the intellectual property rights covered by this Directive', and it is *these* procedures which must be fair and equitable. The obligation in IPRED I would therefore not seem to be confined to the particular enforcement procedures laid out in the directive itself, but to any procedures deemed 'necessary' to ensure enforcement of IP.

[22] ACTA Article 6.3; IPRED I (above n 20) Art 3.2. TRIPS contains references to proportionality in a provision on destruction of infringing copies and implements (Art 46) and the right of information (Art 47). The obligation regarding proportionality differs in strength as between IPRED I and ACTA. IPRED I (Art 3.2) requires measures, procedures and remedies to be 'effective, *proportionate* and dissuasive'. ACTA contains a lesser requirement that parties implementing ACTA '*take into account the need for proportionality* between the seriousness of the infringement, the interests of third parties, and the applicable measures, remedies and penalties'. A disproportionate measure could breach IPRED I but comply with ACTA if proportionality was considered but prioritised below other goals such as deterrence.

[23] However, note that parties to these agreements remain subject to the general obligations in TRIPS.

chapters of preferential trade agreements negotiated by the US in 2000–07 set out detailed obligations concerning enforcement, but do not have general safeguards. The *WIPO Copyright Treaty* Art 14(2) and Art 23(2) of the *WIPO Performances and Phonograms Treaty* follow the pattern of the Berne and Paris Conventions of requiring in the broadest possible term that a contracting party ensure that effective enforcement procedures are available.

Two questions of interpretation arise on the recent texts requiring fair and equitable procedures. The first is whether this obligation has any content beyond the specific elaborations found in those agreements and in TRIPS Articles 41 and 42. The second, interrelated issue is assuming there *is* room for additional content, whether it is legitimate to turn to other bodies of jurisprudence, such as that which has developed under human rights instruments obligations to provide a right to a fair trial, or even domestic understandings of 'due process'; to reach beyond the *lex specialis* to the *lex generalis*.

On one view, the obligation to provide fair and equitable treatment is codified in TRIPS Articles 41 and 42. Under Art 41 of TRIPS:

- decisions on the merits should preferably be in writing and reasoned;
- decisions should be made available 'at least' to the parties without undue delay;
- decisions on the merits must be based only on evidence on which the parties were offered the opportunity to be heard; and
- judicial review must be available in respect of final administrative decisions; appeals from trial court decisions are also required at least on points of law.

Art 42 provides:

- an obligation to make civil judicial procedures to rights-holders;
- a right of the defendant to written notice and timely and sufficiently detailed information inclusive of relevant facts and the legal basis for the claim;[24]

[24] While timeliness is contingent on the specifics of a case, the principle of efficiency in Art 41.2 leans against an overly generous interpretation of the concept. Commonly considered criteria include 'the extent and complexity of the procedure, the domicile of the defendant and the potential necessity of employing a legal representative': Vander, *infra.* n. 31, 704. A possible baseline period for straightforward cases could be a minimum term of 14 days: ibid., 705.

- a right for the defendant to independently selected legal representation for all activities and in all procedural stages;[25]
- an obligation on the state not to impose onerous requirements for personal appearances by parties in the proceedings;
- the right (of all parties) to present relevant evidence; and
- the protection of confidential information, subordinate to any contrary constitutional requirements.[26]

This is an elaborate list. Interestingly, neither ACTA[27] nor IPRED I repeat this list – a fact that could suggest that the drafters of these later instruments were treating the obligation to provide 'fair and equitable' procedures as comprehending this list of requirements and no more.

Gervais explicitly treats Art 42 as a codification of the Art 41(2) obligation.[28] His approach seems to be endorsed, less explicitly, by Correa,[29] Taubman[30] and Vander,[31] who confine their discussion of Art 41(2) to an examination of Art 42. This approach receives some support from the TRIPS *travaux preparatoires*. During early negotiations, states put forward lists of procedural protections they considered necessary,[32]

---

[25] Vander, *infra*. n. 31, 705.

[26] For example, a prohibition against secrecy in civil procedures has a constitutional basis in some South American countries and in South East Asia. See Vander, *infra*. n. 31, 707.

[27] Noting the absence of limitations embedded into the procedural provisions of ACTA, see Kamperman-Sanders et al., *The Anti-Counterfeiting Trade Agreement (ACTA): An Assessment* (Directorate-General for External Policies Policy Department, 2011), 48.

[28] Daniel Gervais, *The TRIPS Agreement: Drafting History and Analysis* (Sweet & Maxwell, 3rd ed., 2008) 441.

[29] Carlos M. Correa, *Trade-Related Aspects of Intellectual Property Rights: A Commentary on the TRIPS Agreement* (Oxford University Press, 2007) 413–18.

[30] Antony Taubman, *A Practical Guide to Working with TRIPS* (Oxford University Press, 2011) 112–13.

[31] Sascha Vander, 'Section 1: General Obligations' in Peter-Tobias Stoll, Jan Busche and Katrin Arend (eds), *Trade-Related Aspects of Intellectual Property Rights* (Martinus Nijhoff, 2009) vol 7, 692.

[32] The following documents are particularly important: US proposal dated 13 October 1988 (MTN.GNG/NG11/W/14/Rev.1) pp12ff; European Communities proposal dated 30 May 1989 (MTN.GNG/NG11/W/31) pp4–5; Submission from Canada dated 5 September 1989 (MTN.GNG/NG11/W/42); Communication from India dated 5 September 1989 (MTN.GNG/NG11/W/40); Proposal by Japan dated 12 September 1989 (MTN.GNG/NG11/W/43); Communication from the Republic of Korea dated 26 October 1989 (MTN.GNG/NG11/W/48). See also the Synoptic Table produced by the Secretariat on enforcement provisions

under various rubrics from 'due process' to 'natural justice and fair play'.[33] A majority of the specific protections mentioned in these early discussions came to be enumerated in Articles 41 and 42, and the most obvious omission, a requirement that foreign and domestically produced goods be subject to the same procedures, is covered by TRIPS Art 3 (national treatment).

On the other hand, not all commentators think that the list in Art 42 confines the scope of Art 41.2. Bronckers, Verkade and McNelis state that 'the requirement that enforcement procedures should be fair and equitable is a very general principle, corresponding to principles enshrined in the human rights conventions, and elaborated in more detail both in those conventions as well as in further articles of the enforcement provisions, particularly in Article 42.'[34]

A procedure could tick every box in Articles 41 and 42 and still be unfair or inequitable. This becomes clearer if we look at other related international provisions. Article 14 of the *International Covenant on Civil and Political Rights*, embodying the human right to a fair trial, provides (in relation to civil proceedings) that:

> 1. *All persons shall be equal before the courts and tribunals.* In the determination of … his rights and obligations in a suit at law, everyone shall be entitled to a *fair and public hearing by a competent, independent and impartial tribunal established by law.* The Press and the public may be excluded from all or part of a trial for reasons of morals, public order (*ordre public*) or national security in a democratic society, or when the interest of the private lives of the parties so requires, or to the extent strictly necessary in the opinion of the court in special circumstances where publicity would prejudice the interests of justice; but any judgement rendered… in a suit at law shall be made public except where the interest of juvenile persons otherwise requires or the proceedings concern matrimonial disputes or the guardianship of children [emphasis added].

Article 6 of the *European Convention on Human Rights*[35] sets out a 'right to a fair trial' in similar terms. These texts provide two additional

---

dated 7 June 1989 (MTN.GNG/NG11/W/33) which collects and synthesises the early Japanese, EC and US proposals.

[33] The early US and Japanese proposals (cited in preceding footnote) use 'due process'. 'Natural justice and fair play' comes from the Indian proposal.

[34] M.C.E.J. Bronckers, D.W.F. Verkade and N.M. McNelis, *TRIPs Agreement: Enforcement of Intellectual Property Rights* (European Communities, 2000) 33.

[35] *Convention for the Protection of Human Rights and Fundamental Freedoms*, opened for signature 4 November 1950, 213 UNTS 221 (entered into force

requirements beyond TRIPS Art 42. Fair trial requires *equality before courts and tribunals* and an entitlement to a hearing before *an independent and impartial tribunal established by law*.[36] Both would be useful additions to our armoury in assessing recent and potential future procedural innovations. It is possible that some possible streamlined structures for online copyright enforcement, in particular graduated response using private forms of arbitration, could breach a requirement that rights be determined by a 'competent, independent and impartial tribunal':[37] although much would depend on the particular rules and whether they preserve access to the courts. Arguments that were put before the Constitutional Council in France against the original version of its law for the termination of the internet access of file-sharers[38] could be reframed as breaching the requirement for a competent, independent and impartial tribunal. It is not hard to imagine other circumstances in which, seeking expeditious and effective enforcement procedures, policymakers might, in the construction of expert administrative tribunals, skirt the boundaries between expertise and partiality by appointing experts with a real or perceived interest in the subject matter of enforcement. The ICCPR's conception of the right to a fair trial stands as a reminder of the permissible limits of such attempts.

Perhaps more important is the concept, stated in the very first sentence of ICCPR Art 14, that all persons shall be equal before the courts and tribunals. Equality in procedure is a concept explored in the literature concerning

---

3 September 1953), as amended by *Protocol No 14 to the Convention for the Protection of Human Rights and Fundamental Freedoms, Amending the Control System of the Convention*, opened for signature 13 May 2004, CETS No 194 (entered into force 1 June 2010).

[36] It is arguable that one aspect of the right to a competent, independent and impartial tribunal established by law is reflected in TRIPS Art 41.4, which requires review by a judicial authority of final administrative decisions: even if a tribunal failed to meet the ICCPR standard, the judicial authority on appeal would likely comply.

[37] See generally Nic Suzor and Brian Fitzgerald, 'The legitimacy of graduated response schemes in copyright law' (2011) 34 *UNSW Law Journal* 1; Annemarie Bridy, 'Graduated Response American Style: "Six Strikes" Measured Against Five Norms' (2012) 23 *Fordham Intellectual Property, Media and Entertainment Law Journal* 1; Mary LaFrance, 'Graduated Response by Industry Compact: Piercing the Black Box' (2012) 30 *Cardozo Arts & Entertainment Law Journal* 165, 183.

[38] *Loi 2009-1311 du 28 octobre 2009 relative à la protection pénale de la propriété littéraire et artistique sur internet* Arts 6 and 7, 251 Journal Officiel de la République Française, 29 October 2009, 18290.

procedural justice. One way to understand this concept of equality is as a requirement of even-handedness: courts and legal institutions should treat competing interests equally and show equal concern for opposing litigants. As Zuckerman has articulated such a requirement:

> The machinery of justice, the process by which rights are enforced, must not, for instance, confer an advantage on one litigant at the expense of another litigant, who has a claim to equal respect. It must not favour defendants over plaintiffs, or vice versa, just as it must not favour the state over private litigants.[39]

One problem with recent developments in IP procedure is that a single-minded focus on effective and efficient enforcement can lead to reforms that systematically favour IP owners. Strong presumptions that copyright subsists, or that patents or trade marks are validly granted, could violate this requirement.[40] ACTA's provisions on provisional measures (which lack procedural safeguards) arguably provide a systematic advantage to IP owners.[41]

More broadly, some innovations in border enforcement could violate a principle of equality. A full analysis would require more space, but can be briefly summarised. As Zuckerman argues, provisional measures of all kinds must necessarily favour one side or the other, because you have to act as if one side or the other will win the case on the merits.[42] Seizure at the border gives an IP owner part of their remedy in advance of proving their case, and interferes, perhaps irreversibly, with the defendant's rights to their property and to conduct their business without interruption. It also creates leverage: an IP owner's consent to release of goods becomes a bargaining chip in negotiations. *Failure* to seize alleged infringing

---

39 A.A.S. Zuckerman, 'Interlocutory Remedies in Quest of Procedural Fairness' (1993) 56 *Modern Law Review* 325, 325.

40 Not all presumptions would violate a requirement of even-handedness: simple rebuttable presumptions may convey little forensic advantage and may therefore be considered fair; on the other hand, strong presumptions (or even irrebuttable presumptions) could convey considerable forensic advantage on a party and hence 'tilt the balance' too far to be considered equitable. Or consider s 115(5)–(6) of Australia's *Copyright Act 1968* (Cth), which allows an Australian court, in a case of online infringement, to 'have regard' to the fact that infringements beyond those proven are likely to have occurred. Does this put an onus on the defendant to prove the *absence* of broader infringement, and, if so, does that make a copyright-owner's case easier to prove in a way that is more than academic or theoretical?

41 See Kamperman-Sanders et al., above n 27.

42 Zuckerman above n 39.

goods at the border, however, gives the importer a partial 'win' and the power to affect the plaintiff's interests, maybe permanently, because it will be hard, perhaps impossible, to retrace all the goods and get them out of the market and prevent them harming the plaintiff's business and reputation. The TRIPS framework for seizures weighs the process in favour of the IP owner, but a concern with even-handedness should lead us to minimise the risks of severe or incorrect interference with the importer's rights. TRIPS seeks to minimise these risks by confining seizures to cases where IP infringement can be most easily determined, such as trade mark counterfeiting and not infringement generally, and by imposing strict time limits, to minimise the severity of the interference.[43]

More recent innovations in both Europe[44] and Australia have tipped the balance further towards IP claimants. The range of infringements that can lead to seizure has been extended beyond straightforward counterfeiting to include, for example, alleged trade mark infringement through the adoption of confusingly similar marks.[45] This is troubling because it may give one side in a genuine trade mark dispute a distinct, strong, forensic advantage in the form of seizure and holding of goods, in circumstances where, unlike other drastic provisional measures involving seizures and interference with the defendant's business (for example injunctions, Mareva orders, and so on), there is no requirement to weigh up the merits of the case, or consider whether, if goods are released, the harm suffered cannot be compensated in money.

In addition, both countries now require an importer whose goods have been seized to lodge a claim for release, failing which goods may be forfeited and destroyed without any legal proceedings to determine infringement and without explicit consent from the owner of the goods.[46] This arguably contravenes principles of even-handedness. You might argue that requiring an importer to claim their goods proactively is 'equitable' in that *both* parties are required to engage actively with the process: first the importer to claim their goods and then the IP owner to

---

43 See TRIPS Articles 51–60, especially Arts 55 and 56.

44 European Union Regulation 608/2013 concerning customs enforcement of intellectual property rights, repealing Regulation (1383/2003). Regulation 608/2013 applies from 1 January 2014.

45 It should be noted that this is not a recent innovation in Australia: seizures of allegedly infringing, but not counterfeit, trade mark goods have been allowed since at least the 1995 *Trade Marks Act*.

46 *Copyright Act 1968* (Cth) s 135AEA (claim for release), with 'claim period' defined in the *Copyright Regulations 1969* (Cth) Reg 22A as meaning 10 working days; *Copyright Act 1968* (Cth) s 135AEB (forfeiture).

institute proceedings. The EU even characterises forfeiture in these circumstances as being the result of the importer's 'implied consent' (that implication arising from the failure to claim the goods). But this ignores the fact that border measures are in the nature of provisional measures: they allow for an interference with the importer's undoubted personal property rights in their imports on the basis of the IP owner's mere allegation and without any judicial determination of the rights and wrongs. In essence, the new procedure allows for forfeiture and destruction, without consent, and without any proof beyond the right-holder's mere assertion that there is infringement.

These examples show the potential uses of an interpretation of the obligation to provide fair and equitable procedures informed by the right to a fair trial. But is the ICCPR relevant in interpreting TRIPS? Under the *Vienna Convention on the Law of Treaties*,[47] which has attained the status of customary international law,[48] the interpretation of treaties is first and foremost a matter of ascertaining in good faith the ordinary meaning of terms in their context and in light of the treaty's object and purpose.[49] The general object and purpose of TRIPS is not likely to be particularly helpful, however, when it comes to assessing the specifics of civil adjudication of IP rights and Part III of TRIPS. Not only is TRIPS' 'object and purpose' rarely adverted to by WTO dispute settlement bodies in interpreting the treaty,[50] but none of the Preamble, Art 7 ('Objectives') or Art 8 (Principles) have much to say about internal civil enforcement procedure beyond requiring 'effective and appropriate means for … enforcement … taking into account differences in national legal systems'. At most, the objects and purposes of TRIPS, which make clear that IP is to be understood in a general societal context and that protection of IP rights should contribute to society 'in a manner conducive to social and economic welfare, and to a balance of rights and

---

[47] *Vienna Convention on the Law of Treaties*, opened for signature 23 May 1969, 1155 UNTS 331 (entered into force 27 January 1980) ('VCLT').

[48] See, e.g., *Arbitral Award of 31 July 1989 (Guinea-Bissau v Senegal) (Judgment)* [1991] ICJ Rep 53, 70 and *Land, Island and Maritime Frontier Dispute (El Salvador/Honduras: Nicaragua intervening)* [1992] ICJ Rep 351, 582.

[49] VCLT above n 47 Art 31.1.

[50] Henning Grosse Ruse-Khan, 'The (non) use of treaty object and purpose in intellectual property disputes in the WTO', *Max Planck Institute for Intellectual Property and Competition Law Research Paper*, No 11–15.

obligations', suggests that an interpretation of the enforcement provisions *only* by reference to 'effectiveness' or IP policy is not required.

It may therefore be appropriate to refer to the context of TRIPS. The context of a treaty includes the 'relevant rules of international law applicable in the relations between the parties'.[51] Consequently, a treaty *in pari materia*, that is, an instrument with identical subject matter and same or similar terms to the treaty being interpreted, may be regarded as relevant to the context, particularly where the treaty being interpreted has been drafted based on the initial treaty in question.[52] The Vienna Convention permits recourse to supplementary means of interpretation, including the preparatory work of the treaty and the circumstances of the treaty's conclusion, in prescribed circumstances where the primary means of interpreting a treaty's terms prove insufficient.[53] A treaty *in pari materia* may also be regarded as part of the circumstances of conclusion of the treaty being interpreted,[54] particularly if averted to during negotiations. Given that the term 'supplementary means of interpretation' is not exhaustively defined in the *Vienna Convention*, a treaty *in pari materia* may constitute supplementary means.[55] Finally, it is worth noting the general interpretive canon that parties to a treaty do not intend the treaty to be incompatible with customary international law as a supplementary means of interpretation,[56] which may bring TRIPS into alignment with international human rights law more indirectly.

A difficulty with treating the ICCPR as *in pari materia* is that general human rights provisions like Art 14 of the ICCPR relating to legal process do not have identical subject matter. Where TRIPS seeks to address enforcement generally, including both judicial and administrative proceedings, leading human rights instruments are concerned chiefly with rights to fair *trial* (that is, with judicial proceedings). Further, the text is dissimilar. On the other hand, it is clear that although TRIPS

---

[51] VCLT Art 31.3(c).

[52] Ulf Linderfalk, *On the Interpretation of Treaties: The Modern International Law as Expressed in the 1969 Vienna Convention on the Law of Treaties* (Springer, 2007) 255.

[53] VCLT Art 32.

[54] Linderfalk, above n 52, 255; Richard K Gardiner, *Treaty Interpretation* (Oxford University Press, 2008), 342.

[55] Anthony Aust, *Modern Treaty Law and Practice* (Cambridge University Press, 2nd ed., 2007) 200.

[56] Ibid.

specifically countenances that administrative processes may be used *instead* of judicial proceedings in the enforcement context (a recognition that Member States have many and varied legal and juridical structures), it is also clear that TRIPS takes court processes as its ideal model, with administrative processes, if used, required to meet similar standards. Article 14 of the ICCPR and Art 6 of the ECHR are concerned, at heart, with fairness and equity in legal processes. Insofar as the jurisprudence around these provisions elaborates on the concept of what constitutes 'equality' and 'fairness' in legal process, they can and should be used to help us understand the content of the IP treaties.

A further source of content for the obligation to provide fair and equitable procedures could be *domestic* notions of due process, such as the jurisprudence developed in the US under the 5th and 14th Amendments. We might draw, for example, on US concepts of due process to impose limits on statutory damages.[57] Such arguments would be much more of a stretch. While the terminology of 'due process' was used in early negotiations for TRIPS,[58] such language appears to have been abandoned in favour of the more general requirement of 'fairness and equity',[59] in part owing to

---

[57] E.g. Pamela Samuelson and Tara Wheatland, 'Statutory Damages in Copyright Law: A Remedy in Need of Reform' (2009) 51 *William & Mary Law Review* 439.

[58] See e.g. Note by the Secretariat MTN.GNG/NG11/4 (17 November 1987) [8]; [19]; Note by the Secretariat, MTN.GNG/NG11/9 (13 October 1988) at [47] (using 'due process' as a compendious term for some of the specific protections mentioned in Articles 41 and 42 plus others); also Note by the Secretariat MTN.GNG/NG11/12 (13 June 1989) [10] (talking about the need for due process '*comprising inter alia*' specific protections later included in Articles 41 and 42 as well as others); Note by the Secretariat MTN.GNG/NG11/13 (16 August 1989) at 7 [16] (noting that judicial procedures are 'an important safeguard … at least to the extent that judicial procedures conformed to the principles commonly referred to as *due process of law*, which were outlined in the proposal' of the European Communities NG11/W/31) and at 22 [30] (assertion by the US that 'the fundamental tenets of due process would apply to all procedures') and at 26 [31] (delegate affirming that enforcement measures 'should be guided by a set of broad and pragmatic criteria such as effectiveness, appropriateness *and due process of law*'); Note by the Secretariat MTN.GNG/NG11/15 (26 October 1989), 22 (Japanese delegate discussing the principle of due process of law).

[59] The language of 'fairness and equity' seems to have developed through proposals from Canada (Submission from Canada dated 5 September 1989 (MTN.GNG/NG11/W/42)) and the European Communities (European Communities, Draft Agreement on Trade-Related Aspects of Intellectual Property Rights, 29 March 1990 (MTN.GNG/NG11/W/68)), with the latter's provisions on enforcement including the requirement for fair and equitable procedures being

concerns from some negotiating parties that there was no *internationally accepted* understanding of 'due process'.[60]

3.2 Is the Obligation Enforceable?

I have argued that procedural innovations can and should be analysed for their fairness and equity, drawing on jurisprudence and literature developed in the context of the right to a fair trial and civil procedural justice generally. This has rhetorical force in domestic debates over particular reforms. We must acknowledge, however, that there are significant legal and practical barriers in the way of any attempt to enforce the obligation against a state.

It is clear that the general requirement of fairness could not be used to qualify specific provisions. Thus no dispute resolution body would entertain an argument that the procedures actually agreed to by all WTO Members in TRIPS are 'unfair' and hence contrary to Art 41(2).[61]

Secondly, in the case of TRIPS and ACTA, provisions allowing individual countries considerable freedom in domestic implementation must also be taken into account. As is clear from the *travaux preparatoires*, TRIPS was drafted with the specific intention of accommodating

---

adopted almost wholesale by the US in its draft text dated 11 May 1990 (MTN.GNG/NG11/W/70).

[60] E.g. Note by the Secretariat, MTN.GNG/NG11/6 (6 April 1988) [18]. Other language is also used, e.g. an early Indian proposal discusses 'natural justice, fair play, prior notice, adequate opportunities for defence etc' as being 'well-recognised principles defined by each country according to its legal traditions': Note by the Secretariat, MTN.GNG/NG11/15 (26 October 1989), at 22.

[61] By analogy, see *Canada-Pharmaceutical Patents* WTO DS114(2000), in which the WTO Panel considered the impact of TRIPS Art 8.1, which allows parties to adopt 'measures necessary to protect public health and nutrition, and to promote the public interest in sectors of vital importance to their socio-economic and technological development'. The Panel held that while Art 8.1 has interpretive force, it does not alter the specifically negotiated balance of rights and interests found in TRIPS Art 30. A more interesting question might arise in interpreting ACTA, which has a series of specific provisions but which also states in Art 1 that nothing in ACTA 'shall derogate from any obligation of a Party with respect to any other Party under existing agreements, including the TRIPS Agreement'. Could a specific obligation in ACTA be treated as 'unfair'? It seems unlikely. The relative generality of the provisions of ACTA may render this a moot point.

Members with a wide range of judicial and administrative systems.[62] The TRIPS preamble recognises the need for new rules concerning enforcement 'taking into account differences in national legal systems'. TRIPS Art 1.1 allows Members to provide more extensive protection to IP than is required by the text of TRIPS, and states that Members 'shall be free to determine the appropriate method of implementing the provisions [of TRIPS] within their own legal system and practice'. ACTA Art 2.1 mirrors this provision. Moreover, under TRIPS, no Member is obliged to provide a better enforcement system for IP rights than domestic law in general. Thus the fact that a given set of procedures adopted by one state might be considered 'unfair' by some or even many other states is not decisive in establishing a breach of the obligation to provide fair and equitable procedures: factors such as civil procedure in other kinds of proceedings in the defending state and the resources and social priorities of the individual state would all be relevant.[63]

Thirdly, obligations in ACTA or TRIPS cannot be litigated directly by plaintiffs or defendants at an international level.[64] A state party to the agreement would have to raise any complaints. A state has no legitimate complaint unless the potential injury *to the interests of that state* could credibly rise to the level of a claim for nullification or impairment of

---

[62] Gervais, above n 28, 442–3; Taubman, above n 30, 110; Paul Goldstein and Bernt Hugenholtz, *International Copyright: Principles, Law and Practice* (Oxford University Press, 2nd ed., 2010) 79; Jerome H. Reichman, 'Universal Minimum Standards of Intellectual Property Protection under the TRIPS Component of the WTO Agreement' in Carlos M. Correa and Abdulqawi A. Yusuf (eds) *Intellectual Property and International Trade: The TRIPS Agreement* (Wolters Kluwer, 2nd ed., 2008) 69. Concerns about 'unwelcome effort[s] to harmonise national judicial procedures' are dotted throughout the *travaux* (e.g., Note by the Secretariat, MTN.GNG/NG11/20 (24 April 1990) at 17 [25]; Note by the Secretariat MTN.GNG/NG11/13 (16 August 1989) page 7 [16]).

[63] WTO, *China – Measures Affecting the Protection and Enforcement of Intellectual Property Rights: Report of the Panel*, WT/DS362/R (26 January 2009). One suggestion in the *travaux preparatoires* is that 'in assessing expectations regarding the administration of justice, the appropriate standard was the justice accorded to nationals. A State should not be held responsible for denial of justice to foreigners if they had been granted all the benefits the national legal system granted to nationals': Note by the Secretariat, MTN.GNG/NG11/7 (21 June 1988) [49]; see also Note by the Secretariat, MTN.GNG/NG11/10 (30 November 1988) [23].

[64] TRIPS Agreement Arts 1(1), 64 (dispute settlement procedures), Restatement (Third) Foreign Relations Law (1987) S 713.

benefits under the WTO Agreement.[65] This would be difficult to prove: isolated instances of unfairness in enforcement would not be a cause for complaint.[66]

Despite these practical difficulties, it is still important to determine the content of the fair and equitable obligation. A specific enforcement procedure adopted by a state, which appeared to violate due process concerns in a particularly egregious manner, could ground a complaint. In addition, the meaning and content of the obligation could be relevant in a broader trade dispute over a state's obligation to provide effective enforcement. A state accused of shirking its obligation to provide for effective enforcement could counter with the 'defence' that it is implementing its obligation to provide for 'fair and equitable' procedures. For example, a country might be accused of failing to take sufficiently quick action against online piracy if it requires a court procedure prior to the cancellation of internet access, but might respond that effective judicial protection is an essential procedural right. Finally, arguing inconsistency with the obligation could be an important rhetorical device in domestic law reform debates for stakeholders concerned that procedures are too favourable to certain interests.[67]

3.3 In a World of Privatised Enforcement, is the Obligation Moot?

Another issue is whether privatisation of IP enforcement has the potential to circumvent the obligation to provide fair and equitable enforcement procedures. Is a state entitled, despite the international instruments, to delegate enforcement to private schemes and private agreements, and if it does so, is it obliged to ensure that the procedures embodied in such arrangements are fair and equitable?

At both an international and a domestic level, policymakers today put considerable emphasis on the desirability of private cooperation as an alternative to state involvement in enforcement. For example, Art 27.3 of ACTA provides:

---

[65] Cf. John H. Jackson, *The World Trading System* (1990) 263–64; World Trade Organisation, *Guide to GATT Law and Practice* 241–48.

[66] UNCTAD-ICTSD, *Resource Book on TRIPS and Development* (Cambridge UP 2005), 580–81, 582.

[67] See e.g. Horten, above n 16, where the right to a fair trial more generally became an important part of the debate over the introduction of certain online enforcement procedures.

> Each Party shall endeavour to promote cooperative efforts within the business community to effectively address trademark and copyright or related rights infringement while preserving legitimate competition and, consistent with that Party's law, preserving fundamental principles such as freedom of expression, fair process, and privacy.

We see a similar trend in many states. Privatised enforcement is not new: the US *Digital Millennium Copyright Act 1998* included a requirement that internet safe harbours be conditioned on online service providers having a policy for the termination of repeat infringers.[68] This is a clear example of a penalty for infringement being applied by a private party outside of any judicial or administrative process, although, as the case law has made clear, the exact form of any such policy is left to the discretion of the internet service provider.[69] More emphasis has been placed on such moves recently. In Australia, the government has consistently expressed its hope that industry players will agree a code of conduct for managing mass online infringement, and has sought to facilitate industry meetings.[70] A Memorandum of Understanding on the topic has already been agreed in the US between major internet access providers and copyright-owners.[71] The US government has also asserted that one of three planks of its online enforcement strategy is to 'support[] voluntary efforts by the private sector'.[72] The *Stop Online Piracy Act* in

---

[68] 17 USC §512(i)(1)(A). This provision has been exported to other countries through the US free trade agreements: see e.g. *Copyright Act 1968* (Aust.) s 116AH (1) Table item 1.

[69] *Corbis Corp v Amazon.com, Inc* 351 F Supp 2d 1090, 1101 (WD Wash 2004); see also *UMG Recordings, Inc v Veoh Networks Inc* 665 F Supp 2d 1099 (C D Cal 2009). The same applies in Australia: the Australian Parliament was unequivocal in setting out that the policy was 'to be determined by the carriage service provider': Explanatory Memorandum to the US Free Trade Agreement Implementation Bill 2004 (Cth), 161 [699].

[70] For a recent iteration of this desire, see Mitchell Bingemann, 'Brandis calls time on online piracy', *The Australian,* 28 October 2013. The expectation that industry codes of conduct would be negotiated is reflected in Australia's copyright law: see *Copyright Act 1968* (Cth) ss 36 and 101 (making industry codes relevant to the assessment of authorisation liability); also s 116AH (internet safe harbours).

[71] 'Memorandum of Understanding of 7 June 2011 between Content Owner Representatives and Participating ISPs, Participating Content Owners Group', available at http://www.copyrightinformation.org/wp-content/uploads/2013/02/Memorandum-of-Understanding.pdf.

[72] 2013 Joint Strategic Plan; also Department of Commerce Internet Policy Task Force *Copyright Policy, Creativity, and Innovation in the Digital Economy*

the US (which was proposed but never enacted) embodied obligations of cooperation in legislation, including a provision requiring intermediaries to cooperate with copyright-owners[73] and a provision specifically indemnifying internet intermediaries who take action outside the statutory framework envisaged in that Act.[74]

Is the fairness or equity of privatised enforcement measures outside the purview of international IP instruments?[75] The general principle in international law is that states are internationally responsible only for acts attributable to the state.[76] Treaties are generally intended to impose obligations on the state, not on private parties, and complaints brought under international trade agreements must relate to the conduct of the state and its organs. Further, the treaty language in TRIPS, ACTA and similar instruments could be interpreted as requiring only that measures adopted and implemented by the state are covered. First, the word 'enforcement' may itself suggest official activity only.[77] Secondly, the treaties mostly seem to confine their provisions to procedures and remedies provided by the state. ACTA Art 6(2) provides that the obligation to ensure fairness and equity is limited to 'procedures adopted,

(July 2013), 42. See also at 67, where Task Force 'encourages stakeholders to continue to work together to develop identification and filtering systems that are consistent with rights to due process and free expression'. Also at 74 talking about private/voluntary graduated response; noting the need to protect due process, prevent over-breadth and ensure proportionality, but also speaking in favour of 'the progress that has been made through the cooperative efforts of right holders, ISPs, payment processors, ad networks and search engines to develop… voluntary initiatives', and 'we encourage interested stakeholders to continue identifying and developing voluntary solutions that benefit all parties and that are consistent with the principles of privacy, free speech, competition and due process'.

[73] *Stop Online Piracy Act*, HR 3261 (112th Congress (2011)), §103. For a detailed summary of the SOPA proposals, see Kimberlee Weatherall, 'Evaluating SOPA: Who Should Enforce IP Online?' (2012) 62(4) *Telecommunications Journal of Australia* 59.1.

[74] *Stop Online Piracy Act*, HR 3261 (112th Congress (2011)), §104.

[75] This is a different question from whether such privatised enforcement systems may be contrary to the rule of law, or even breach domestic constitutional requirements: cf. Suzor and Fitzgerald, above n 37.

[76] International Law Commission *Draft Articles on State Responsibility*; *United States Diplomatic and Consular Staff in Tehran, Judgment, ICJ Reports 1980* p3, at p 29 [56]; *Military and Paramilitary Activities in and against Nicaragua (Nicaragua v United States of America), Merits, Judgment, ICJ Reports 1986,* p14, pp117–18 [226].

[77] UNCTAD-ICTSD, above n 66, 575.

maintained, or applied to implement the provisions of this Chapter'. The EU's IPRED I Article 3.1 also requires that Member States 'shall provide for the measures, procedures and remedies' necessary for enforcement and that 'those' measures, procedures and remedies, that is, the ones provided by the Member State, shall be fair and equitable. TRIPS is less specific, stating that 'procedures concerning the enforcement of intellectual property rights shall be fair and equitable'. It is arguable, however, that the concept of 'procedures concerning ... enforcement' implies legal or administrative procedure and not activities which are described in ACTA Art 27(3) as 'cooperative efforts within the business community to effectively address' infringement. It seems therefore that private and voluntary measures adopted by private parties – such as the US Memorandum of Understanding – are not likely to be affected by a state's obligation to provide that enforcement procedures are 'fair and equitable'.[78]

The legal position could be more complicated, however, in situations where the state adopts private cooperative efforts. The proposal in SOPA, for example, not only encouraged cooperation but would have granted a general immunity so that no cause of action could be brought against a service provider for taking action against infringing sites either under the legislation or for 'otherwise voluntarily blocking access to or ending financial affiliation with' infringing websites.[79] A case where state law deprives individuals of claims they might otherwise have, on the basis of decisions made by unfair procedures, involves state action and hence would be subject to international law.

4. THREE FINAL PROVOCATIONS

As international IP treaties have included more detailed provisions on IP enforcement, it has become important to consider the scope of states' obligations to implement procedural reforms, and the constraints, if any, that international law may impose on the choices states make, particularly if states choose implementations that are more favourable to one party in litigation. I have argued here that there is a 'ceiling' on the IP

---

[78] Although, as the literature points out, they could well fail those standards if they did apply: see in particular the analysis of Annemarie Bridy, above n 37, especially 51–58 (analysing the fairness of the US MOU procedure).

[79] SOPA above n 73 §104.

owner-friendly procedural reforms that a state can introduce.[80] I have also argued that our usual tools for analysis as IP scholars are peculiarly inappropriate for thinking about these developments, and we have much to learn from sources outside the IP toolbox. The chapter raises as many questions as it answers, and leaves much room for further development and thinking. I want to end with three final provocations for IP scholars:

1. Thinking about enforcement procedures should become part of regular IP scholarship. Some scholarship is developing, but it needs to be more generally integrated. Enforcement procedures, to some extent, make the whole system tick. They warrant our attention.
2. IP theories are largely blind to the interests, or personhood, of parties other than creators, and have very little useful to say about these developments. Using our usual instrumental or utilitarian-style analysis runs the risk of reducing infringers and defendants to dot points in a broader cost–benefit analysis. Procedural scholarship focuses, usefully, on the personhood and interests of all parties to a dispute.
3. Despite many challenges in doctrinal analysis and practical enforceability, there may be some scope for using case law and theory around the right to a fair trial and civil procedural justice to develop the content of IP treaties. Given the poverty of IP thinking in this area, it may be a necessity.

---

[80] Annette Kur and Henning Grosse Ruse-Kahn, 'Enough is enough – the notion of binding ceilings in international intellectual property protection', in Annette Kur (ed.), *Intellectual property rights in a fair world trade system* (Edward Elgar, Cheltenham: 2011), 359–407; Thomas Jaeger, Henning Grosse Ruse-Khan, Josef Drexl and Reto M. Hilty, 'Statement of the Max Planck Institute for Intellectual Property, Competition and Tax Law on the Review of EU Legislation on Customs Enforcement of Intellectual Property Rights', Max Planck Institute for Intellectual Property, Competition and Tax Law Research Paper Series No. 10-08, paragraph 13. Dinwoodie has also referred to the possibility of 'substantive maxima' in international IP agreements: Graeme Dinwoodie, 'The International Intellectual Property Law System: New Actors, New Institutions, New Sources' (2006) 10 *Marquette Intellectual Property Law Review* 205, at 214.

10. A "bundle" of national patents v a European patent with unitary effect: A jurisdictional comparison

Torsten Bjørn Larsen

1. INTRODUCTION

The purpose of this chapter is to compare the rules of jurisdiction that apply to litigation of certain claims based on the existing "bundle" of national patent rights within the EU – that is, where there are two or more corresponding national patent rights within the EU – with the rules of jurisdiction that apply to the same claims made on the basis of the future European patent with unitary effect (hereinafter EPUE). The former rules are found in the Brussels I Regulation (hereinafter BR) if the defendant is domiciled in the EU,[1] in the Lugano Convention if the defendant is domiciled in the EFTA,[2] or in the Member States' own private international laws if the defendant is domiciled outside the EU/EFTA.[3] The latter rules are found exclusively in the Agreement on a

[1] Council Regulation (EC) No 44/2001 of 22 December 2000 on jurisdiction and the recognition and enforcement of judgments in civil and commercial matters (OJ L 12/1). Council Regulation 44/2001 is replaced by Council Regulation (EC) No 1215/2012 of 12 December 2012 on jurisdiction and the recognition and enforcement of judgments in civil and commercial matters (OJ L 351/1) on 10 January 2015 cf. art. 81.

[2] Convention on jurisdiction and the enforcement of judgments in civil and commercial matters signed in Lugano on 30 October 2007. The Convention must be interpreted in line with the BR. Cf. Art. 1, Protocol No. 2 to Convention on jurisdiction and the enforcement of judgments in civil and commercial matters signed in Lugano on 30 October 2007; Ulrich Magnus and Peter Mankowski, European Commentaries on Private International Law, Brussels I Regulation, 2nd Revised Edition, 2012, p. 21.

[3] Art. 4(1) BR.

Unified Patent Court (hereinafter AUPC).[4] This chapter is limited to cases where the defendant is domiciled in the EU.[5] But it examines the jurisdictional rules governing national patent rights regardless of whether they have been applied for via a centralized procedure such as the European Patent Convention[6] or the Patent Corporation Treaty[7] systems or on a Member State-by-Member State basis. I have not covered the Unified Patent Court's (UPC) competence on European patents,[8] unless the parties choose to opt out.[9]

The BR and the AUPC rules of jurisdiction are compared in three situations, namely:

- in infringement actions where invalidity is not raised
- in infringement actions where invalidity is raised, and
- in non-infringement actions[10] where invalidity is not raised

---

[4] Council Agreement on a Unified Patent Court (2013/C 175/01) of 20 June 2013.

[5] The EU is defined as every Member State except Croatia, Poland and Spain given that those countries are not parties to the AUPC. Cf. http://ec.europa.eu/internal_market/indprop/patent/ratification. In order to not compare 'apples with oranges', Croatia, Poland and Spain are therefore disregarded.

[6] Convention on the Grant of European Patents of 5 October 1973 as revised by the Act revising Art. 63 EPC of 17 December 1991 and the Act revising the EPC of 29 November 2000 (EPC).

[7] Patent Corporation Treaty done at Washington on June 19, 1970 as amended on September 28, 1979 as modified on February 3, 1984 and on October 3, 2001 (PCT).

[8] Art. 1; cf. Art. 2(e) AUPC.

[9] Art. 83 AUPC.

[10] In non-infringement actions the infringer acts as the plaintiff and the rightholder acts as the defendant and so the parties trade places. The idea of bringing any such action is not to impose any liability on the rightholder. Rather the idea is to rule out the infringer's own liability by seeking a finding that his/her conduct does not infringe the rightholder's patent right. A non-infringement action is known under various terms. *Firstly*, the term 'negative declaration' is used by the Court of Justice in Case C-133/11, *Folien Fischer AG, Fofitec AG v. Ritrama SpA*, para. 56 and by legal scholars, inter alia, James J. Fawcett and Paul Torremans, Intellectual Property and Private International Law, second edition, Oxford Private International Law Series, 2011 at 5.37; Ulrich Magnus and Peter Mankowski, European Commentaries on Private International Law, Brussels I Regulation, 2nd Revised Edition, 2012, p. 229; Anna Gardella, Torpedoes and Actions for Negative Declarations in International IP Law Litigation published in Arnaud Nuyts (ed.), International Litigation in Intellectual Property and Information Technology, Kluwer Law International, 2008, p. 181

The rules of jurisdiction in the BR are briefly examined in Section 2 of this Chapter and the rules of jurisdiction in the AUPC are briefly outlined in Section 3. In Section 4, a conclusion is drawn.

2. RULES OF JURISDICTION IN THE BRUSSELS REGULATION

Infringement actions where invalidity is not raised can be heard at the defendant's domicile[11] having cross-border jurisdiction[12] (hereinafter unlimited full jurisdiction). A second option is to bring the action including threatened infringements at forum delicti.[13] This option encompasses two possible places for jurisdiction, namely a "place of action" (being the place of the conduct of the defendant)[14] and a "place of effects" (being the place of registration).[15]

The scope of jurisdiction when based upon place of the conduct of the defendant is (despite the decision of the Court of Justice in *Wintersteiger*) likely to be national jurisdiction (hereinafter limited forum jurisdiction).[16]

---

and Ulf Maunsbach, Jurisdiction in Relation to Online Cross-Border Infringements: The Code and the Law published in Internationalisation of Law in the Digital Information Society, Dan Jerker B. Svantesson and Stanley Greenstein (editors), p. 182. *Secondly*, the term "declaratory action" is also used, inter alia, in the Principles on Conflict of Laws in Intellectual Property (CLIP Principles) Commentary, European Max Planck Group on Conflicts of Laws in Intellectual Property, Oxford University Press, 2013, p. 173 (2:602.C01) *et seq*. *Thirdly*, the term "action for declaration of non-infringement" is used, inter alia, in arts. 96(b) Council Regulation (EC) No. 207/2009 of February 26, 2009 on the Community trade mark, 81(b) Council Regulation (EC) No. 6/2002 of December 12, 2001 on the Community design, in art. 32(1)(b) AUPC and by legal scholars, inter alia, Marta Pertegás Sender, Cross-border enforcement of patent rights, Oxford private international law series, 2002, at 4.81.

[11] Art. 2 BR.

[12] Ulrich Magnus and Peter Mankowski, European Commentaries on Private International Law, Brussels I Regulation, (2d rev. ed, Sellier European Law Publishers, 2012) p. 77 *et seq.*

[13] Art. 5(3) BR.

[14] Case C-523/10, *Wintersteiger AG v Products 4U Sondermaschinenbau GmbH*, ECLI:EU:C:2012:220 (hereinafter *Wintersteiger*) para. 38.

[15] *Wintersteiger* para. 29.

[16] Axel Metzger, Jurisdiction in Cases Concerning Intellectual Property Rights on the Internet, Brussels-I-Regulation, ALI-principles and Max-Planck Proposals in Intellectual Property and Private International Law (Stefan Leible and Ansgar Ohly, Mohr Siebeck, 2009) p. 261 at note 42; James C. Fawcett and

The place of registration is (despite *Wintersteiger*'s reference to "all the damage")[17] likely also subject to any such forum jurisdiction.[18] A third option is to bring the action at the defendant's branch.[19] The multiple defendants' rule[20] does not apply since the Court of Justice has held that parallel claims based upon a bundle of national patents do not come within the meaning of the provision.[21]

If invalidity is raised during the infringement action, the courts of the Member State that issued the patent are exclusively competent to address the invalidity question.[22] If therefore a company based in Germany has allegedly infringed a French patent and the infringement action is brought in Germany, the German courts are competent to address the infringement question (following Art. 2 BR), whereas the French courts must address invalidity of the French patent if such a claim is raised by the German company (following Art. 22.4 BR). Thus, the case must be split up. Non-infringement actions can be heard at the defendant's

---

Paul Torremanns, Intellectual Property and Private International Law, Oxford Private International Law Series, (2d ed. Oxford University Press, 2011) at 5.58 cf. 5.62 and 5.86; Conflict of Laws in Intellectual Property, The CLIP Principles and Commentary, European Max Planck Group on Conflicts of Laws in Intellectual Property (Oxford University Press, 2013) p. 85 (2:203.C03).

[17] *Wintersteiger*, para. 28.

[18] *See* Annette Kur, Jurisdiction and Enforcement of Foreign Judgments – The General Structure of the MPI Proposal in Intellectual Property and Private International Law, Heading for the Future, 2005, p. 29; Axel Metzger, Jurisdiction in Cases Concerning Intellectual Property Infringements on the Internet in Intellectual Property and Private International Law (Stefan Leible and Ansgar Ohly, eds 2009) p. 260; Arnaud Nuyts, Suing at the Place of Infringement: The Application of Article 5(3) of Regulation 44/2001 to IP Matters and Internet Disputes, in Arnaud Nuyts, International Litigation in Intellectual Property and Information Technology, Kluwer Law International, 2008, p. 127 *et seq.*; S. Bariatti, La giurisdizione e l'esecuzione delle sentenze in material di brevetti di invenzione nell'ambito della C.E.E, 1982, RDIPP 518 and Hess, Rechtsfolgen von Patentverletzungen im Europäischen Patentrecht, Duncker und Humblot, 1987, 32.

[19] Art. 5(5) BR.

[20] Art. 6(1) BR.

[21] Case C-539/03, *Roche Nederland BV and Others v. Frederick Primus and Milton Goldenberg* ECLI:EU:C:2006:458 (hereinafter *Roche*) para. 31.

[22] Art. 22(4) BR cf. case C-4/03, *Gesellschaft für Antriebstechnik mbH & Co. KG v. Lamellen und Kupplungsbau Beteiligungs KG* ECLI:EU:C:2006:457 (hereinafter *Gat Luk*) para. 32.

domicile,[23] at forum delicti[24] and at the defendant's branch[25] and thus the above applies *mutatis mutandis*.

In sum, infringement and non-infringement actions can be brought at the defendant's domicile, at forum delicti or at the defendant's branch. If invalidity is raised during the infringement proceedings, the case may be split up due to Art. 22(4) BR as interpreted by the Court of Justice in *GAT v. LuK*. The resulting jurisdictional picture can be illustrated as shown in Figure 10.1.

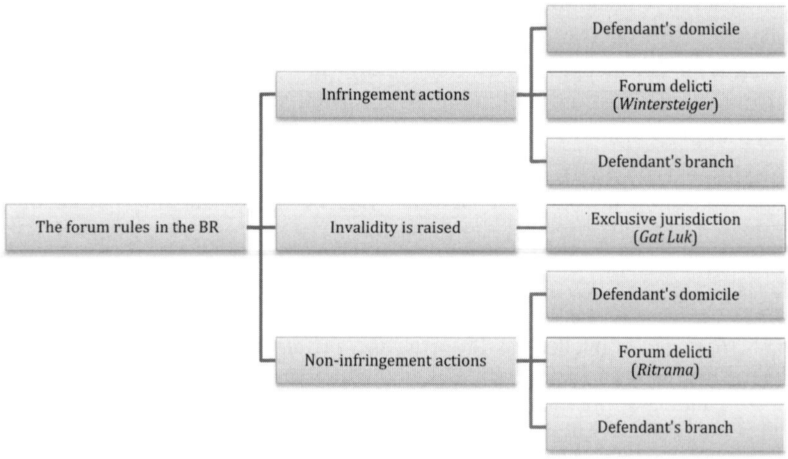

Figure 10.1 The forum rules in the BR

3. RULES OF JURISDICTION IN THE AUPC

Infringement actions where invalidity is not raised[26] can be heard at the defendant's domicile[27] which, contrary to Art. 2 BR, speaks of "residence". This term is new and it is not clear whether it covers the defendant's branch. Like Art. 5(3) BR, such actions can also be brought at the forum delicti.[28] The provision here expressly allows for jurisdiction

[23] Art. 2 BR.

[24] Art. 5(3) BR cf. case C-133/11, *Folien Fischer AG and Fofitec AG v Ritrama SpA* ECLI:EU:C:2012:664 (hereinafter *Ritrama*), para. 56.

[25] Art. 5(5) BR.

[26] Art. 32(1)(a) AUPC.

[27] Art. 33(1)(b) AUPC.

[28] Art. 33(1)(a) AUPC.

based upon threatened infringements. The impact of the forum delicti rule in Art. 33(1)(a) AUPC is unknown. However, it seems likely that the provision must be construed independently of Art. 5(3) BR, inter alia, because the UPC is not bound by Art. 5(3) BR case law of the Court of Justice and *since* the unitary nature of the patent does not favour a distinction between a "place of action" and a "place(s) of effect(s)" given that the former will always coincide with the latter. Finally, the claim may be brought where one of more defendants is domiciled.[29] Like Art. 6(1) BR (as understood by the Court of Justice in *Roche*), the wording of the pertinent provision in the AUPC requires the same set of facts to be involved.[30] Contrary to Art. 6(1) BR and *Roche*, the provision does not condition jurisdiction on the same legal question being involved – but this is obviously met due to the unitary character of the patent. In all three instances, the court will have unlimited full jurisdiction.[31]

If invalidity is raised during the infringement action,[32] a flexible variation of Art. 22(4) BR and *GAT v. LuK* has been introduced. The court where invalidity is raised may either decide the case (meaning that the court will decide both the infringement and the invalidity questions), send the case to the central division if the parties agree (meaning that the central division will decide both the infringement and the invalidity questions), or bifurcate (meaning that the invalidity question will be referred to the central division and the infringement question will be either suspended or decided).[33]

In non-infringement actions[34] a distinction must be drawn depending on whether an infringement action is pending between the same parties relating to the same patent before a local/regional division. If any such action is pending, the non-infringement action must be brought at the same local/regional division; if an infringement action is not pending, the non-infringement action must be brought at the central division,[35] which will be located in Paris, London or Munich depending on the subject matter.[36] Interestingly, the central division is obliged to stay the non-infringement

[29] Art. 33(1)(b)(last sentence) AUPC.
[30] Art. 33(1)(b)(last sentence) AUPC.
[31] Art. 34 AUPC.
[32] Art. 32(1)(e) AUPC.
[33] Art. 33(3) AUPC; cf. James J. Fawcett and Paul Torremans, Intellectual Property and Private International Law (2d ed. Oxford Univ. Press 2011) at 8.141.
[34] Art. 32(1)(b) AUPC.
[35] Art. 33(4) AUPC.
[36] Annex II AUPC.

action if the potential rightholder brings an infringement action no later than three months after the non-infringement action has been brought.[37] Thus, under the AUPC, a non-infringement action must be stayed pending an infringement action, whereas under the BR the situation is quite the opposite, namely, that an infringement action must be stayed pending the non-infringement action.[38] Where, therefore, the AUPC rule favours the potential rightholder, the BR rule favours the alleged infringer. Having said that, the overall purpose of the AUPC rule seems to limit the problem which exist(ed) under the BR where an alleged infringer may bring a non-infringement action (fire a 'torpedo') at a slow-moving court system and have an infringement action stayed against him/her following the *lis pendens* rule.[39] This is not possible under the AUPC since the AUPC gives a three-month priority to the potential rightholder. The above can be illustrated as shown in Figure 10.2.

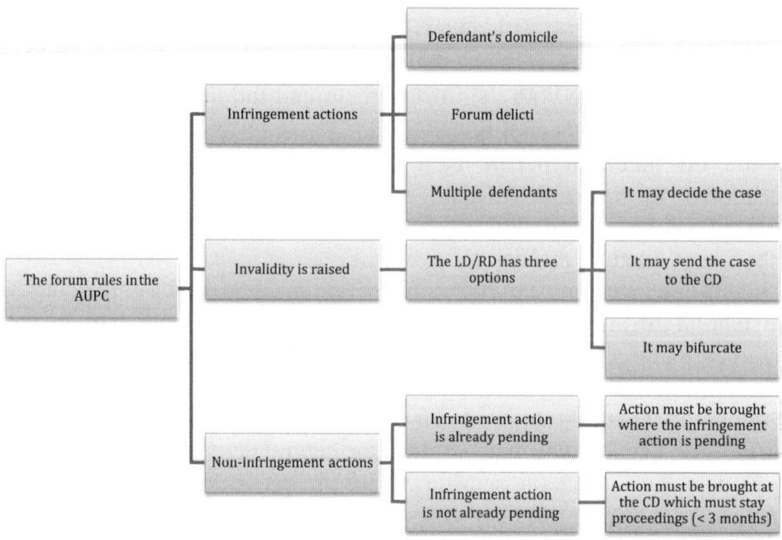

Figure 10.2 The forum rules in the AUPC

---

[37] Art. 33(6) AUPC.

[38] Art. 27 BR cf. James J. Fawcett and Paul Torremans, Intellectual Property and Private International Law, second edition, Oxford Private International Law Series, 2011 at 5.174–5.175.

[39] Art. 27 BR.

4. CONCLUSION

In infringement actions where invalidity is not raised, four relevant rules of jurisdiction can be identified.

The first one is the rule of the defendant's domicile. The rule is found in both the BR and in the AUPC. The rules are similar since they are both subject to unlimited full jurisdiction, but differ because the AUPC introduces the new term 'residence', which may/may not be interpreted to cover a defendant's branch. Subject to any such reservation, the AUPC rule seems not to favour one party at the expense of the other.

The second one is the forum delicti rule. The rule is also found in both the BR and in the AUPC. The rules are similar since they both allow for threatened infringements but differ because the BR rule covers two heads of jurisdiction, which the AUPC rule may likely not do. Moreover, the BR rule is subject to limited forum jurisdiction; this is contrary to the AUPC rule, which confers unlimited full jurisdiction. Thus, the AUPC rule may favour the potential rightholder.[40]

The third one is the branch rule. The rule applies under the BR but not under the AUPC unless the defendant's 'residence' rule is interpreted to that effect. Subject to any such reservation, the AUPC rule favours the alleged infringer since one less forum is available for the potential rightholder.

The final one is the multiple defendants' rule. The rule does not apply under the BR contrary to the AUPC. Thus, the AUPC rule favours the potential rightholder since one more forum is available for him/her.

If invalidity is raised the exclusive jurisdiction rule applies under the BR, whereas a flexible version has been introduced under the AUPC. Thus, the risk that a case must be split up as under the BR due to invalidity being raised has been limited under the AUPC, which in turn is an advantage for the potential rightholder.

Non-infringement actions can be brought at the defendant's domicile, forum delicti or at the defendant's branch under the BR. Under the AUPC, non-infringement actions must be brought at the local/regional division where the infringement action is pending (which can be in a defendant's domicile, forum delicti or multiple defendants' court depending on where the plaintiff has brought the infringement action) or if an infringement action is not already pending, at the central division (which

---

40 In practice, unlimited full jurisdiction is not always considered an advantage for the potential rightholder given that any such full jurisdiction create risks that he/she loses it all on the floor "in one blow".

can be in either Paris, London or Munich depending on the subject matter). Interestingly under the AUPC, non-infringement actions brought with the central division must be stayed if the potential rightholder brings an infringement action against the alleged infringer within three months. Any such rule is unknown under the BR. The three-month rule favours the potential rightholder since it allows him/her to choose the forum.

Overall it seems that the future rules of jurisdiction under the AUPC favour the potential rightholder at the expense of the alleged infringer, whereas the existing rules of jurisdiction under the BR are more balanced.

11. IP, disability, culture and exceptionalism: Does copyright law deal with difference?

Abbe Brown and Charlotte Waelde

INTRODUCTION

This chapter explores the extent to which human rights laws relating to disability and copyright conflict or complement each other. Does copyright consider itself *lex specialis*? If one sees the human rights and disability treaties as governing only general obligations, and copyright the specific, does copyright override what human rights and disability would otherwise dictate? Focusing on two case studies which involve human rights from different perspectives – one considers creation (the disabled dancer and her dance), and one considers use (people with visual impairments and access to books) – this chapter will look to developments in policy, international instruments, European and some domestic (UK) law to explore the relationship between these areas of law.

PROBLEMS

Both creators and users of copyright works have an interest in the human rights and disability instruments and activism, and the agenda which results. Consider a choreographer and dancer with disability, who is recognised as a leader in the field of dance, or blind or partially sighted person wishing to access and enjoy the latest books in the bestseller list. How does copyright treat the disabled creator and the disabled user: the disabled dancer and her dance, and the blind reader and the books she would like to read? Is there any element of 'oppression, discrimination, inequality and poverty' – the key inequities that disability rights seek to eradicate[1] – in the application of copyright when faced with these types of impairment?[2] Does copyright law recognise difference? More fundamentally, how do the copyright and the human rights disability agendas intersect? What is the reality when the disabled dancer seeks equality with her non-disabled counterpart; and the blind reader seeks access to books?

To address these questions two case studies will be used: the first is that of authorship and ownership of dance made by a disabled dancer – specifically that of Caroline Bowditch[3] and the dance *Love Games* choreographed by Joan Clevillé, which was first performed in Scotland in 2011 by Naomi Watts and then by Caroline at the Pathways to Profession Scottish Dance Theatre event in Dundee in January 2012 and in terms of which the underlying question was whether an able-bodied dancer could cover for a disabled dancer. A recording of the performance can be viewed on YouTube which shows clips from the 2011 and 2012 performances side by side,[4] in both cases with the same male dancer.[5] The second case study will be used to explore access to books by the blind with particular regard to the finalisation in 2013 under the auspices of WIPO of the Marrakesh Treaty to Facilitate Access to Published Works

---

[1] M Oliver 'The Individual and Social Models of Disability' Paper presented at Joint Workshop of the Living Options Group and the Research Unit of the Royal College of Physicians July 1990 <disability-studies.leeds.ac.uk/files/library/Oliver-in-soc-dis.pdf> last accessed 14 October 2013 *'the real issues in disability which are about oppression, discrimination, inequality and poverty'*.

[2] Here, a preliminary point should be made. The disability conventions speak of utilising creative potential for personal and community benefit; to access cultural material and activities in accessible forms; and to access places where cultural performances and services are offered. This comment is concerned with the first two – but not with physical access. See United Nations Convention on the Rights of Persons with Disabilities art. 30; and General comment Committee on Economic, Social and Cultural Rights Forty-third session 2–20 November 2009 General comment No. 21.

[3] Caroline Bowditch's profile on the Dance4 website <dance4.co.uk/profile/associate-artist/caroline-bowditch> last accessed 14 October 2013.

[4] 'Casting Exploration by Scottish Dance Theatre' <youtube.com/watch?v=6YEtEyr6N4g> last accessed 14 October 2013.

[5] This part of the chapter will build on discussions carried out from the dance, copyright, human rights and ethics perspective, in S Whatley et al. 'Validation and Virtuosity: Perspectives on Difference and Authorship/Control in Dance' submitted to and accepted by *Choreographic Practices* to be published in 2015. This paper formed part of 'InVisible Difference: Dance, Disability, Law,' a project funded by the AHRC on which the authors are Co-Investigators. See project website http://www.invisibledifference.org.uk.

for Persons Who Are Blind, Visually Impaired, or Otherwise Print Disabled (the Marrakesh Treaty). This contains copyright exceptions and limitations for the print disabled.

A fundamental preliminary point arises in respect of the different models of disability that have developed over the years. These have a strong bearing on the way in which we can think about how copyright responds to difference. While there are a number of different models, two influential ones are the medical model and the social model. Broadly put, the medical model sees disability as a consequence of impairment and something to be 'cured' by an appropriate professional. By contrast the social model sees disability as a product of the failure of society to accommodate the needs of people with impairments.[6] The medical model held sway for many years, but was challenged in the mid-1970s by the disabled community, who offered the social model. Different aspects of different laws reflect these different approaches, while some seek to reconcile them, and this is considered below, particularly in respect of the Marrakesh Treaty.[7] A second preliminary point concerns the existing debate among scholars concerning IP and human rights.[8] This is something that is increasingly recognised: for example, the United Nations Sub-Commission for the Promotion and Protection of Human Rights in 2000 and 2001 issued resolutions stating that the manner in which countries had chosen to implement their international obligations under the TRIPS agreement was inconsistent with international human rights obligations;[9] and the English

[6] UPIAS, *Fundamental principles of Disability* (London Union of the Physically Impaired, 1976) at 14; see also Sheila McLean and Laura Williamson *Impairment and Disability: law and ethics at the beginning and end of life* (2007 Routledge Cavendish); Alastair Campbell *The body in Bioethics* (2009 Routledge Cavendish).

[7] Sheila McLean and Laura Williamson *Impairment and Disability: law and ethics at the beginning and end of life* (2007 Routledge Cavendish).

[8] Peter K Yu 'Intellectual property and human rights in the non-multilateral era' 64 *Fla. L. Rev.* July 2012 no 4 1045; Laurence Helfer 'The New Innovation Frontier? Intellectual Property and the European Court of Human Rights' 49 *Harv. Int'l. L. J.* 1(2008); Wojciech Sadurski 'Allegro without Vivaldi: trademark protection, freedom of speech, and constitutional balancing' *E.C.L. Review* 2012 8(3) 456–492; and see also Christophe Geiger *Research Handbook on Human Rights and Intellectual Property* (forthcoming, Edward Elgar).

[9] UN High Commissioner for Human Rights, Intellectual Property and human rights, Sub-Commission on Human Rights Resolution 2000/7 <http://www.unhchr.ch/Huridocda/Huridoca.nsf/0/c462b62cf8a07b13c12569700046704e?Opendocument> last accessed 21 October 2013; and United Nations Commission on Human Rights, Sub-Commission on the Promotion and Protection of

Court of Appeal in *Ashdown*,[10] the European Court of Human Rights in *Ashby Donald*,[11] and the US Court in *Time v Geis*[12] reveal acceptance that in some (rare) cases, rights to freedom of expression can prevail over copyright.[13] This chapter does not aim to contribute directly to this discourse, but rather to discuss the impact this potential conflict can have in the scenarios discussed, the implications for exceptionalism and the clashes between IP, human rights and disability.[14]

Human Rights. Economic, Social and Cultural Rights, Intellectual property rights and human rights. Report of the Secretary-General. E/CN.4/Sub.2/2001/12 14 June 2001 <http://www.unhchr.ch/Huridocda/Huridoca.nsf/(Symbol)/E.CN.4.Sub.2.2001.12.En?Opendocument> last accessed 21 October 2013.

[10] *Ashdown v Telegraph Ltd* [2001] EWCA Civ 1142 [2002] Ch. 149.

[11] In French *Ashby Donald v France* (2013) http://hudoc.echr.coe.int/sites/eng/pages/search.aspx?i=001-115979 and comment Copyright vs Freedom of Expression (22 January 2013) at <http://echrblog.blogspot.co.uk/2013/01/copyright-vs-freedom-of-expression.html> last accessed 21 October 2013.

[12] *Time Inc v Geis* 293 F. Supp 130.

[13] See C Geiger and E Izyumenko 'Copyright on the human rights' trial: redefining the boundaries of exclusivity through freedom of expression' *IIC* 2014, 45(3), 316–342.

Although frequently copyright will still prevail over human rights arguments see *Harper & Row v Nation Enterprises* 471 U.S. 539; and *HRH Prince of Wales v Associated Newspapers Ltd* [2006] EWHC 522 (Ch) [2006] E.C.D.R. 20. Human rights arguments are still not yet omnipresent in intellectual property litigation, and, there are some cases where a possible human rights argument is not pursued, for example the use of a photograph of drugs in a campaign warning against them, as was considered in *Hoffman v Drug Abuse Resistance Education (UK) Ltd* [2012] EWPCC 2.

[14] This chapter will not explore questions of the extent to which IP is a human right, including in respect of being a form of property, or is a form of delivery of human rights – in respect of which see article 15(1)(c) ICESCR; article 17(2) UDHR; Office of the High Commissioner for Human Rights Committee on Economic, Social and Cultural Rights 'The right of everyone to benefit from the protection of the moral and material interests resulting from any scientific, literary or artistic production of which he or she is the author' General Comment No. 17 (2005), http://tbinternet.ohchr.org/_layouts/treatybodyexternal/TBSearch.aspx?Lang=en&TreatyID=9&DocTypeID=11 last accessed 3 December 2014; *Anheuser-Busch Inc v Portugal* (73049/01) [2007] E.T.M.R. 24 (2007) 45 E.H.R.R. 36; *Smith Kline & French Laboratories Ltd v Netherlands (Admissibility)* (12633/87) October 4, 1990 Eur Comm HR 70; *Levi Strauss & Co v Tesco Stores Ltd* [2002] EWHC 1625 (Ch) [2002] 3 C.M.L.R. 11 [2003] R.P.C. 18; Audrey Chapman 'Approaching intellectual property as a human right: obligations related to Article 15(1)(c)' Copyright Bulletin, vol XXXV No. 3,

IF ONE STARTS WITH HUMAN RIGHTS …

As indicated in the introduction, this chapter proceeds from the assumption that human rights is a *lex generalis* and therefore the appropriate starting point. Legal and political theory, which can be traced back across many centuries and in respect of which debate continues, reveals strong support for the existence of human rights.[15] The present set of human rights instruments stem from the aftermath of World War II, and a determination that obligations would be imposed on states to ensure that atrocities against humankind should not happen again.[16] Has this resulted in rights which are relevant to enjoyment of and participation in culture? This is worthy of consideration given contemporary arguments that there has been an expansion of human rights and an application of them to situations which were not envisaged, as can be seen in particular from discussions in the UK regarding the place of the Human Rights Act 1998.[17] Yet it is clear from the international instruments that culture and related rights were considered worthy of attention in the post-war activity.

July-September 2001 UNESCO Publishing, Paris, France; Jonathan Griffiths 'Constitutionalising or harmonising? The Court of Justice, the right to property and European copyright law' 2013 *ELR* 65.

[15] See e.g. Declaration of the Rights of Man and the Citizen, (1789); John Locke, *Two Treatises of Government* (work first published 1690, The Legal Classics Library 1994); Jeremy Bentham, *An Introduction to the Principles of Morals and Legislation* (work first published 1789 The Hafner Library of Classics Hafner Publishing Co 1963); for ongoing arguments, see e.g. John Rawls, *A Theory of Justice* (Clarendon Press 1972) (see 225 regarding freedom of expression of interest here); Ronald Dworkin, *Taking Rights Seriously* (Duckworth 1977) (see 277 regarding freedom of expression); Michael Ignatieff (ed.), *Human Rights as Politics and Idolatry* (Princeton University Press 2001); Wiktor Osiatynski, *Human Rights and their limits* (CUP 2009); and Andrew Fagan, *Human Rights: Confronting Myths and Misunderstandings* (Edward Elgar 2011).

[16] See e.g. J Symonides (ed.), *Human Rights: Concepts and Standards* (Dartmouth Publishing Co Ltd and UNESCO 2000); Y Donders and V Volodin, *Human Rights and Educational, Social and Cultural Developments and Challenges* (UNESCO Publishing and Ashgate 2007); Brian Galligan and Charles Sampford (eds), *Rethinking Human Rights* (The Federation Press 1997).

[17] The UK Commission on a Bill of Rights, established by the UK Government, did not come to any clear decision. See http://www.justice.gov.uk/about/cbr> last accessed 21 October 2013; see also 'Protecting Human Rights in the UK' proposal of the UK Conservative Party 2014, https://www.conservatives.com/~/media/Files/Downloadable%20Files/HUMAN_RIGHTS.pdf.

Article 15(1)(a) of the International Covenant on Economic, Social and Cultural Rights ('ICESCR') (1966)[18] sets out the right of everyone to take part in cultural life.[19] Article 15(2) refers to steps being taken as necessary to develop and diffuse culture. In terms of how this might apply to books and dance, it is interesting to note that the UN's Committee on Economic, Social and Cultural Rights' General Comment on persons with disabilities of 1994[20] identifies that there has been discrimination in respect of cultural life,[21] articulates the right to full participation and appeals for the elimination of communication barriers to the greatest extent possible. The General Comment refers to the need for talking books, adapted theatre, and to education of the general public of the fact that persons with disabilities have as much right as other persons to make use of cultural venues.[22] Likewise, the UN's Committee on Economic, Social and Cultural Rights' General Comment from 2009[23]

The suggestion that there should be a replacement of the regime was resisted strongly by the Scottish Human Rights Commission. <http://scottishhumanrights.com/news/latestnews/article/billofrightsnov11news> last accessed 21 October 2013. Yet dance and the arts were absent from the lengthy Scottish Human Rights Commission *Getting it Right? Human Right in Scotland* (Edinburgh: SHRC, 2012).

[18] Regarding states who have ratified the international human rights treaties, see Office of the United Nations High Commissioner for Human Rights 'Status of Ratifications of the Principal Human Rights Treaties as of 14 July 2006', available at http://www2.ohchr.org/english/bodies/docs/status.pdf last accessed 21 October 2013.

[19] See discussion in R Stavenhagen 'Cultural Rights: A Social Science Perspective' and A Eide 'Cultural Rights as Individual Human Rights' both in Asbjorn Eide, Catarina Krause and Allan Rosas (eds) *Economic, Social and Cultural Rights: A Textbook*, Revised Second Edition (Martinus Nijhoff, 2012); and L Shaver 'The Right to Science and Culture' 10 *Wis. L. Rev.* 212. In December 2014 as this collection went to press, the UN Special Rapporteur in the field of cultural rights published a report 'Copyright policy and the right to science and culture', http://www.ohchr.org/EN/Issues/CulturalRights/Pages/AnnualReports.aspx, which refers to disability in paras 67 and 115, 116.

[20] Office for the High Commissioner for Human Rights Persons with Disabilities General Comment 5, <http://www.unhchr.ch/tbs/doc.nsf/0/4b0c449a9ab4ff72c12563ed0054f17d> last accessed 21 October 2013.

[21] Office for the High Commissioner for Human Rights Persons with Disabilities General Comment 5, Para 15, <http://www.unhchr.ch/tbs/doc.nsf/0/4b0c449a9ab4ff72c12563ed0054f17d> last accessed 21 October 2013.

[22] <http://www.unhchr.ch/tbs/doc.nsf/0/4b0c449a9ab4ff72c12563ed0054f17d> last accessed 21 October 2013, General Comment 5, Paras 37, 38.

[23] 'Right of everyone to take part in cultural life' (General Comment 21) E/C.12/GC/21 accessible via http://tbinternet.ohchr.org/_layouts/treatybody

recognises that culture evolves.[24] For present purposes, it could thus cover reading by the visually impaired in an online format, or to dancing by people with disabilities.[25] Further, the General Comment states that culture includes non-verbal communication (such as dance),[26] and for people who want to observe and share in dance by people with disabilities or to read books in whatever format, it provides for 'the encouragement and promotion of … participation, to the extent possible, in recreation, leisure and sporting activities';[27] and refers to accessibility of culture without discrimination, particularly in respect of disability.[28]

From the disability perspective, article 2 ICESCR guarantees that rights will be exercised without discrimination in respect of 'other status' as to cultural rights. This provision was also considered in a General Comment in 2009,[29] which makes clear that disability is a relevant 'other status'.[30] It also refers to the possibility or obligation on states to adopt special measures to address discrimination provided these are reasonable, objective and proportionate and might exceptionally be permanent, including reasonable impairment for sensory impairments.[31] This could be relevant to permanent requirements regarding, say, the sharing of books and their information in different formats over the internet, or on new handheld devices.

If the ICESCR right in respect of culture fits directly with the rights of persons with disabilities to dance and to share in dance and in books, the

---

external/TBSearch.aspx?Lang=en&TreatyID=9&DocTypeID=11 last accessed 22 October 2013.

[24] General Comment 21, Para 11.

[25] Which might have been (or still be) considered unusual by some. A review by Michael Scott appeared in *Vancouver Sun*, 20 May 1999. Scott commented with a specific reference to Candoco company member David Toole: 'There is a horrific, Satyricon quality to CandoCo that heaves up in the chest – nausea at the moral rudderlessness of a world where we would pay money to watch a man whose body terminates at his ribcage, moving about the stage on his hands.'

[26] General Comment 21, see note 23 Para 13.

[27] General Comment 21 Para 31.

[28] General Comment 21 Paras 16(b), 30 and also makes a general reference to non-discrimination including 'on … other status' para 21.

[29] 'Non-discrimination in economic, social and cultural rights' (General Comment 20) E/C.12/GC/20 accessible via http://tbinternet.ohchr.org/_layouts/treatybodyexternal/TBSearch.aspx?Lang=en&TreatyID=9&DocTypeID=11 last accessed 22 October 2013.

[30] General Comment 20 Paras 11, 15 (regarding non-exhaustive), 16, 28 (which refers back to General Comment 5).

[31] General Comment 20, Para 9.

International Covenant on Civil and Political Rights ('ICCPR') (1966)[32] has a less direct but highly relevant right. This is freedom of expression and information, in article 19(2), with the right expressed, *inter alia*, to be subject to respect for the rights of others. This right was considered by the Human Rights Committee in its General Comment from 2011.[33] This stresses the importance of cultural and artistic expression,[34] of expression in non-verbal form and over the internet[35] and also of the need for proportionate implementation.[36] This makes no specific reference, however, to disabilities.

Yet there has been significant action in respect of persons with disabilities elsewhere. The General Comment on persons with disabilities discussed above was written against the backdrop of the Standard Rules on Equalization of Opportunities for Persons with Disabilities.[37] These Rules led in 2006[38] to the Convention on the Rights of Persons with Disabilities (CRPD),[39] which springs from the disability movement and has at its core the social model of disability.

> It takes to a new height the movement from viewing persons with disabilities as 'objects' of charity, medical treatment and social protection towards viewing persons with disabilities as 'subjects' with rights, who are capable of claiming those rights and making decisions for their lives based on their free and informed consent as well as being active members of society.[40]

The CRPD imposes explicit obligations on states to ensure that persons with disabilities have the opportunity to 'develop and utilize their creative, artistic and intellectual potential, not only for their own benefit,

---

[32] 999 UNTS 171 ('ICCPR') Regarding states who have ratified the international human rights treaties, see Office of the United Nations High Commissioner for Human Rights 'Status of Ratifications of the Principal Human Rights Treaties as of 14 July 2006', available at http://www2.ohchr.org/english/bodies/docs/status.pdf last accessed 21 October 2013.

[33] General Comment No. 34 on article 19 http://www2.ohchr.org/english/bodies/hrc/docs/GC34.pdf last accessed 22 October 2013.

[34] General Comment 34 Para 11.

[35] General Comment 34 Para 12.

[36] General Comment 34 Para 34.

[37] Annexed to UNGA resolution 48/96 of 20 December 1993.

[38] See Louise Arbour, UN High Commissioner for Human Rights, General Assembly Ad Hoc Committee 8th session, New York, 5 December 2006.

[39] See United Nations Convention on the Rights of Persons with Disabilities <http://www.un.org/disabilities/convention/conventionfull.shtml> last accessed 21 October 2013.

[40] United Nations Enable – The Convention in Brief <http://www.un.org/disabilities/default.asp?navid=15&pid=162> last accessed 21 October 2013.

but also for the enrichment of society' and states that intellectual property should not be an obstacle to this.[41]

So, persons with disabilities seeking to dance, to read books, and to view the output of dancers with disabilities, do have rights. These are – consistent with the international human rights framework – rights against states, rather than, say, private dance companies who may decide not to employ dancers with disabilities, theatres who may choose not to book disabled dance companies, or early stage providers of tablet eReader products which did not include software to assist the blind in accessing the text.[42] So what might a dancer in the UK concerned about state withdrawal of funding from a disabled dance company actually do?[43] This is highly problematic. The means of ensuring that states respect these rights – and to ensure for present purposes that there is opportunity to dance and to read books with appropriate steps taken to enable this to be done by people with disabilities – operates through a system of monitoring and reporting rather than any more tangible form of enforcement. For the ICCPR, the Human Rights Committee has a monitoring role,[44] as does the Committee on Economic, Social and Cultural Rights

---

[41] Article 30(2) Convention on the Rights of Persons with Disabilities (2006). This is noted, although not considered in detail, in the Committee on the Rights of Persons with Disabilities General Comment No. 2 (2014) on Article 9: Accessibility, article 45 (see also articles 21, 22, 28, 44).

[42] See A Brown, S Harmon and C Waelde 'Do You See What I See? Disability, Technology, Law and the Experience of Culture' 2012 *IIC* (8) 901–930, at 909–913.

[43] Such as when the company Blue Eyed Soul lost its public funding. <disabilityartsonline.org.uk/Blue-Eyed-Soul-Dance-Company> last accessed 21 October 2013. See discussion in Alfredsson, Gudmundur et al. (2009) *International Human Rights Monitoring Mechanisms: Essays in Honour of Jakob Th. Moller* (Martinus Nijhoff, Netherlands, 2009); AR Chapman 'Development of Indicators for Economic, Social and Cultural Rights. The rights to Education, Participation in Cultural Life and Access to the Benefits of Science' 111 in Y Donders and V Volodin (2007) *Human Rights and Educational, Social and Cultural Developments and Challenges* UNESCO Publishing and Ashgate, Aldershot, Hampshire, UK and Burlington, VT, USA; and WA Schabas 'Study of the Rights to Enjoy the Benefits of Scientific and Technical Progress and its Applications' 273 in Donders and Volodin (n 43). See consideration of the impact of different rights approaches and models, and practical application, in P Harpur 'Embracing the new disability rights paradigm: the importance of the Convention on the Rights of Persons with Disabilities' 2012 27(1) *Disability & Society* 1.

[44] Human Rights Committee <http://www2.ohchr.org/english/bodies/hrc/> last accessed 21 October 2013.

in respect of the ICESCR.[45] So a concerned individual or group could hope that this issue would be identified and addressed by a Committee – but with little opportunity for ensuring that this happens, or that it would engage with their own situation.[46] There are opportunities under both international treaties, through optional protocols, for individuals or groups to complain about state conduct.[47] Yet the UK is not a member of either protocol.[48] It is also interesting to note that there has been very limited activity in respect of cultural and discrimination rights at international level.[49]

Little is likely to come, therefore, from the general cultural and expressive rights. In terms of more specific rights, the CRPD has an optional protocol enabling complaints to its Committee;[50] and this time the UK is a signatory.[51] Yet in terms of ultimate outcomes, this will once again lead only to identification of an issue, monitoring, encouragement of action and support. If the UK considers that it has insufficient funds to dedicate to, say, dancers with disabilities, further action is unlikely.[52]

---

[45] Committee on Social, Economic and Cultural Rights <http://www2.ohchr.org/english/bodies/cescr/> last accessed 21 October 2013.

[46] See N Pillay, 'A report by the United Nations High Commission for Human Rights. Strengthening the United Nations human rights treaty body system' (June 2012) <http://www2.ohchr.org/english/bodies/HRTD/docs/HCReportTBStrengthening.pdf> last accessed 21 October 2013.

[47] http://www.ohchr.org/Documents/HRBodies/CESCR/OProtocol_en.pdf (CESCR 2008) last accessed 22 October 2013; http://www.ohchr.org/EN/ProfessionalInterest/Pages/OPCCPR1.aspx (ICCPR 1966) last accessed 22 October 2013.

[48] See United Nations Treaty Collection <http://treaties.un.org/Pages/Treaties.aspx?id=4&subid=A&lang=en> last accessed 21 October 2013.

[49] See R Stavenhagen 'Cultural Rights: A Social Science Perspective' and A Eide 'Cultural Rights as Individual Human Rights' in Eide, Krause, Rosas (n 19); and L Vanhala *Making Rights a Reality? Disability Rights Activists and Legal Mobilization* (CUP, 2013).

[50] Committee on the Rights of Persons with Disabilities <http://www.ohchr.org/en/hrbodies/crpd/pages/crpdindex.aspx> last accessed 21 October 2013.

[51] Optional Protocol to the Convention on the Rights of Persons with Disabilities, articles 4, 6, 7 <http://www.ohchr.org/EN/HRBodies/CRPD/Pages/OptionalProtocolRightsPersonsWithDisabilities.aspx> last accessed 21 October 2013.

[52] See <http://www.ohchr.org/en/hrbodies/crpd/pages/crpdindex.aspx> last accessed 21 October 2013, for link to CRPD Committee response to the Human Rights Treaty body consultation, see also note 46.

In summary, this discussion has identified rights which are relevant to participation, sharing and supporting dance and to access to books for disabled people.[53] There are legal limits on these rights, with the references in freedom of expression to the rights of others, and the reminder of the power of intellectual property in the cultural life provision of the CRPD,[54] which has echoes of the balancing acts discussed in the cases and resolutions referred to above. And there are also practical limits on enforcing these human rights. This should provide a useful comparator with the position in respect of copyright, which is considered in the next section.[55] This brief overview and discussion of priorities suggests, however, that there may be significant differences in how one approaches books and dance from the perspective of copyright and its international legal obligations than from that in respect of human

---

[53] Note also that comparable rights exist in the European Convention on Human Rights (articles 10, 14), Charter of Fundamental Rights of the European Union OJ C 326 26.10.2012 391–407 (article 21); Treaty on the Functioning of the European Union OJ C 326 26.10.2012 1–390 (articles 10 and 19); and there is also in the UK the Equality Act 2010, see in particular sections 13(4), 15, 19, 21, 29. The practical impact of these instruments is considered in A Brown and C Waelde 'Human Rights, persons with disabilities and copyright' in Christophe Geiger *Research Handbook on Human Rights and Intellectual Property* (forthcoming, Edward Elgar). Note also growing use of these European based human rights in private actions for copyright infringement in respect of internet service providers, see e.g. *Productores de Musica de Espana (Promusicae) v Telefonica de Espana SAU* (C-275/06) [2008] E.C.R. I-271; *Scarlet Extended SA v Societe Belge des Auteurs, Compositeurs et Editeurs SCRL (SABAM)* (C-70/10) [2012] E.C.D.R. 4; *Sky Osterreich GmbH v Osterreichischer Rundfunk* (C-283/11) [2013] E.C.D.R. 6; *UPC Telekabel Wien GmbH v Constantin Film Verleih GmbH* (C-314/12) [2014] E.C.D.R. 12; Kevin O'Sullivan, 'Enforcing copyright online: internet service provider obligations and the European Charter of Human Rights' *E.I.P.R.* 2014, 36(9), 577–583.

[54] Even though it is clearly intended there that the rights of the person with disabilities shall prevail.

[55] Since intellectual property came under the umbrella of the WTO in 1994, if a state is concerned about another state's action or inaction in respect of IP it can make a complaint to the WTO dispute settlement system, which could lead ultimately to trade sanctions. Strong arguments have also been made that if IP owners are concerned, they are encouraging states to complain (see GC Shaffer *Defending Interests: Public-Private Partnerships in WTO Litigation* (Brookings Institution Press, Washington, USA, 2003)). Scholars have argued that these complaints are made less frequently than had been feared, and outcomes have also been more balanced – see J Pauwelyn 'The dog that barked but didn't bite: 15 years of intellectual property disputes' (2010) 1 *JIDS* 2, 389–429.

rights and disabilities, the *lex generalis*. This, and then the implications for conflict and complementarity, will now be considered.

STARTING WITH COPYRIGHT …

How does copyright law deal with disability and difference? How does it reflect the rights of the disabled dancer to access and use their talents for the benefit of themselves and their communities, and of the blind to read books? And is this a fitting outcome?

The Copyright/Disability Interface

Copyright rules[56] mostly recognise and build rights around works and performances developed by the able-bodied and perceived by the senses, especially the eyes and ears. Indeed, copyright has its origins in text – the protection of the book and booksellers.[57] Until recently, mention of disability has been largely conspicuous by its absence in international treaties dealing with copyright: there is nothing for instance in the Berne Convention,[58] the WCT, or TRIPS. European Directives make no mention of disability – with the exception of the InfoSoc Directive,[59] which provides in the recitals:

---

[56] Derived from a web of international treaties, and, for European Union member states, from Regulations and Directives. Examples include: Berne Convention for the Protection of Literary and Artistic Works 1886 as revised; WIPO Copyright Treaty 1996; Copyright in the Information Society Directive 2001/29/EC of the European Parliament and of the Council on the harmonisation of certain aspects of copyright and related rights in the information society OJ L 167 12.6.2001 10–19; Term of Protection Directive 2006/116/EC of the European Parliament and of the Council of 12 December 2006 on the term of protection of copyright and certain related rights OJ L 372 27.12.2006 12–18; Rental Right Directive 2006/115/EC of the European Parliament and of the Council of 12 December 2006 on rental right and lending right and on certain rights related to copyright in the field of intellectual property (codified version) OJ L 376 27.12.2006 28–35.

[57] Statute of Anne 1709.

[58] Berne Convention for the Protection of Literary and Artistic Works 1886 as revised.

[59] Directive 2001/29/EC of the European Parliament and of the Council of 22 May 2001 on the harmonisation of certain aspects of copyright and related rights in the information society (n 56).

> (43) It is in any case important for the Member States to adopt all necessary measures to facilitate access to works by persons suffering from a disability which constitutes an obstacle to the use of the works themselves, and to pay particular attention to accessible formats.

This is reflected in the Articles of the InfoSoc Directive as permission to provide an exception or limitation in national law for:

> uses, for the benefit of people with a disability, which are directly related to the disability and of a non-commercial nature, to the extent required by the specific disability.[60]

The influence of both the social and medical models of disability on the policy thinking underpinning this measure is evident in the references to *obstacles* to the use of works, and that persons *suffer* from disability (emphasis added).

In some domestic laws, some concessions have been given for people with disabilities – perhaps exploiting the flexibility offered by the silence in most treaties on this point but the scope as between different jurisdictions differs.[61] For instance as a result of joint lobbying in the UK by the publishing industry, the Royal National Institute of Blind People (RNIB), and the National Library for the Blind (NLB), an exception to copyright was introduced in the Copyright (Visually Impaired Persons) Act 2002 (CVIPA 2002),[62] which amends the Copyright Designs and Patents Act 1988 (CDPA), to the effect that accessible copies of a literary, dramatic, musical, or artistic work may be made by or for visually impaired persons without the consent of the copyright owner.[63] In 2013, in domestic UK law the Government signalled an intention to broaden the exceptions for the disabled in terms of type of work, scope and beneficiaries. This led to a consultation,[64] and ultimately to regulations.

---

60 Ibid. article 3 (b).

61 SCCR, Study on Copyright Limitations and Exceptions for the Visually Impaired, WIPO <wipo.int/meetings/en/doc_details.jsp?doc_id=75696> last accessed 22 October 2013.

62 In force 31 October 2003. For commentary by the introducer of that Bill, particularly interesting with the benefit of hindsight, see D Bradshaw, 'Making books and other copyright works accessible, without infringement, to the visually impaired: a review of the practical operation of the applicable, and recently-enacted, UK legislation' *IPQ* 2005, 4 335–360.

63 Subject to a host of limitations: see ss. 81–83, Copyright Designs and Patents Act 1988.

64 See consultation details, ipo.gov.uk/techreview-disability-exceptions.pdf Last accessed 22 October 2013. This closed in September 2013.

These allow for the making of accessible copies for personal use of all types of work, for people with all types of disability (mental as well as physical) so long as the person or an authorised body had lawful possession or use of that work, and it was not available on reasonable commercial terms.[65]

The pinnacle in this framework at present is the Marrakesh Treaty, which concerns the access of visually impaired people to books. The negotiation period leading up to the signing of the Treaty was challenging, as a range of different interests needed to be accommodated. The tensions that arose will be explored below, as will the text of the Treaty relevant to this discussion.

So on the copyright side, some policy-makers and legislators have shown themselves anxious at some levels to build a framework that would enable the disabled user to gain access to copyright-protected works for a range of reasons. The impact of this on the disabled dancer and her creation will be considered, and then that in respect of books and the blind.

THE CASE OF THE DISABLED DANCER: AUTHORSHIP AND OWNERSHIP OF THE DANCE

The question for this section is how copyright law treats the disabled dancer and her dance, with a particular focus on authorship and ownership of the copyright in the dance. Does the approach of copyright accord with the disability agenda which has been discussed? Or does it follow its own path? If discrimination and inequality are to be avoided, then, on matters of authorship and ownership, the disabled dancer needs to be treated not only the same as others, but any barriers to inclusion should be broken down. As there is nothing explicit in copyright law about disability and dance, what is the reality of the position of the disabled dancer as compared with her non-disabled colleagues in matters of authorship and ownership? This contribution will focus on the UK position.[66]

---

65 The Copyright and Rights in Performances (Disability) Regulations 2014: No 1384 (para 2, introducing section 31A CDPA. See UK IPO 'Exceptions to Copyright: Accessible Formats for Disabled People' (October 2014), https://www.gov.uk/government/uploads/system/uploads/attachment_data/file/375952/Accessible_formats_for_disabled_people.pdf.

66 Legally, this is an underexplored area although has been the subject of some attention recently. F Yeoh 'The copyright implications of Beyoncé's

Copyright Subsistence – The New Regime

The author is the central figure in the copyright regime. It is around her that the framework is built. The Berne Convention accords copyright protection, ownership[67] and moral rights[68] to a qualifying author[69] for literary and artistic works including choreographic works[70] for a fixed period of time.[71] These rules are reflected to a greater or lesser extent in European Directives and national law.[72]

Since 2008, there have been developments in the case law of the Court of Justice dealing with the criteria for the subsistence of copyright – which in turn have impact on laws in member states. Through a series of cases, the Court of Justice has stressed that the European scheme of protection for copyright,[73] based on obligations to be found in the international regime, provides that works are to be protected where the subject matter is original in the sense of being the author's intellectual

"borrowings"', *Choreographic Practices* 2013 Volume 4 No. 1, 95–117; F Yeoh 'Choreographers' moral right of integrity,' *Journal of Intellectual Property and Practice*, 2013, Vol. 8, No. 1. 43–58; F Yeoh 'Choreographer's Copyright Dilemma,' *Entertainment Law Review*, 2012, Issue 7, 201–208; F Yeoh 'The Choreographic Trust: Preserving Dance Legacies,' *Dance Chronicle*, 2012, 35.2, 224–249. There is more in the US where there has been some important litigation in relation to ownership of dance around the Martha Graham estate; see e.g. A. Braveman 'Duet of Discord: Martha Graham and Her Non-Profit Ballet over Worth for Hire' *Loyola of Los Angeles Entertainment Law Review* (2005) Vol. 6 Issue 1, pp 471–498; N Kim, 'Martha Graham, Professor Miller, and the Work for Hire Doctrine: Undoing the Judicial Bind Created by the Legislature' *Journal of Intellectual Property Law* (2006) Vol 13, p 337; S Kutner and H Rich, 'Dirty Dancing: Attributing the Moral Right of Attribution to American Copyright Law: The Work for Hire Doctrine and the Usurping of the Ultimate Grand Dame and Founder of Modern Dance, Martha Graham' *Hofstra Lab. & Emp. L.J.* (2005) Issue 22, pp 325–351; CJS Picart, 'A Tango Between Copyright And Choreography: Whiteness As Status Property In Balanchine's ballets, Fuller's Serpentine Dance And Graham's Modern Dances' *Cardozo Journal of Law & Gender* (2012) Issue 18, pp 685–724.

67 Berne Convention article 5.

68 Berne Convention article 6 *bis*.

69 Berne Convention article 3.

70 Berne Convention article 2.

71 Berne Convention article 7.

72 In the UK, the Copyright Designs and Patents Act 1988 as amended.

73 J Pila 'An intentional View of the Copyright Work' 71 *Mod. L. Rev.* (2008); C Handig '*Infopaq International A/S v Danske Dagblades Forening* (C-5/08): is the term "work" in the CDPA 1988 in line with the European Directives?' (2010) *EIPR* 32(2), 53.

creation.[74] What the work is called, whether a literary, dramatic or musical work, is irrelevant. The standard of originality for all types of work is one of intellectual creation.[75]

To reach this level the author should:

- express her creative ability in an original manner by making free and creative choices[76]
- stamp her 'personal touch' on the work.[77]

Where choices are dictated by technical considerations, rules or constraints which leave no room for creative freedom, these criteria are not met.[78]

What does this mean for dance? While there are debates among dance professionals as to what constitutes a dance, many of these focus on a personal view of the quality of the work. Those in the dance community

---

[74] Case C-5/08 *Infopaq International A/S v Danske Dagblades Forening* (*Infopaq*) paras 33, 38; see also Case C-393/09 *Bezpečnostní softwarová asociace* para 45. What is not protected is expression, which is limited by its technical function Case C-406/10 *SAS Institute Inc. v World Programming Ltd* paras 38–40. Case C-145/10, *Painer v Standard VerlagsGmbH et al*; in the UK see *SAS Institute Inc. v World Programming Ltd* [2013] EWHC 69 (Ch) para 27.

[75] Case C-5/08 *Infopaq International A/S v Danske Dagblades Forening*, Case C-393/09 *Bezpečnostní softwarová asociace* [45]; Joined Cases C-403/08 and C-429/08 *Football Association Premier League and Others*; E Rosati 'Originality in a work, or a work of originality: the effects of the *Infopaq* decision' *E.I.P.R.* 2011, 33(12), 746–755; E Derclaye 'Wonderful or Worrisome? The Impact of the ECJ Ruling in Infopaq on UK Copyright Law' (2010) *EIPR* 32(5), 248.

[76] *Infopaq International A/S v Danske Dagblades Forening* (C-5/08), [45]; Case C-393/09 *Bezpečnostní softwarová asociace*, [50]; and Case C-145/10, *Painer v Standard VerlagsGmbH et al*, [89] and Case C-604/10 *Football Dataco v Yahoo!* [2012] 2 CMLR 24 [38].

[77] Case C-145/10, *Painer v Standard VerlagsGmbH et al*, [92]; Case C-604/10 *Football Dataco* [38].

[78] Case C-393/09 *Bezpečnostní softwarová asociace*, [48]–[49]; Cases C-403/08 and C-429/08 *Football Association Premier League and Others,* [98]; and Case C-604/10 *Football Dataco* para 39. A number of articles have discussed the implications of these cases. These include: M van Eechoud 'Along the road to uniformity – diverse readings of the Court of Justice Judgments on copyright work' 3 (2012) *JIPITEC* 1 para 60; C Handig 'The "sweat of the brow" is not enough! – more than a blueprint of the European copyright term "work"', 2013, *EIPR* 1; A Rahmatian 'Originality in UK copyright law: the old "skill and labour" doctrine under pressure', *IIC* 2013, 44(1), 4–34; E Rosati 'Towards an EU-wide copyright? (Judicial) pride and (legislative) prejudice', 2013, *IPQ* 46.

are not always in agreement. Nijinsky said of work by Duncan: '… her performance is spontaneous and is not based on any school of dancing and so cannot be taught … It is not art.'[79] Others talk of the difficulty in identifying the work in postmodern dance: 'One major aspect of post-modernism in dance is the nature of the works created: its structure and form challenge the traditional and consequently it is difficult to fix its identity as the works are prone to have many identities: each instantiation is a "token" of the work.'[80] Despite these reservations, from the perspective of the law it would seem that there would not be a difficulty in showing the necessary intellectual creation for these to qualify as original works for the purposes of copyright.

There could perhaps be challenges for some dances in relation to the 'dictated by technical considerations' proviso. Some works which have historically been protected may no longer receive copyright status because they are limited by their technical function. An example from music is the skill, labour and effort exerted in updating musical scores to recreate the music of a baroque composer: the input may be considered to be dictated by technical requirements and may therefore not now be capable of protection by copyright.[81] By analogy, would the recreation of a historic dance to conform to an original production now earn its own copyright protection? Arguably not, if its re-creation was dictated by the technical requirements of the original choreographer. The question of how much of the dance should be considered personal to the dancer as opposed to fixed on the body by a more contemporary choreographer, or by an interpretation of the choreographer's intent, will be considered below.

Dance: Fixation

Although there is no requirement of fixation in the international framework for copyright to subsist,[82] the law in the UK does require that the work be fixed in some material form:[83] copyright only arises on fixation. What form fixation takes is left open and needs only to be 'in writing or

[79] D Jowitt *Time and the Dancing Image* (Berkeley and Los Angeles: University of California Press) 1988, p76.

[80] F Yeoh *Copyright law does not adequately accommodate the art form of dance*, PhD thesis, Birkbeck College 2012.

[81] *Sawkins v Hyperion Records Ltd,* [2005] EWCA 565.

[82] Berne Convention article 2.2 leaves fixation to members of the Union.

[83] This is so the extent of the monopoly claimed may be known to others – *Tate v Fulbrook* 1908 1 KB 821 at 832.

otherwise'.[84] Traditionally fixation has been thought of as being in writing, reflecting the historical text-based roots of copyright law. For dance, one of the notation systems, such as Laban or Benesh, might be deployed, both of which have relatively modern origins, having been invented in the mid-20th century. More modern examples of dance fixation might include film and video, computer animation, motion capture and holography. But for dance, meeting the requirement of fixation is perhaps too easily assumed. These methods might fix the work but may not capture the essence of the dance.[85] Choreographers voice different opinions as to what amounts to fixation as well as challenging the requirement itself. As to the dance, some view its fugitive nature as presenting particular problems for capture; others point to the technicalities of the art form occupying both space and time as being too challenging for fixation.[86] Yet others assert that the dance is fixed or 'set' in the 'memories and bodies of the dancers', where the bodies are considered material objects.[87] For others the idea of any form of record is an anathema: the dance is meant only to be ephemeral – to exist at the time of performance where fixation ossifies the work.[88]

With the current state of the law, in the UK the expectations and practices of those who would see fixation on the body are unlikely to be met. A court refused to accept that Adam Ant's make-up was the subject of copyright protection because it was painted on his face and not fixed to a surface, saying that a painting is an object and not an idea.[89] The court wanted to

---

84 Copyright Designs and Patents Act 1988 as amended (CDPA) s. 3(2).

85 Each of which may have separate protection in their own right. It is interesting to note that dance notation systems remain largely inaccessible to dance artists because of their technicality as well as their cost, and that the other forms of fixation do not offer the accuracy of fixation of Laban and Benesh, particularly regarding the three-dimensional aspect of performances: Lauren B Kramer, 'Copyright Protection for Choreography: Can It Ever Be "En Pointe"?' (2010) *Syracuse Journal of legislation and policy*, Issue 1, 148–150; K.L. De Quintana, 'The Balancing Act: How Copyright and Customary Practices Protect Large Dance Companies over Pioneering Choreographers' *Villanova Sports & Entertainment Law Journal* (2004) Issue 11, 150–151.

86 M Cook 'Moving to a new beat: copyright protection for choreographic works' 1977 24 *UCLA L Rev* 1287; Yeoh n 80 pp 96–100.

87 M Traylor (1981) 'Choreography, Pantomime and the Copyright Revision Act of 1976' *New England Law Review* 16: 227, 237.

88 See for instance P Théberge 'Technology Creative Practice and Copyright' in S Frith and L Marshall (eds) *Music and Copyright* (Edinburgh: Edinburgh University Press 2004 2nd ed) 139, 140.

89 *Merchandising v Harpbond* (1983) FSR 32.

separate the idea in the work from the expression of the idea, as copyright protects only expression and not ideas.[90] For performative works it would seem that the idea and expression may fuse into one – as in the fixation of the dance on the bodies and in the memories of the dancers.

So Who has Authored the Dance?

What of the dance performance by Caroline Bowditch discussed above: does it meet the requirements for copyright protection? And if so, who has authored the dance? The requirement of fixation is clearly met. Whatever may be thought of fixation, these dances, or at least the parts that are available on YouTube, have been fixed in a form that is sufficient to meet this prerequisite. What also seems unarguable is that intellectual creation has been expressed in the work in an original manner through making free and creative choices. The key question is *who* has expressed this creative ability and stamped their personal touch on the work? There is a clear assumption in the dance community that the choreographer is the author of the dance and first owner of the copyright in the work. This comes through clearly from interviews with choreographers,[91] in the literature both by[92] and about choreographers.[93] The one case in the UK jurisdictions to have considered the question, *Massine v de Basil*,[94] was decided under the 1911 Act, which in turn included a reference to 'choreographic work',[95] as did the 1956 Act.[96] By contrast the CDPA says nothing about choreography or choreographic work. Is it therefore

---

90 *Designers Guild Ltd v Russell Williams (Textiles) Ltd* [2001] FSR 11, paras 24, 25.

91 C Waelde and P Schlesinger 'Music and Dance: Beyond Copyright Text?' (2011) 8:3 SCRIPTed 257 <http://script-ed.org/?p=83> last accessed 22 October 2013.

92 A De Mille *And Promenade Home* (Boston, Toronto: Little, Brown and Company, 1956), at 256. '[T]he choreographer is glued immobile as a fly in a web and must watch his own pupils and assistants, suborned to steal his ideas and livelihood. Several dancers made paying careers out of doing just this.'

93 See generally G McFee (2011) *The Philosophical Aesthetics of Dance: Identity, Performance and Understanding* (Alton: Dance Books).

94 [1936–45] MacG CC 223.

95 Copyright Act 1911 s. 35(1). 'Dramatic work' includes any piece for recitation, choreographic work or entertainment in dumb show, the scenic arrangement or acting form of which is fixed in writing or otherwise, and any cinematograph production where the arrangement or acting form or the combination of incidents represented give the work an original character.

96 Copyright Act 1956 s. 45(1). L Carrière 'Choreography and Copyright: some comments on choreographic works as newly defined in the Canadian

the choreographer who would be recognised as the author under the CDPA? Or Caroline, the dancer? Or both?

By analogy it is useful to look at the subsistence of copyright in music. A distinction exists between composition and arrangement. Copyright can subsist in an original musical composition[97] and a separate copyright can exist in an arrangement of the composition so long as the correct type of originality has been expended.[98] Why can the dancer not be considered as an arranger of the choreography?[99] The dance may be 'placed on the body' by the choreographer, but is there not room in interpretation and arrangement on and through the body for authorial intent sufficient for copyright? This is particularly so if we look at Caroline's virtuoso interpretation of the dance, interpreting the choreographic intent, but visibly different from that performed by Naomi, the other female dancer. It seems unarguable that Caroline's personal touch is stamped on her arrangement of *Love Games*. It is only Caroline who knows how her body operates. It is only Caroline who could produce the dance in the form that she has. In terms of who then is the author of the dance, it seems perfectly plausible that there are two: one in the composition (the choreographer) and one in the arrangement (the dancer). If on the other hand the two contributions are considered indistinguishable, the dance could be considered a work of joint authorship.[100]

Some have said that this is not a plausible argument:[101] copyright focuses on the work, and not on the personal attributes of the author who

---

Copyright Act' 2003, available at <http://www.robic.ca/admin/pdf/279/105-LC.pdf> last accessed 22 October 2013.

[97] First recognised in *Bach v Longman*, 98 ER [1777] 1274.

[98] *Austin v Columbia*, [1917–1923] MacG CC 398; *Robertson v Lewis* [1976] RPC 169; *Redwood Music v Chappell & Co Ltd.* [1982] RPC 109. Although the case law which has considered copyright in arrangements tends to leave the line between composition and arrangement rather fuzzy *Godfrey v Lees* [1995] EMLR 307; *Beckingham v Hodgens* [2002] EMLR 45; *Hadley v Kemp* [1999] EMLR 589; *Fisher v Brooker* [2009] UKHL 41. See also R Arnold 'Reflections on The Triumph of Music: Copyrights and Performers' Rights in Music' (2010) *IPQ* 153; R Arnold 'Are Performers Authors? *Hadley v Kemp*,' (1999) *EIPR* 21(9), 464.

[99] *Redwood Music Ltd v Chappell & Co Ltd* [1982] R.P.C. 109; *Fisher v Brooker* [2009] UKHL 41.

[100] *Fisher v Brooker* [2009] UKHL 41; *Brighton v Jones* [2004] EWHC 1157 (Ch); *Stuart v Barrett* [1994] EMLR 449; *Hadley v Kemp*, [1999] EMLR 589.

[101] Conversation with participants at ATRIP Oxford 2013 after the presentation on which this contribution is based.

makes that work; others argue that it is an interpretation of a work and thus in the nature of performance, and thus more apt to be protected by performers' rights than by copyright.[102] The points raise tricky questions that lie at the interface between the authorial input necessary to be considered an author for the purposes of copyright, and when the input instead interprets a work and is in the nature of performance. There is no case law on dance, and only limited case law considering the authorial requirements in respect of dramatic works. *Brighton v Jones*[103] considered whether a director and playwright were the joint authors of a play. One argument was in respect of the contributions made during the course of rehearsals. The court noted that one contributor, Ms Jones, the defendant, had contributed the plot of the play in advance of rehearsals. Ms Brighton, the claimant, had contributed ideas to the dialogue, with the decisions on whether these were taken up for Ms Jones. The ideas were found by the court to be 'contributions to the interpretation and theatrical presentation of the dramatic work'[104] rather than to contributions to the work itself.[105] There was therefore no joint authorship. In *Coffey v Warner*[106] a musical work, voice expression, pitch contour and syncopation were found to be elements in the 'interpretation or performance characteristics by the performer' which was not 'the legitimate subject of copyright protection in the case of a musical work, rather than [...] composition, which is.'[107]

A number of observations can be made. *Brighton v Jones* was not concerned with the input into the work by the performers, but rather by those in charge of realising the performance. Further, it is quite accepted that where a performer interprets the work of another, such as where a chamber orchestra interprets a score, then performers' rights are the appropriate mechanism to protect their interests. But there is a real difference between that type of performance and a performance where the performer brings her own intellectual creation to the work of interpretation: it is her skill as a dancer through having developed her techniques through which she interprets and delivers the arrangement of the dance that makes Caroline's contribution suitable for protection by

[102] Although it seems unarguable that a work can be protected by both copyright and by performers' rights; R Arnold 'Reflections on The Triumph of Music: Copyrights and Performers' Rights in Music' (2010) *IPQ* 153.

[103] [2004] EWHC 1157 (Ch).

[104] Ibid. [56].

[105] Citing *Fylde Microsystems Ltd v Key Radio Systems Ltd* [1998] FSR 449.

[106] *Coffey v Warner/Chappell Music Ltd* [2005] EWHC 449.

[107] Ibid. [6].

copyright. While *Coffey v Warner* seems to rule out certain elements of musical performance as suitable for copyright protection, finding analogies within dance seems problematic. Might a *battement développé* be considered equivalent to voice expression? Or an *elevé* equivalent to syncopation? It seems difficult to equate these. Further, in *Coffey* the elements were found to be not 'the legitimate subject of copyright protection in the case of a musical work'. With the new case law from the Court of Justice mentioned above in respect of intellectual creation, it seems that the concept of work may not be relevant. If so, this may lead the way for hitherto unprotected elements to be considered as suitable for protection by copyright. One more question arises: suppose Caroline gives an *ex tempore* performance which is then recorded? Does this mean that no copyright would exist in the dance at all?[108] Or copyright would exist in the dance but there would be no author? Does a dance really have to exist in the mind of a choreographer or be fixed in some other form by another party before it can be protected by copyright? It seems implausible; but that seems the logical outcome if Caroline is to be denied copyright protection in her creativity in her arrangement of the dance on her body.

So where does this take us when thinking about the disability agenda, the disabled dancer and her dance and copyright? Does copyright consider itself exceptional in this regard? The argument suggests not. Copyright, with its focus on the work rather than the author, is blind to difference. Copyright supports the creative effort expended by those with impairments in the same way as those who are able-bodied; indeed, copyright may be *more* sympathetic to the work produced by the disabled dancer because of its very particular expression and because of the virtuoso nature of the arrangement. As is argued by Anes, in responding to the claim that the trained and disabled dancer's body is the ideal of aesthetic beauty: 'it is exactly the disability and its marks of symptom – its signs of pathology – that produces a new and radical aesthetic. An able-bodied virtuoso cannot produce this aesthetic and the site of resistance to interpellation that is found in this kind of performance.'[109] By recognising the disabled dancer as an author, she would become a

[108] Copyright would subsist in the sound recording and film of the dance; Copyright Designs and Patents Act ss. 5A and 5B and for detailed consideration on this, see C Waelde et al 'Let's dance! – but who owns it?' 2014 *EIPR* 217.

[109] M Anes 'Performing between intention and unconscious daily gesture. How might disabled dancers offer us a new aesthetic sensibility?' *About Performance* No 11, 2012, 143, 143.

co-owner of the copyright in the work. This would confer equality with co-owners and status within the dance community and beyond.

So it would seem that for the disabled dance artist in her capacity as creator, the human rights, disability and copyright converge, showing support for the artist and her creation. Can the same be said for disability and human rights in relation to books, where the concern is for the user rather than the author?

BOOKS AND THE BLIND

It has been noted above that where disability is included in the copyright framework at European and domestic level, its focus is on accessibility for the disabled user. Historically, this has been done through relying on the medical model of disability, but more recently emphasis has been on the social model. However, the reality for disabled people seems not to have lived up to the aspirations within the legislation. It has long been argued that there is a 'book famine', despite the legislation.[110] There have been and continue to be notable numbers of private initiatives seeking to make works available, including through audio books, text-to-voice software and newer technologies which convert words, images and graphics into words and oral descriptions to which a blind person may listen.[111] Yet high hurdles remain.

For the last 30-odd years attempts have been made to break down these hurdles at international level to provide a mechanism which would result in meaningful ways in which the blind could access books. When the disability agenda reached the international copyright policy-making stage in the early 1980s, both visual and auditory impairments were considered. However, in 1981, a Working Group created by WIPO and

---

[110] Annex 111 SCCR/20/5 WIPO Standing Committee on Copyright and Related Rights Twentieth Session Geneva, 21–24 June 2010, at 2. In 2004, despite the 2002 VIP Copyright Act, no discernible increase in the number of accessible publications could be detected.

[111] See discussion on RNIB website 'Talking Books and Daisy Players' <rnib.org.uk/livingwithsightloss/readingwriting/Talkingbooksanddaisyplayers/Pages/talking_books_daisy.aspx> last accessed 22 October 2012. For links to some sources, see http://talkingbookstore.net/ and <www.amazon.co.uk/Audio-CDs-Books/b?ie=UTF8&node=267859> last accessed 22 October 2013. In tandem with the proposals discussed below, extensive informal efforts have been made at international level to develop licensing schemes to facilitate access to works and WIPO established the TIGAR project see <http://www.visionip.org/tigar/en/faq.html> last accessed 22 October 2013.

UNESCO to look at access by the visually and auditory impaired to protected works accepted the findings of a report which argued that captioning (which involves capturing and condensing text and making it available in written form) involves an 'adaptation' of the work which does not fall under the Berne Convention's 'minor reservations' doctrine.[112] As a result the Working Group abandoned their remit of addressing auditory impairment.[113] At the related 1982 Intergovernmental Committee meeting, it was noted that there was support for finding ways to facilitate making works accessible to the blind, but that there was a concern for the legitimate interests of authors (as opposed to rightholders more broadly). Delegates were in favour of reproduction into Braille, but were not in favour of reproduction into large print or sound recording or broadcasting. Braille, it was reasoned, would be accessible only to the blind, while reproduction by other means would be difficult to limit to the blind, so there 'would be much danger that [the author's]

[112] The Working Group on Access by the Visually and Auditory Handicapped to Material Reproducing Works Protected by Copyright met in Paris on 25–27 October 1982, and its report, Report d IV, was published in 1985 in conjunction with that of the ensuing Intergovernmental Committee: see Executive Committee of the International Intergovernmental Committee of the Union for the Protection of Literary and Universal Copyright Convention on Artistic Works (Berne Union), Twenty-Fourth Session Sixth Ordinary Session of the (9th Extraordinary) Committee of the 1971 Convention PARIS (17–25 June 1985) B/EC/XXIV/10 IGC/VI/11, Paris, 12 March 1985. Regarding the scope of the minor reservations doctrine, see WTO DSS 160 Section 110(5) US Copyright Act, http://www.wto.org/english/tratop_e/dispu_e/cases_e/ds160_e.htm and consideration in S Ricketson *International Copyright and Neighbouring Rights: the Berne Convention and Beyond* (OUP, 2006), chapter 13

[113] The Working Group agreed with the submission that the making of captions involves the right of adaptation. Thus, it opined that it would be incompatible with both international copyright treaties and the national legislation of many countries to provide for any kind of exceptions or non-voluntary licensing in respect of such use: see Berne Union, ibid., at 354. For more on minor reservations for religious ceremonies, military bands and the educational needs of children and adults, and its revisions in 1948 and 1967, see Standing Committee on Copyright and Related Rights, Nineteenth Session Geneva, 14–18 December 2009, Study on the Limitations and Exceptions to Copyright and Related Rights for the Purposes of Educational and Research Activities in Latin America and the Caribbean, SCCR/19/4, 30 September 2009, at para 1.1.1.

interests might be prejudiced'.[114] In a report in 1985, 'Copyright Problems Raised by the Access by Handicapped Persons to Protected Works',[115] two key issues were identified as being barriers to access. These were (a) the lack of an exception or limitation in domestic laws that would allow reproduction of the works to make them accessible; and (b) the absence of a mechanism whereby accessible works once made could be distributed across borders. These two problems, it was argued, could be solved by an international treaty.[116]

Notwithstanding this, and while the disability agenda gained momentum in other fora,[117] there was little obvious activity within the copyright sector. The next major, but general (in the sense that it is not a culture-specific treaty but rather deals with a range of human rights and equality issues of people with disabilities, including culture), milestone was the negotiation of the CRPD in 2006, which was discussed above. No doubt as a result at least in part of the obligations undertaken in this Convention, further activity ensued in the copyright space. The European Commission established a stakeholder forum to examine issues of access by the blind to cultural works,[118] and the World Blind Union (WBU)

---

[114] Executive Committee of the International Union for the Protection of Literary and Artistic Works (Berne Union) Paris (17–25 June 1985) B/EC/XXIV/10, para. 12, and p 3 of ANNEX I.

[115] Ms Wanda Noel, IGC(1971)/VI/11 – B/EC/XXIV/10 ANNEX II – pp 25–26.

[116] See WIPO, *Supplementary Information on Studies on Limitations and Exceptions for Educational Activities* (document SCCR/20/3); WIPO, *Second Analytical Document on Limitations and Exceptions* (document SCCR/20/4); WIPO, *Examples of Practices and Other Measures at National Level for the Benefit of Persons with Print Disabilities* (document SCCR/20/5); WIPO, *Third Interim Report on the Stakeholders Platform* (document SCCR/20/6); WIPO, *Report on the Questionnaire on Limitations and Exceptions* (document SCCR/20/7). See also J Sullivan *Study on Copyright Limitations and Exceptions for the Visually Impaired* (Geneva: WIPO, 2007), which demonstrated that there is a legal patchwork of exceptions for visually impaired people worldwide, and that transferring a book to country B which has been made accessible under a copyright exception in country A remains a legal 'grey area'. For the US, which has just embraced international exhaustion for works lawfully made under the US Copyright Act, the emphasis may change; see *Kirtsaeng v John Wiley & Sons, Inc.*, 568 U.S. (2013).

[117] See A Brown and C Waelde 'Human Rights, persons with disabilities and copyright' in Christophe Geiger *Research Handbook on Human Rights and Intellectual Property* (forthcoming, Edward Elgar).

[118] See European Commission, Communication: Copyright in the Knowledge Economy, Brussels, 19.10.2009 COM(2009) 532 final. In this Communication,

succeeded in placing the issue of a specific treaty containing exceptions and limitations for the blind on WIPO's agenda,[119] which eventually resulted in the Marrakesh Treaty in 2013. Full details of the views of people with disabilities of the brouhaha over these negotiations are not clear. Yet it is clear is that there was fierce lobbying over large principles and over small words. Some of the issues that arose included whether the proposal should take the form of a Treaty imposing obligations or a recommendation regarding permitted action;[120] what types of disabilities should be included;[121] what rights should be included;[122] the class(es) of beneficiaries; the works to be included and the extent of rights in relation to those works; the extent of relaxations to be provided for developing countries; and, tellingly, the relationship to the Berne three-step test.[123] Finally, in July 2013 agreement was reached. Some note that because of the publicity surrounding the negotiations this was the only possible outcome because: 'members will feel pressure to do whatever it takes to

---

the Commission notes that, despite the UN Convention on the Rights of Persons with Disabilities, only 5 per cent of books were available in formats accessible to the blind, accepts that the exceptions and limitations in Member State legislation are piecemeal and not conducive to cross-border trade, and agrees that technical protection measures may cause problems for changing formats. However, it is not clear whether this stakeholder forum has yet been constituted, as there appears to be no publicly available information.

[119] The WBU managed to persuade Brazil, Ecuador and Paraguay to table a proposal for a WIPO Treaty for Improved Access for Blind, Visually Impaired and Other Reading Disabled Persons at WIPO 2009, which proposal was debated at the WIPO Standing Committee in 2010: see Standing Committee on Copyright and Related Rights, Eighteenth Session, Geneva, 25–29 May 2009, Proposal by Brazil, Ecuador and Paraguay Relating to Limitations and Exceptions: Treaty Proposed by the World Blind Union, SCCR/18/5, 25 May 2009.

[120] The US was the last country holding out against a Treaty but eventually agreed that the initiative should take that form. http://www.ip-watch.org/2013/09/20/negotiators-stakeholders-tell-tale-of-wipo-marrakesh-treaty-negotiation-look-to-implementation/.

[121] For example, the African delegation and the WBU sought to include those unable to turn pages, those unable to move their eyes (and so requiring reformatting as opposed to re-writing), and those suffering from physical, mental, sensory, or cognitive incapacity. Standing Committee on Copyright and Related Rights, Twentieth Session Geneva, 21–24 June 2010, Draft Report Prepared by the Secretariat, SCCR/20/13 PROV, 6 August 2010.

[122] The African delegation also wanted to extend the treaty to any work in which copyright subsists, whereas the US proposed that it should be limited to works that had been published, and the EU to those which had been published in print.

[123] See Document SCCR/23/7.

conclude a treaty because whoever stands in the way of this effort for blind people "will be branded as a villain".'[124] The World Blind Union has welcomed the final Treaty and sees it as a promising base for future action.[125]

The Treaty itself is more obviously embedded in the social model of disability and in human rights rhetoric than any of the previous measures. This is evident from the preamble: the link between disability and human rights is emphasised:

> Recalling the principles of non-discrimination, equal opportunity, accessibility and full and effective participation and inclusion in society, proclaimed in the Universal Declaration of Human Rights and the United Nations Convention on the Rights of Persons with Disabilities.[126]

The preamble also notes that the Treaty is rooted in the social model of disability:

> Aware of the barriers of persons with visual impairments or with other print disabilities to access published works in achieving equal opportunities in society, and the need to both expand the number of works in accessible formats and to improve the circulation of such works.

In terms of content, the Treaty requires States to introduce limitations or exceptions to facilitate the reproduction, dissemination and making available[127] of literary and artistic works[128] in accessible formats to beneficiaries defined as people who are blind, have a visual impairment which cannot be improved or who are unable to hold or manipulate a

---

[124] W New 'Mixed Reaction Among Participants in WIPO Talks on Treaty for the Blind' (Intellectual Property Watch, 22 April 2013) <http://www.ip-watch.org/2013/04/22/mixed-reactions-among-participants-in-wipo-talks-on-treaty-for-the-blind/> last accessed 22 October 2013.

[125] See D Pescod 'What the Marrakech Treaty means for Blind People' WIPO Magazine (August 2013) <http://www.wipo.int/wipo_magazine/en/2013/04/article_0002.html> last accessed 22 October 2013; and statement of World Blind Union to WIPO General Assemblies, 26 September 2013.

[126] Marrakesh Treaty to Facilitate Access to Published Works for Persons who are Blind, Visually Impaired, or otherwise Print Disabled. Preamble, First para. For consideration of the human rights perspective, see also J Li and N Selvaurai 'Reconciling the enforcement of copyright with the upholding of human rights: a consideration of the Marrakesh Treaty to Facilitate Access to Published Works for the Blind, Visually Impaired and Print Disabled' 2014 *EIPR* 653.

[127] Marrakesh Treaty Preamble, first para.

[128] Marrakesh Treaty Preamble, fourth para.

book to read it; it has also been argued that these provisions are consistent with the Berne three-step test.[129] This avoids questions of the extent to which states can in fact implement them, and wider issues of the impact of general provisions on solutions developed to specific problems (similar to those explored throughout this collection). The Treaty also allows for cross-border exchange of works in accessible format via a system of authorised entities[130] thus eliminating costly duplication in effort, and holding out the possibility of access by those in developing countries to accessible format collections from elsewhere. By September 2013 there were 53 signatories to the Treaty, which comes into force three months after 20 eligible parties have deposited their instruments of ratification or accession.[131] By November 2014, only two countries have ratified the treaty and the World Blind Union has stated that it sees encouraging ratification as its next sphere of activity.[132] Further, to move on from the international achievements, much depends on the next stage – domestic implementation of the provisions, in which the World Blind Union is also active. Ratification and domestic action might also be stimulated from the reference to the Marrakesh Treaty in a 2014 General Comment on the CRPD on the question of "Accessibility".[133] Given the newness of the Treaty, and the rather ponderous processes needed for ratifying the treaty and then implementing Treaty

---

[129] Marrakesh Treaty, article 3; and see S Vezzoso, 'The Marrakesh spirit – a ghost in three steps?' 2014 *IIC,* 45(7), 796–820.

[130] Marrakesh Treaty, article 5; for consideration of this, see M Trimble, 'The Marrakesh Puzzle' 2014 *IIC* 45(7) 768–795, in which the author aims to assist legislative and executive experts, and which considers interpretation and questions of practicality.

[131] Marrakesh Treaty, article 18.

[132] See note 126. For the long list of contracting parties, as at November 2014, see the list at http://www.wipo.int/treaties/en/ShowResults.jsp?lang=en&treaty_id=843. As at November 2014, the treaty has been ratified by El Salvador and India. For consideration and criticism of delay, in this respect see K Koklu, 'The Marrakesh Treaty – time to end the book famine for visually impaired persons worldwide' 2014 *IIC* 45(7) 737–739.

[133] See World Blind Union website, http://www.worldblindunion.org/English/Pages/default.aspx. Regarding the level of national change which is likely required, see J Li, 'Copyright exemptions to facilitate access to published works for the print disabled – the gap between national laws and the standards required by the Marrakesh Treaty' 2014 *IIC* 45(7) 740–767, in particular from 764; see also consideration of the treaty and possible practical obstacles which could arise, in J Li and N Selvaurai (n126). General Comment: Committee on the Rights of Persons with Disabilities General Comment No. 2 (2014) on Article 9: Accessibility, article 45 (see also n 41).

provisions into domestic law where not self-executing, it is still likely to take some time before we witness changes that have the potential to make practical differences. One would hope, however, that the time period is not excessive.

So where does this take us when thinking about the disability agenda, and its impact on the disabled user of books and copyright? Unlike the position in respect of dance, the protracted nature of negotiations relating to the Marrakesh Treaty suggests that copyright does consider itself exceptional. The Marrakesh Treaty does suggest a balance between copyright, human rights and disability concerns:

> Recognizing the need to maintain a balance between the effective protection of the rights of authors and the larger public interest, particularly education, research and access to information, and that such a balance must facilitate effective and timely access to works for the benefit of persons with visual impairments or with other print disabilities.[134]
>
> Emphasizing the importance of copyright protection as an incentive and reward for literary and artistic creations and of enhancing opportunities for everyone, including persons with visual impairments or with other print disabilities, to participate in the cultural life of the community, to enjoy the arts and to share scientific progress and its benefits.[135]

These recitals indicate that in respect of one group of people with certain specified disabilities, the three fields can once again complement each other. The nature of the negotiations suggests, however, that it was something of a 'shotgun' wedding. It is only when there are national laws and they start to be used by the beneficiaries and those who help them to access books that the real and tangible impact of these words will be known. That will be the point at which we will have a deeper understanding of the relationships between disability, human rights and copyright, and of the extent to which they support and complement each other, or are in conflict.

CONCLUSION

So what then is the conclusion about the intersections between the disability, human rights and copyright? Where the focus is on the creator and her creation, the systems can seem well aligned. Copyright is blind to difference in the individual and treatment of the able-bodied and the

---

134 Marrakesh Treaty Preamble, ninth para.
135 Marrakesh Treaty Preamble, third para.

disabled is equal. Yet is this blindness, or perhaps wilful ignorance, sufficient? Should there be more open and robust discussions between the fields to enable the reality of disabled dance to form part of the copyright framework, rather than relying on creative legal arguments to bring it within its scope? In respect of users and books, while the Marrakesh Treaty, rightfully, has been hailed as a historic success, the real test will be as to how it is implemented into domestic laws and then how it is used in practice. Only then will we know whether disability as underpinned by a human rights agenda and instruments is actually powerful enough to displace the control conferred by copyright and the sway that the copyright lobby holds over policy-makers.

This is only the start of the exploration into the disability, human rights and copyright ecosystem. Our focus has been on two particular case studies: one of creation and one of use. There are many other intersections that need to be explored. While we chose to look at issues of ownership and authorship in relation to Caroline Bowditch's performance in *Love Games*, the intention of the choreographer of that piece was to explore whether a disabled dancer could 'cover' a non-disabled dancer. While feedback we understand was generally positive, anecdotal evidence suggests that there were some who did not agree. The right of the disabled artist to take part in cultural performance is a pressing issue. While there are notable inclusive companies such as Candoco in respect of dance and Graeae in respect of theatre, is there any disabled performer in say the Royal Ballet? Or in Ballet Rambert? And of interest to this collection, what role might copyright play in contributing to exclusion? In respect of the position of users, what of other forms of disabilities and other works which are not covered by the Marrakesh Treaty? And what of the role of copyright in excluding disabled people from our cultural heritage, such as producing touchable copies of works of art?

This chapter has identified clear differences in priority and substance between disability, human rights and copyright. In some policy discussions and in some court cases, they have moved closer together and, using the arguments made here, they could move closer still. There remains, however, a significant power imbalance. Human rights and disabilities treaties make clear the rights to be accorded to people with disabilities, but enforcement systems are limited. A significant body of law which relates to culture makes very limited reference to the position of people with disabilities. This field of law, copyright, has robust enforcement procedures and has well-organised and well-funded lobbyists to protect its interests. Copyright appears to consider itself a *lex specialis*; and the (largely) legitimate arguments which can be made in favour of it enable it to disregard in many cases the interests of others –

notwithstanding that these interests are recognised by rights in international treaties. This seems not to have been, at least until auditory impairment was excluded from WIPO, the result of a deliberate decision. More concerning, it came from being inward looking and disregarding those who do not seem sufficiently relevant to warrant attention, be that through exceptions to copyright or conferring copyright's protection. Marrakesh is a triumph – but it is not the end: it is a fine beginning.

Index